AI in Healthcare

This book addresses the urgent need for AI healthcare insights in a post-pandemic and swiftly progressing world in which the use of advanced health technologies is becoming the norm. It explores the rapidly evolving AI landscape affecting health systems and provides practical, evidence-informed guidance drawn from practice, theory, and research.

Covering a wide range of topics—from digital health technologies to data analytics and interoperability—it offers a thorough examination of advancements in these areas, giving readers a comprehensive understanding of the health sector's transformation. The book goes beyond theory, showcasing practical applications of AI solutions, discussing both advantages and possible disadvantages. Real-world case studies and expert perspectives drawn from recent developments equip readers with actionable insights for implementation in various healthcare settings. With a holistic approach, the book explores not only technological aspects but also ethical considerations, regulatory challenges, and the human impact of digital transformation.

This invaluable resource is essential for academics, practitioners, and policymakers in healthcare management, information systems management, healthcare policy, and public health.

AI in Healthcare

A Transparent Approach to Informatics

Edited by
Philip Eappen, Virginia Gunn, Dimitrios Zikos, and
Narasimha Rao Vajjhala

CRC Press
Taylor & Francis Group
Boca Raton London New York

CRC Press is an imprint of the
Taylor & Francis Group, an **informa** business
A CHAPMAN & HALL BOOK

First edition published 2026
by CRC Press
2385 NW Executive Center Drive, Suite 320, Boca Raton FL 33431

and by CRC Press
4 Park Square, Milton Park, Abingdon, Oxon, OX14 4RN

CRC Press is an imprint of Taylor & Francis Group, LLC

ISBN: 9781041036876 (hbk)
ISBN: 9781041036883 (pbk)
ISBN: 9781003624875 (ebk)

DOI: 10.1201/9781003624875

Typeset in Times
by Deanta Global Publishing Services, Chennai, India

Access the Support Material: http://www.routledge.com/9781041036876

Dedication

To my treasured dad, **Eappen**—*a gentle spirit whose steadfast guidance, immense resilience, and limitless kindness continue to light my journey even though he has departed. He existed with a sincere heart that welcomed all people without bias or animosity, recognizing only the goodness within humanity. While his physical presence is no longer among us, his precious principles of unconditional affection and embrace give meaning to every chapter of this endeavor.*

May his heritage of dedication and compassion continue to motivate coming generations!

Dr Philip Eappen

Contents

Contributors

Edward A.A.
Africa College of Healthcare Administrators (AfCHCA), South Africa

Zainab Almukhtar
Cape Breton University, Canada

Prakash Agarwal
Indian Institute of Information Technology Dharwad, India

Lalit Banger
GNA University, India

Ekta Bhaggi
GNA University, India

Anushka Chaurasia
National Institute of Technology, India

Sudeepto Chatterjee
Indian Institute of Information Technology Dharwad, India

Ranney D.J.
Africa College of Healthcare Administrators (AfCHCA)

Philip Eappen
Cape Breton University, Canada

Adam Elliott
Cape Breton University, Canada

Ruiling Guo
Idaho State University, USA

Virginia Gunn
Cape Breton University, Canada

Hilary Hall
Western University, Canada

Rajendra Hegadi
Indian Institute of Information Technology Dharwad, India

Ashis J. Kalathil
Indian Institute of Information Technology Dharwad, India

Karen Kennedy
Cape Breton University, Canada

Deepak Kumar
National Institute of Technology, India

Matthew MacLeod
Cape Breton University, Canada

Krishnendhu Manoharan
Cape Breton University, Canada

Kelsey Morrison
Cape Breton University, Canada

Christopher Partridge
Idaho State University, USA

Prathamesh P. Pai
Indian Institute of Information Technology Dharwad, India

Simran Kaur Sandal
GNA University, India

Wasswa Shafik
Universiti Brunei Darussalam, Brunei

Vismaya Annie Vinod
Cape Breton University, Canada

Narasimha Rao Vajjhala
American University, Bulgaria

Yogita
National Institute of Technology Kurukshetra, India

Dimitrios Zikos
Texas Tech University Health Sciences Center, USA

Preface

The rapid advancement of artificial intelligence (AI) in healthcare has reached a critical inflection point. While AI technologies promise unprecedented improvements in diagnostic accuracy, treatment personalization, and operational efficiency, their implementation raises fundamental questions about transparency, accountability, and the preservation of human-centered care. This book emerges from the urgent need to bridge the gap between AI's technical capabilities and the ethical frameworks necessary for its responsible deployment in healthcare settings.

Healthcare systems worldwide face mounting pressures from aging populations, chronic disease burdens, and resource constraints. Simultaneously, algorithmic management systems are increasingly replacing human decision-making processes across healthcare organizations, from staff scheduling to clinical protocols. The confluence of these trends demands careful examination of how AI technologies can enhance rather than compromise the quality, equity, and humanity of healthcare delivery.

The concept of transparency in healthcare AI extends far beyond technical explainability. As demonstrated throughout this volume, transparency encompasses accountability in algorithmic scheduling decisions, fairness in resource allocation, clarity in clinical decision support systems, and openness about the limitations and biases inherent in AI models. When algorithmic scheduling systems operate as "black boxes," they may obscure critical questions about staff-to-patient ratios and worker well-being. When AI diagnostic tools lack transparency, they risk undermining the trust essential to effective patient-provider relationships.

This book presents a comprehensive examination of AI applications across the healthcare spectrum, from foundational ethical considerations to cutting-edge technical implementations. The contributing authors—spanning clinical practice, academic research, and technological innovation—bring diverse perspectives to the challenge of developing AI systems that are not only technically sophisticated but also ethically sound and practically beneficial.

Part I, "Transparency and Accountability in Healthcare AI" establishes the critical foundation by examining how algorithmic management affects healthcare workers and exploring the ethical frameworks necessary for responsible AI implementation. These chapters reveal that algorithmic scheduling, while offering efficiency gains, may contribute to deteriorating job quality for health workers when implemented without sufficient transparency or consideration of employment conditions. The ethical implications discussed here—encompassing patient privacy, data security, algorithmic bias, and fair access—provide essential guidance for healthcare professionals, administrators, technologists, and policymakers.

Part II, "Transformative Technologies and Patient-Centered Care" explores how emerging technologies can advance patient-centered care while maintaining the foundational principles of respect for patient preferences, needs, and values. These chapters examine the transformative potential of artificial intelligence, blockchain,

Internet of Things devices, wearable technologies, robotics, and telehealth in creating more personalized, responsive, and data-driven care models. Critically, they also address the challenges of privacy concerns, equity issues, cybersecurity risks, and algorithmic bias that must be navigated to ensure inclusive technological adoption.

Part III, "AI Applications in Healthcare Practice" provides concrete examples of AI implementation across diverse healthcare contexts. From disease preparedness strategies that leverage AI for pandemic response to personalized healthcare applications that predict disease and enable early detection, these chapters demonstrate both the remarkable potential and inherent limitations of AI systems. The emphasis on data quality, privacy concerns, and the need for human interaction underscores that effective AI implementation requires careful attention to both technical and human factors.

Part IV, "Advanced AI Technologies and Clinical Applications" showcases sophisticated technical implementations while maintaining focus on transparency and accountability. The deep learning approaches to abdominal trauma diagnosis, transparent drug classification systems using neural networks with explainability analysis, and wearable IoT applications for patient monitoring represent the cutting edge of AI healthcare technology. Importantly, these chapters demonstrate how advanced technical capabilities can be developed with built-in transparency mechanisms, such as SHAP analysis for understanding model decisions.

Throughout this volume, several critical themes emerge that define responsible AI implementation in healthcare. The preservation of human oversight remains paramount—AI systems must serve as enablers rather than replacements for clinical judgment. The imperative for transparency extends beyond technical explanations to encompass clear communication about system limitations, potential biases, and decision-making processes. Equity considerations must be embedded from the outset, ensuring that AI advances do not exacerbate existing healthcare disparities but instead promote more inclusive and accessible care.

The global perspective represented in these chapters—from pandemic preparedness strategies for low- and middle-income countries to advanced diagnostic technologies—reflects the universal nature of both healthcare challenges and AI opportunities. The authors consistently emphasize that while AI can provide valuable insights and recommendations, the accuracy and reliability of these systems depend fundamentally on data quality, ethical implementation, and ongoing human oversight.

Perhaps most importantly, this book argues that transparency in healthcare AI is not merely a technical requirement but a moral imperative. As AI systems become increasingly integrated into clinical workflows, understanding their mechanisms, acknowledging their limitations, and maintaining accountability for their decisions becomes essential for preserving the trust that forms the foundation of effective healthcare delivery.

The COVID-19 pandemic has demonstrated both the potential of AI technologies to accelerate medical discovery and the critical importance of robust, transparent systems for health emergency preparedness. The lessons learned during this global health crisis inform many of the perspectives presented in this volume, emphasizing the need for AI systems that can rapidly adapt to emerging challenges while maintaining ethical standards and transparency.

Looking toward the future, we envision a healthcare landscape where AI technologies are seamlessly integrated with patient-centered values, creating systems that are not only efficient and predictive but also compassionate, inclusive, and empowering. Achieving this vision requires the thoughtful integration of technical innovation with ethical frameworks, robust governance structures, and meaningful stakeholder collaboration.

This book serves multiple audiences: healthcare professionals seeking to understand AI's role in clinical practice, administrators evaluating AI implementation strategies, technologists developing healthcare AI systems, policymakers crafting regulatory frameworks, and students preparing for careers in an AI-enhanced healthcare environment. Each chapter provides both theoretical foundations and practical guidance for navigating the complex landscape of healthcare AI implementation.

We extend our gratitude to Professor William Bertrand for his thoughtful foreword and to all contributing authors who have shared their expertise across this interdisciplinary landscape. Their collective wisdom illuminates pathways toward AI implementations that enhance rather than compromise the fundamental values of healthcare: healing, caring, and serving the needs of all patients with dignity and respect.

The future of healthcare will undoubtedly be shaped by artificial intelligence. Our responsibility is to ensure that this transformation strengthens rather than weakens the human connections that define quality care, promotes rather than hinders equity in health outcomes, and maintains the transparency necessary for accountability and trust.

Dr Philip Eappen
Dr Virginia Gunn
Dr Dimitrios Zikos
Dr Narasimha Rao Vajjhala

Foreword

The information technology revolution of recent decades has brought unprecedented transformation to healthcare. In the wake of the global pandemic, one truth has crystallized: traditional care and research models alone cannot bear the weight of the complex, interconnected challenges we face. It is within this moment of uncertainty and urgency that Artificial Intelligence (AI) has emerged—not as a distant promise, but as a practical and powerful tool fundamentally reshaping how we understand, deliver, and experience prevention and care.

This book, *AI in Healthcare: A Transparent Approach to Informatics*, arrives at precisely the right moment. It avoids the trap of celebrating technology for technology's sake. Instead, it adopts a measured, thoughtful approach—balancing enthusiasm with critique and possibility with responsibility. Through its comprehensive case studies, global perspectives, and concrete examples, the book illustrates not merely what AI can accomplish, but how it is already being applied to enhance diagnostics, personalize treatment, optimize resource management, and even anticipate outbreaks before they spread.

What distinguishes this work is its recognition that the story of AI in healthcare encompasses not only algorithms and data, but also people—patients, practitioners, policymakers, and communities. The book addresses the essential ethical questions: How do we safeguard privacy in an era of digital medicine? How do we ensure equity and prevent the replication of bias in machine learning systems? How do we prepare a workforce to collaborate with, rather than compete against, intelligent technologies?

By skillfully weaving together foundational knowledge with practical guidance, **Dr Eappen** and his colleagues as editors have assembled a work that provides both clarity and direction. They remind us that AI is not a panacea, but rather a sophisticated set of tools that, when deployed transparently and humanely, can extend the reach and compassion of medicine itself.

As you explore the pages ahead, I invite you to approach this book not only as a guide to emerging technologies, but also as a roadmap to the future of healthcare—a future in which innovation and humanity advance hand in hand.

Prof. William Bertrand
Emeritus Wisner Professor of Public Health
Tulane School of Public Health and Tropical Medicine

Acknowledgments

We are privileged to introduce *AI in Healthcare: A Transparent Approach to Informatics*, a unified endeavor forged through the combined knowledge, commitment, and forward-thinking perspective of a global network of researchers, clinicians, and pioneers. This publication embodies both technological progress and our collective dedication to establishing a more open, responsible, and fair healthcare framework for tomorrow.

I wish to extend my profound appreciation to everyone who contributed to making this initiative a reality. To my co-editors—**Dr Virginia Gunn**, **Dr Dimitrios Zikos**, and **Dr Narasimha Rao Vajjhala**—I am grateful for your collaboration, insightful contributions, and steadfast encouragement throughout this endeavor. Your guidance and varied specializations have enhanced this work beyond measure, ensuring its applicability across the intricate terrain of healthcare AI deployment.

We want to convey our sincere thanks to **Professor William Bertrand** from **Tulane University** for your perceptive foreword, which establishes crucial background for the challenges and possibilities we examine within these pages. Your knowledge and viewpoint have deepened our comprehension of AI's transformative potential in healthcare delivery.

Our appreciation goes to all contributing authors, whose varied viewpoints—encompassing clinical expertise, scholarly investigation, technological advancement, and policy formulation—have produced an extensive resource that connects the technical and moral aspects of healthcare AI. Your dedication to openness, responsibility, and patient-focused care shines through this work and establishes a standard for ethical AI development in healthcare settings.

We offer sincere thanks to the institutions and organizations globally that endorsed this project. The worldwide reach of this partnership mirrors the universal character of healthcare obstacles and AI possibilities, and we appreciate the institutional backing that enabled this international academic collaboration.

To the medical professionals, patients, and communities whose real-world experiences shape the practical implementations discussed in this publication, we recognize that your everyday challenges fuel our determination to create AI systems that genuinely address human requirements. The transparency and responsibility principles we champion ultimately aim to enhance your experiences and results.

We acknowledge the trailblazing researchers and ethicists whose groundbreaking contributions in AI transparency, algorithmic responsibility, and healthcare informatics have laid the groundwork for the conversations presented here. Your work in the field has created the scholarly foundation that supports this publication.

Above all, I express deep gratitude to my family for their affection, understanding, and encouragement sustained us during this process. To my cherished wife **Figgi** and dear son **Evan**, whose patience through numerous hours of writing and cooperation enabled this achievement. To beloved mum **Baby**, whose prayers and support provided continual inspiration, and to my extended family and friends whose backing remained constant.

This publication is affectionately dedicated to honoring my treasured dad **Eappen**, whose deep wisdom, steadfast principles, and caring nature continue to guide our journey. His conviction that learning should benefit humanity and his commitment to assisting others have influenced not only the core of this work but also our shared mission to ensure human worth, advance fairness, and maintain the confidence vital to therapeutic relationships.

Within these chapters, we pay tribute to all who have enhanced our knowledge of how technology can fulfill humanity's greatest hopes for health and wellness. Their influence motivates us to keep developing healthcare AI that is not merely technically advanced but also transparent, responsible, and genuinely focused on human needs.

Dr Philip Eappen

Editors

Dr Philip Eappen is an accomplished Healthcare Executive, Academic, and Researcher currently serving as Assistant Professor in the Department of Professional Studies, School of Nursing; Director, Research in Medicine | CBMC | Dalhousie University Adjunct Faculty in Healthcare Management, Shannon School of Business at Cape Breton University; and Associate Scientist with the Maritime SPOR SUPPORT Unit. With over a decade of experience spanning hospital operations, healthcare education, and strategic leadership, he has consistently advanced innovation and excellence across diverse healthcare systems in Canada, the United States, and internationally.

Dr Eappen's clinical leadership experience includes progressive roles at the Breton Ability Centre in Sydney, Nova Scotia, where he advanced to Director of Clinical Services and Transition to Community, leading person-centered care initiatives and community transition services. His academic career encompasses appointments at the University of Toronto, Southern Alberta Institute of Technology, and Fanshawe College. Internationally, he served as Director of Health Services and Chief Administrator of Healthcare Operations at the American University of Nigeria, where he spearheaded clinical transformation, emergency preparedness, and inclusive health initiatives, including programs supporting survivors of Boko Haram abductions.

Dr Eappen holds a Doctorate in Healthcare Administration and Post-Graduate Certificate in International Health from Central Michigan University, complemented by an MBA in Healthcare Management and Bachelor of Nursing. He has developed and taught curricula across undergraduate and graduate levels in healthcare leadership, innovation, and health systems analytics, while leading the program development of Cape Breton University's Master of Healthcare Innovation and Leadership program.

An active contributor to national and global health dialogues, Dr Eappen serves on the boards of the American College of Healthcare Executives, Myeloma Canada, Aplastic Anemia and Myelodysplasia Canada, and the Network of Rare Blood Disorder Organizations (NRBDO). He chairs research and ethics committees, reflecting his commitment to governance, evidence-based practice, and health equity.

Dr Eappen has published extensively on artificial intelligence in healthcare, digital health transformation, and health workforce development. His recent editorial work includes *Healthcare Informatics Innovation Post COVID-19 Pandemic* (Taylor & Francis). He has presented at major international conferences including ICN 2025, ICIMTH, and INTED. As a Certified Health Executive (CHE) through the Canadian College of Health Leaders and Fellow candidate of the American College of Healthcare Executives (FACHE), Dr Eappen continues pursuing the highest standards of professional excellence in healthcare leadership. His research agenda focuses on digital innovation, rare diseases, and global workforce integration, continuing to shape policy, practice, and pedagogy in healthcare management.

Dr Virginia Gunn is an Associate Professor in the School of Nursing at Cape Breton University and an Affiliate Researcher at the Unit of Occupational Medicine, Institute of Environmental Medicine, Karolinska Institute, Sweden. As a public health researcher with interdisciplinary training in health and social sciences, Dr Gunn earned her doctoral and master's degrees from the Lawrence Bloomberg Faculty of Nursing and completed a Collaborative Doctoral Specialization in Global Health from the Dalla Lana School of Public Health, University of Toronto.

Dr Gunn combines her academic background with extensive professional experience as a health practitioner, with expertise spanning public health, acute care, and long-term care settings. She has assumed various leadership roles—including project lead, committee chair, board director, finance officer, and co-founder of interest groups—through which she has spearheaded initiatives to improve health systems and promote evidence-informed decision-making.

As a dedicated researcher, Dr Gunn maintains an active record of engagement in international, national, and regional projects and collaborations. Her established research program examines the intersection of advanced technologies, including artificial intelligence, with social determinants of health—particularly employment, migration, and gender—and their role in shaping health inequities. Through this work, she contributes to understanding how technological advancement can address or exacerbate existing health disparities in diverse populations.

Dr Dimitrios Zikos is an Associate Professor in the Department of Healthcare Management and Leadership at Texas Tech University Health Sciences Center (TTUHSC). He is a core faculty member in the Master of Science in Healthcare Administration (MSHA) program, where he teaches graduate-level courses in health informatics, research methods, and statistics. Dr Zikos brings extensive academic and leadership experience, having previously served as Director of the Health Administration Division and Interim Program Director of the Master of Health Administration at Central Michigan University. During his tenure there, he led the program's successful accreditation by the Commission on Accreditation of Healthcare Management Education (CAHME).

Dr Zikos holds a Ph.D. in Health Informatics from the National and Kapodistrian University of Athens in Greece and a Bachelor's degree in Nursing. His professional background spans both Europe and the United States, with applied research and academic contributions focused on the intersection of health data, workforce management, and patient safety.

His research is centered on leveraging data analytics to improve clinical and administrative decision-making in healthcare. He specializes in the secondary analysis of medical claims data, comorbidity modeling, and the evaluation of inpatient outcomes such as mortality and length of stay. Dr Zikos is particularly interested in the use of digital tools to enhance healthcare access for underserved populations, and the development of data-driven systems to support evidence-based care and decision-making. He is also active in the field of medical education technology, working on simulation-based tools that enhance the accessibility and usability of health information for both clinicians and patients.

A dedicated mentor, Dr Zikos has chaired over twenty doctoral dissertations, supporting students who aim to apply informatics and analytics to solve complex, real-world healthcare challenges. He has authored numerous peer-reviewed articles, book chapters, and conference presentations in health informatics, healthcare management, and digital health systems.

Dr Narasimha Rao Vajjhala is a distinguished Academic and Researcher currently serving as Professor and Chair of the Department of Computer Science at the American University in Bulgaria (AUBG). With over two decades of experience in higher education, Dr Vajjhala has held senior academic leadership positions, including Dean of the Faculty of Engineering and Architecture at the University of New York Tirana (UNYT), Albania, and Chair of Computer Science and Software Engineering programs at the American University of Nigeria (AUN).

Throughout his career, Dr Vajjhala has taught a comprehensive range of undergraduate and graduate courses in computer science, database systems, and programming across institutions in Europe and Africa. He serves as Editor-in-Chief of the *International Journal of Risk and Contingency Management* (IJRCM) and maintains active membership as a Senior Member of both the Association for Computing Machinery (ACM) and the Institute of Electrical and Electronics Engineers (IEEE), as well as membership in the Project Management Institute (PMI).

Beyond academia, Dr Vajjhala has provided technology consulting services for various European firms and participated in numerous EU-funded research and innovation projects. He holds a Doctorate in Information Systems and Technology from the United States, an M.Sc. in Computer Science and Applications from India, and an MBA with specialization in Information Systems from Switzerland. His interdisciplinary expertise spans computer science, information systems, and project management, with significant contributions to research, education, and industry practice across international contexts.

Part I

Transparency and Accountability in Healthcare AI

1 The Rise of AI in Healthcare

A Transparent Approach to Implementation

Philip Eappen, Virginia Gunn, Dimitrios Zikos, and Narasimha Rao Vajjhala

1.1 INTRODUCTION

Healthcare operations reached a new era of technological revolution. As we continue forging ahead into the 21st century, artificial intelligence (AI) has emerged as one of the most transformative forces reshaping the ways in which we conceptualize, deliver, or manage healthcare. This chapter examines the complex and evolving intersections between healthcare and AI.

The integration of AI into healthcare represents a massive technological upgrade (Apell & Eriksson, 2023; Shimonski, 2020) and it signifies a fundamental shift in the ways in which healthcare workers will approach patient care, decision-making, and health system management in the years to come (Shimonski, 2020). While significant changes brought forth by the adoption of AI in healthcare are underway across the world, we recognize that the pace of change regarding the integration of AI in the health system or other economic sectors is unequally distributed within and between countries (Goralski & Tan, 2020). Collectively, AI technologies are changing the boundaries of possibilities in healthcare (Alowais et al, 2023; Cheng et al., 2024). While AI integration is widespread across clinical areas, it could take multiple and diverse forms, ranging from deep neural networks enabling quicker abdominal trauma diagnosis to transparent drug classification systems using molecular property analysis (Alowais et al., 2023; Cheng et al., 2024). Other examples of advanced applications include AI-enabled bidirectional healthcare systems that facilitate intelligent device-provider communication, wearable Internet of Things (IoT) technologies transforming patient monitoring and chronic care, and adaptive technologies that strengthen clinical decision-making capabilities (Taherdoost, 2024).

In recent years, the use of AI in the healthcare sector has started to mark a significant shift in the ways in which medical practices are managed, emphasizing efficiency, accuracy, and patient-centered care (Faiyazuddin et al., 2025). AI technologies are increasingly being utilized with the intent of optimizing a variety of processes within

DOI: 10.1201/9781003624875-2

healthcare, including diagnostics, treatment planning, and administrative tasks such as scheduling (Faiyazuddin et al., 2025). Nevertheless, these advancements are accompanied by a series of ethical, legal, and social challenges that must be carefully navigated to fully realize the expected benefits of AI technologies while safeguarding public trust and maintaining high standards of care (Al-Hwsali et al., 2023; Gerke, Minssen, & Cohen, 2020; Cohen, Amarasingham et al., 2014).

1.2 NEED FOR AI IN MODERN HEALTHCARE

The healthcare industry faces increasing pressures globally and traditional approaches alone cannot adequately address ongoing challenges related to aging populations, increasing prevalence of chronic diseases, healthcare workforce shortages, and escalating costs, which have created a perfect storm of challenges requiring innovative solutions. The COVID-19 pandemic further exposed critical vulnerabilities in healthcare systems worldwide, accelerating the urgent need for technological interventions that can enhance resilience, efficiency, and accessibility (Filip et al., 2022).

As summarized in this chapter and throughout the book, the rapid advancement of AI in healthcare has reached a critical point, creating extensive debate among actors from various fields. The ability of AI technologies to enhance diagnostic accuracy, personalize treatment options, and improve operational efficiencies presents a great promise for the future of healthcare (Asonganyi et al., 2025). However, realizing this promise is contingent upon addressing several fundamental questions revolving around transparency, accountability, and the preservation of person-centered care. The present landscape suggests that while AI can significantly improve healthcare delivery systems, it is critical to include ethical considerations deeply in the design, implementation, and governance of AI technologies to prevent potential harms (Al-Hashimi & Hamdan, 2021; Aldosari & Alanazi, 2024) to both patients and health workers.

As global healthcare systems are currently grappling with intense pressures affecting their capacity to deliver care that appropriately responds to the increased needs of aging populations, a higher burden of chronic diseases, and both human and financial resource constraints, the search for increased efficiencies has intensified. As a result, a range of AI-based innovations are gradually adopted. For example, management systems driven by algorithms are increasingly supplementing or replacing traditional human decision-making processes across healthcare organizations, in hopes that this approach increases operational efficiencies. Such AI decision systems are applied to various administrative and clinical processes including staff scheduling, aiming to optimize it, or to clinical protocols to capitalize on findings from existing successful approaches to reduce errors and identify potential problems early on based on pattern identification. However, despite their great promise, these applications require careful examination of the ways in which AI technologies can augment, rather than compromise, the quality, equity, and compassion inherent in healthcare delivery (Janssen et al., 2024; Turchioe et al., 2024). While the incorporation of AI into administrative and clinical health systems aims to enhance efficiency, it could inadvertently introduce additional layers of complexity that must be managed with sensitivity to ethical, equity, and legal implications (Subías-Beltrán et al., 2024).

Furthermore, AI offers unprecedented opportunities to address multifaceted challenges in the healthcare industry. AI's ability to process vast amounts of data, identify patterns invisible to human cognition, and provide real-time insights positions it as a powerful ally in improving patient outcomes, streamlining operations, and advancing health and medical knowledge (Cheng et al., 2025). Unsurprisingly, given its significant estimated potential to contribute to healthcare, current estimates suggest that the global AI in healthcare market reached USD 20.9 billion in 2024, with projections indicating growth to USD 148.4 billion by 2029, reflecting a compound annual growth rate of 48.1% (SoluteLabs, 2025).

1.3 TRANSPARENCY AND ETHICAL IMPLICATIONS IN HEALTHCARE AI

The concept of transparency within healthcare AI extends far beyond technical explainability, and it requires a broader engagement with the principles of accountability, fairness in resource allocation, and open communication regarding the limitations of AI models. It could be concerning when algorithmic scheduling systems used to plan staff shifts or book patient appointments operate as opaque "black boxes," thereby creating critical inquiries from providers and patients and potentially creating or perpetuating inequalities (Bieri & Matt, 2025; Samorani & Blount, 2020). Lack of transparency in AI diagnostic tools can have dire repercussions, potentially undermining the foundational trust required for effective patient-provider interactions (Wadden, 2023). Lack of adequate transparency may overshadow the ethical obligations toward ensuring safe and quality care, thus further complicating the healthcare landscape (Jeelani et al., 2024; García-Gómez et al., 2024).

Furthermore, ethical implications present questions related to issues of patient privacy and data security, since healthcare data is inherently sensitive and vulnerable to exploitation (Eappen et al., 2025). As healthcare organizations increasingly rely on AI-driven tools, robust data protection measures should be instituted to safeguard sensitive patient information. Regulatory frameworks, such as the General Data Protection Regulation (GDPR) enacted by the European Union, exemplify the legal structures necessary to address these concerns effectively (Eappen et al., 2025; Morr et al., 2024). Upholding data privacy not only requires stringent security protocols but also encourages the development of AI models that prioritize ethical considerations, thereby fostering mutual trust between patients and care providers (Buitlear et al., 2023).

The integration of AI into clinical practice comes with ethical challenges that require constant oversight. Weiner et al. propose implementing a review process before AI systems are deployed, where interdisciplinary experts assess bias, transparency, and ethical implications. By scrutinizing these elements, the integration of AI in healthcare could avoid exacerbating existing inequities and, instead, foster more equitable delivery of services (Weiner et al., 2025). Such oversight becomes imperative as the reliance on AI technologies increases; without it, healthcare systems risk overlooking critical issues that could adversely affect patient welfare.

Establishing robust ethical frameworks is essential for the responsible deployment of AI in healthcare. Naik et al. argue that clarity regarding those who hold responsibility for AI outcomes is paramount, especially as the line between human and AI decision-making is blurred (Naik et al., 2022). This discussion around accountability should extend to the ways in which AI systems are monitored, assessed, and improved, ensuring that ethical considerations remain at the forefront of AI integration. To promote shared responsibility and trust, all involved actors should continuously engage in conversations regarding the implications of AI decisions for patient care.

1.4 THE ROLE OF PATIENTS AND HEALTH WORKERS IN AI TECHNOLOGY ADOPTION

It is essential to adopt AI initiatives in healthcare that actively and meaningfully involve patients (Banerjee et al., 2022) and health workers (Marinescu et al., 2025) in the research, development, implementation, and evaluation stages. These collaborative relationships could empower patients and health workers while also enhancing the design and efficacy of AI solutions. Banerjee et al. (2022) contend that involving patients in AI research is critical, particularly in contexts where their personal data will inform the development of healthcare applications. Engaging patients will increase the likelihood that the AI technologies developed align more closely with their needs, expectations, and ethical standards (Banerjee et al., 2022). This participatory model promotes transparency, allowing patients to (i) understand how their data is utilized and (ii) benefit from the AI systems expected to affect their healthcare journeys. Further, as healthcare professionals and institutions seek to integrate AI, understanding the factors influencing their acceptance and use of AI technologies is crucial. Marinescu et al. (2025) highlight that perceived control and transparency are significant determinants in the acceptance by health workers of AI-driven clinical decision-support systems (AI-CDSSs). Specifically, professionals who view AI as a flexible tool that could enhance their decision-making rather than replace it are more inclined to embrace its use (Marinescu et al., 2025). Expectedly, this openness fosters an environment where AI systems can be vetted, refined, and improved through feedback, thus encouraging more widespread adoption.

Not unlike other novel technologies, even though AI offers the potential for significant advancements in healthcare delivery, it also faces skepticism from the public. Esmaeilzadeh (2020) identifies a gap between the aspirations for AI in healthcare and the reality perceived by consumers. Engaging with public concerns regarding accountability-related to negligence or errors caused by AI systems is paramount (Esmaeilzadeh, 2020). It is essential to establish a transparent framework that includes multiple involved actors: healthcare providers, AI developers, health and insurance institutions, professional regulatory bodies, and the patients themselves. This multifaceted approach ensures all parties involved share responsibility in safeguarding the integrity of healthcare solutions powered by AI.

1.4.1 Medical Liability and the Complexity of Diagnosis

One of the most debated aspects of AI in healthcare is determining medical liability. Cestonaro et al. (2023) argue that the lack of explainability seen in many AI algorithms raises questions about the soundness of diagnoses generated by these systems. In an environment where providers may unduly trust AI recommendations, the potential for medical malpractice complicates the accountability landscape (Cestonaro et al., 2023). This situation underscores the necessity to adopt only AI tools that offer transparency in their decision-making processes, thus allowing healthcare professionals to discern when they can legitimately rely on AI-generated insights.

1.5 TRUST AND COLLABORATION IN IMPLEMENTATION

Building trust in AI technologies is crucial for effective implementation. Steerling et al. (2023) emphasize that aligning AI systems with human values and addressing the social dynamics within care settings could impact trustworthiness. Particularly, those individuals who are seen as authoritative or influential, such as physicians, nurses, or family members, play a pivotal role in shaping patient perceptions of AI (Steerling et al., 2023). Understanding these dynamics is essential for advancing the acceptance of AI tools within the general public. Establishing trust requires a transparent implementation strategy, wherein the advantages of AI are clearly communicated alongside a demonstration of consistent ethical practices.

In adopting AI technologies, compliance with data protection regulations such as the GDPR and HIPAA must be prioritized to protect patient data and build confidence in AI-driven healthcare solutions. Koo et al. (2024) assert that algorithmic transparency and interpretability are vital components in maintaining ethical standards and ensuring patient safety. In addition, creating a sense of autonomy among both healthcare professionals and patients increases engagement with AI systems and enhances the potential for better health outcomes, especially in an era where AI decisions can significantly impact patient outcomes (Koo et al., 2024).

Furthermore, AI has the potential to augment clinical decision-making by efficiently processing vast amounts of data, leading to tailored recommendations for individual patients. Giordano et al. (2021) illustrate how machine learning algorithms can support clinicians in identifying high-risk patients and making informed decisions about appropriate interventions. By incorporating patient preferences and values into the decision-making process, healthcare systems can utilize AI to facilitate shared decision-making, aligning clinical practices with broader patient-centered care initiatives (Giordano et al., 2021).

1.6 CONSIDERING THE SOCIETAL IMPLICATIONS OF USING AI IN HEALTHCARE

As AI continues to be increasingly integrated in healthcare systems globally, it is essential to consider its wider societal implications. Stroud et al. (2024) emphasize the need to focus on patient information needs when working to create transparent and trustworthy AI systems. By fostering an understanding of the ways in which AI impacts care delivery and by engaging patients in the safety discourse, we could mitigate concerns surrounding inequity and further foster trust in AI solutions (Stroud et al., 2024). The transformation of healthcare through AI technologies must adopt a holistic view, considering public perceptions, ethical considerations, and the potential social ramifications of AI's widespread implementation.

Moreover, achieving an inclusive and responsible AI ecosystem necessitates vigilance regarding equity and diverse representation in dataset development or model training. Hilling et al. (2025) advocate for prioritizing diversity not only among algorithm developers but also in the datasets that inform AI systems. This diversity is crucial to avoid biases that may perpetuate disparities in healthcare outcomes. Effective governance frameworks must be implemented to ensure AI technologies are developed and applied in ways that uphold ethical principles, support the equitable distribution of care, and enhance the overall health landscape (Hilling et al., 2025).

1.7 THE EVOLUTION OF AI TECHNOLOGIES AND FUTURE OUTLOOK

The dynamic nature of AI technologies presents opportunities for continuous innovation in healthcare. However, as AI systems evolve, patients and clinicians should be supported to improve their understanding of AI's ethical implications and governance needs. Vayena et al. (2018) emphasize the necessity for ongoing dialogue regarding data protection, algorithmic transparency, and accountability to earn the trust of both patients and healthcare professionals. Such an evolving framework should embrace feedback from various actors to fine-tune AI systems, ensuring that these cutting-edge tools truly serve the best interests of patient care (Vayena et al., 2018). Furthermore, the critical examination of algorithmic transparency and its implications for workforce management should be investigated, addressing fundamental questions about the ways in which AI-driven systems could impact hiring or employment conditions, including the right to unionize, pay rates, or occupational health and safety (Holland & Hart LLP, 2024). Studies show that the use of algorithms in healthcare raises significant concerns about transparency, accountability, and bias, particularly as these systems increasingly influence critical decisions about resource allocation and patient care (Ananny & Crawford, 2018). The U.S. Department of Health and Human Services has established the first transparency requirements for AI algorithms in certified health IT, recognizing that healthcare professionals require access to consistent, baseline information about the algorithms they use to support decision-making and assess systems for fairness, appropriateness, and safety (Federal Register, 2024).

Emerging AI technologies could further advance patient-centered care through intelligent, adaptive systems that prioritize individual patient needs and outcomes including (i) examination of bidirectional healthcare communication systems that create seamless device-provider interactions, (ii) adaptive technologies that strengthen clinical decision-making skills, and (iii) personalized healthcare approaches that leverage sophisticated AI algorithms (Kumar et al., 2024). Moreover, the transformative potential of AI technologies in healthcare has illustrated that machine learning algorithms can significantly improve diagnostic accuracy, demonstrating remarkable ability in identifying anomalies in medical imaging and predicting disease progression. Furthermore, AI systems, when designed with patient-centered principles at the forefront, can enhance the personalization of treatment plans by building on analysis results from large datasets, which reveal insights that could guide tailored clinical decision-making. Nonetheless, the success of such AI applications is inextricably linked to the availability of high-quality data; therefore, continuous efforts to enhance data collection processes, promote high data standards, and ensure collaborations between technologists and healthcare professionals are essential (Al-Hwsali et al., 2023; Kaur et al., 2023).

The integration of wearable IoT technologies represents a paradigm shift toward continuous, personalized monitoring that supports both chronic care management and independent living. Research indicates that IoT-enabled wearable devices facilitate real-time monitoring of vital signs, including blood pressure, temperature, oxygen levels, and heart rate, with high accuracy and efficiency in predicting new health conditions or changes in existing ones (Gunn et al., 2025; Taherdoost, 2024). These technologies show promise for aging populations and individuals with chronic diseases, enabling remote health monitoring that supports independent living while reducing healthcare costs (Varatharajan et al., 2018).

Furthermore, AI technologies are not limited to predictive analytics and decision-support; they could encompass various innovative applications, including telehealth, wearable devices, and robotic-assisted procedures. The rapid emergence of these technologies necessitates a commitment to maintaining a patient-centered focus and grappling with the ethical challenges they present. Adaptations should be made to ensure that, as systems evolve, they remain inclusive and equitable, particularly for marginalized populations that have historically faced barriers to accessing healthcare resources. Access disparities must be addressed early in the AI development process, to empower all patients equally rather than exacerbate existing inequalities (Jain et al., 2020; Rehburg et al., 2024).

1.7.1 Specialized Clinical Applications and Deep Learning Integration

Innovations in healthcare encompass cutting-edge applications of AI in healthcare, including deep learning approaches for rapid abdominal trauma diagnosis and injury assessment that streamline emergency patient care (Cheng et al., 2024). Recent research demonstrates that deep learning AI models can achieve remarkable accuracy in detecting traumatic abdominal injuries affecting solid organs, with studies showing very high accuracy rates for spleen, liver, and kidney injuries (Cheng et al., 2024). These developments are particularly significant given that traumatic injury causes nearly 4.4 million deaths annually worldwide, which constitute around 8% of total deaths, with rapid and accurate detection being key to effective treatment and favorable patient outcomes (Radiological Society of North America, 2023).

Furthermore, technological advances such as transparent deep neural network systems utilize molecular properties for drug classification while maintaining transparency in clinical decision-making processes. In addition, the 2023 RSNA Abdominal Trauma Detection AI Challenge, featuring over 4,000 CT examinations from 23 sites across 14 countries, has demonstrated the global scope and collaborative potential of AI applications in trauma care (Shen et al., 2024).

1.7.2 Disease-Preparedness and Systemic Healthcare Enhancement

In recent years, AI integration contributed to enhanced disease-preparedness capabilities, leveraging predictive analytics and machine learning to improve healthcare system readiness and response to public health challenges. The COVID-19 pandemic highlighted the critical importance of using AI technologies in healthcare, with over 17 billion IoT-connected devices predicted for 2024, surging to more than 30 billion by 2030, reflecting the rapid expansion of connected medical devices (Healthcare IT News, 2024). The COVID-19 pandemic has underscored both the extraordinary potential of AI technologies and the imperative for well-structured and transparent systems during health emergencies. The effectiveness of AI in predictive modeling, contact tracing, and logistical support during the pandemic has illuminated the necessity for responsive systems that can adapt to new health crises while upholding ethical standards. Health institutions could learn valuable lessons from the COVID-19 experience and aim to integrate the capabilities and insights gained into systemic designs that address both immediate healthcare needs and long-term sustainability of health systems. Efforts to ensure that AI systems remain flexible enough to tackle unforeseen challenges should go hand in hand with robust ethical outlines (Rane et al., 2024; Lima, 2023).

Research indicates that healthcare professionals' express concerns about overreliance on AI systems and the appropriate allocation of responsibility when AI tools are used in clinical decision-making. AI systems can be designed to enhance rather than replace human judgment and compassion in healthcare delivery, ensuring that the human elements that remain central to effective care are preserved and strengthened. Furthermore, transitioning toward a future dominated by AI requires a thoughtful integration of technological innovations with core human values. Healthcare systems that embed ethical considerations into their operational frameworks can achieve systems that are not only efficient and predictive but also compassionate and inclusive. Achieving this vision relies on building governance structures that adapt to technological advancement while ensuring accountability, transparency, and respect for patient autonomy (Rhem, 2023). Meaningful collaboration among healthcare providers, technologists, regulators, and patients will be crucial in developing holistic approaches that address the myriad challenges faced by the healthcare sector.

1.7.3 Ethical Implementation

Multifaceted examination of AI applications throughout the healthcare spectrum shows the pressing need to marry ethical and transparency considerations with technical advancements. The collective wisdom drawn from such insights will serve as a guide for navigating the complex landscape of AI in healthcare. Carefully analyzing the ethical implications of technology applications serves multiple audiences including healthcare decision-makers, health professionals, IT technologists, policymakers, and students, offering them theoretical foundations coupled with practical guidance to ensure that the AI-based technologies adopted are ethical, safe, and patient-centered. When rolling out new AI-based health technologies, those responsible for their implementation should communicate clearly the theoretical aspects of responsible AI deployment but also provide actionable insights that can inform best practices for implementation (Gaudeul et al., 2024). Moreover, institutionalizing a culture of transparency and accountability is imperative for the responsible integration of AI into everyday healthcare practice. Engaging in ongoing dialogues among involved actors will help demystify AI technologies and redress potential biases and ethical concerns before they manifest in detrimental ways. Ultimately, as the healthcare landscape continues to evolve, the emphasis on ethical implementation must remain a guiding principle. The successful navigation of these complexities will rely on fostering an environment of shared responsibility, one that reinforces the principles that resonate with the mission of healthcare: healing, caring, and serving the diverse needs of patients with dignity and respect.

Research evidence indicates that healthcare professionals' express concerns about overreliance on AI systems that are not transparent and the appropriate allocation of responsibility when AI tools are used in clinical decision-making. Accordingly, AI systems should be designed to enhance rather than replace human judgment and compassion in healthcare delivery, ensuring that the human elements that remain central to effective care are preserved and strengthened. Furthermore, transitioning toward a future dominated by AI requires a thoughtful integration of technological innovations with core human values. Healthcare systems that embed ethical considerations into their operational frameworks can facilitate AI applications that are not only accurate and efficient but also compassionate and inclusive. Achieving this vision relies on building governance structures that adapt to technological advancement while ensuring accountability, transparency, and respect for patient autonomy (Rhem, 2023). Meaningful collaboration among healthcare providers, technologists, regulators, and patients will be crucial in developing holistic approaches that address the myriad challenges faced by the healthcare sector.

In summary, the implementation of AI technologies in healthcare presents transformative potential; nevertheless, it also poses significant challenges requiring transparency, accountability, and inclusiveness. The integration of patients and healthcare professionals in the development and deployment of AI systems promotes trust and aligns technological advancements with ethical considerations. By upholding transparency in AI processes and fostering a collaborative environment among involved actors, we have a better likelihood of navigating the complexities of AI in healthcare to ultimately enhance patient care while ensuring responsible and equitable treatment practices. The journey toward a transparent AI system in healthcare is a shared endeavor that calls for vigilance, ongoing dialogue, and a commitment to the values that define compassionate care.

REFERENCES

AL-Hashimi, M., & Hamdan, A. (2021). Artificial intelligence and coronavirus COVID-19: Applications, impact and future implications. In B. Alareeni, A. Hamdan, & I. Elgedawy (Eds.), *The Importance of New Technologies and Entrepreneurship in Business Development: In The Context of Economic Diversity in Developing Countries.* ICBT 2020. Lecture Notes in Networks and Systems, vol 194. Springer, Cham. https://doi.org/10.1007/978-3-030-69221-6_64

Al-Hwsali, A., Alsaadi, B., Abdi, N., Khatab, S., Alzubaidi, M., Solaiman, B., … & Househ, M. (2023). Scoping review: Legal and ethical principles of artificial intelligence in public health. *Studies in Health Technology and Informatics*, 305, 640–643. https://doi.org/10.3233/shti230579

Aldosari, B., & Alanazi, A. (2024). Pitfalls of artificial intelligence in medicine. *Studies in Health Technology and Informatics*, 316, 554–555. https://doi.org/10.3233/shti240474

Alowais, S., Alghamdi, S., Alsuhebany, N., Alqahtani, T., Alshaya, A., Almohareb, S., … & Albekairy, A. (2023). Revolutionizing healthcare: The role of AI in clinical practice. *BMC Medical Education*, 23(1). https://doi.org/10.1186/s12909-023-04698-z

Ananny, M., & Crawford, K. (2018). Seeing without knowing: Limitations of algorithmic transparency. *New Media & Society*, 20(3), 973–989. https://doi.org/10.1177/1461444816676645

Apell, P., & Eriksson, H. (2023). Artificial intelligence (AI) healthcare technology innovations: The current state and challenges from a life science industry perspective. *Technology Analysis & Strategic Management*, 35(2), 179–193. https://doi.org/10.1080/09537325.2021.1971188

Asonganyi, E. (2025). Preparedness of the local population for the uptake of AI and digital one health for home healthcare of emerging and reemerging infectious diseases in southwest and littoral regions of cameroon. *Journal of Tropical Medicine*, 2025(1). https://doi.org/10.1155/jotm/8896234

Banerjee, S., Alsop, P., Jones, L., & Cardinal, R. (2022). Patient and public involvement to build trust in artificial intelligence: A framework, tools, and case studies. *Patterns*, 3(6), 100506. https://doi.org/10.1016/j.patter.2022.100506

Bieri, M., & Matt, C. (2025). Algorithmic fairness in shift scheduling–assessing the fairness perceptions of healthcare workers. *AMCIS 2025 Proceedings*, 17. https://authorconnect.aisnet.org/conferences/AMCIS2025/papers/1274

Buitlear, C., Byrne, A., McEvoy, E., Camara, A., Yılmaz, M., McCarren, A., … & Clarke, P. (2023). Investigating sources and effects of bias in AI-based systems – results from an mlr., 20–35. https://doi.org/10.1007/978-3-031-42307-9_2

Cestonaro, C., Delicati, A., Marcante, B., Caenazzo, L., & Tozzo, P. (2023). Defining medical liability when AI is applied on diagnostic algorithms: A systematic review. *Frontiers in Medicine*, 10. https://doi.org/10.3389/fmed.2023.1305756

Cheng, C. T., Lin, H. H., Hsu, C. P., Chen, H. W., Huang, J. F., Hsieh, C. H., Fu, C. Y., Chung, I. F., & Liao, C. H. (2024). Deep learning for automated detection and localization of traumatic abdominal solid organ injuries on CT scans. *Journal of Imaging Informatics in Medicine*, 37(3), 1113–1123. https://doi.org/10.1007/s10278-024-01038-5

Cheng, C. T., Ooyang, C. H., Liao, C. H., & Kang, S. C. (2025). Applications of deep learning in trauma radiology: A narrative review. *Biomedical Journal*, 48(1), 100743. https://doi.org/10.1016/j.bj.2024.100743

Cohen, I. G., Amarasingham, R., Shah, A., Xie, B., & Lo, B. (2014). The legal and ethical concerns that arise from using complex predictive analytics in health care. *Health Affairs*, 33(7), 1139–1147. https://doi.org/10.1377/hlthaff.2014.0048

Eappen, P., Gunn, V., Singh Brar, H., & Stedman, I. (2025). *Capitalizing on the Transformative Role of AI and Human Capital to Strengthen Cybersecurity in Healthcare*. Taylor & Francis. https://doi.org/10.1201/9781003504979-7

Esmaeilzadeh, P. (2020). Use of ai-based tools for healthcare purposes: A survey study from consumers' perspectives. *BMC Medical Informatics and Decision Making*, 20(1). https://doi.org/10.1186/s12911-020-01191-1

Faiyazuddin, M., Rahman, S. J. Q., Anand, G., Siddiqui, R. K., Mehta, R., Khatib, M. N., … & Sah, R. (2025). The impact of artificial intelligence on healthcare: A comprehensive review of advancements in diagnostics, treatment, and operational efficiency. *Health Science Reports*, 8(1), e70312. https://doi.org/10.1002/hsr2.70312

Federal Register. (2024). Health data, technology, and interoperability: Certification program updates, algorithm transparency, and information sharing. *Federal Register*, 89(6), 1767–2175. https://www.federalregister.gov/documents/2024/01/09/2023-28857/health-data-technology-and-interoperability-certification-program-updates-algorithm-transparency-and

Filip, R., Gheorghita Puscaselu, R., Anchidin-Norocel, L., Dimian, M., & Savage, W. K. (2022). Global challenges to public health care systems during the COVID-19 pandemic: A review of pandemic measures and problems. *Journal of Personalized Medicine*, 12(8), 1295. https://doi.org/10.3390/jpm12081295

García-Gómez, J., Blanes-Selva, V., & Doñate-Martínez, A. (2024). Proposing an AI passport as a mitigating action of risk associated to artificial intelligence in healthcare. *Studies in Health Technology and Informatics*, 316, 547–551. https://doi.org/10.3233/shti240472

Gaudeul, A., Arrigoni, O., Charisi, V., Escobar-Planas, M., & Hupont, I. (2024). Understanding the impact of human oversight on discriminatory outcomes in AI-supported decision-making. *Frontiers in Artificial Intelligence and Applications*, 392, 1067–1074. https://doi.org/10.3233/faia240598

Gerke, S., Minssen, T., & Cohen, G. (2020). Ethical and legal challenges of artificial intelligence-driven healthcare. In *Artificial Intelligence in Healthcare* (pp. 295–336). Academic Press. https://doi.org/10.1016/B978-0-12-818438-7.00012-5

Giordano, C., Brennan, M., Mohamed, B., Rashidi, P., Modave, F., & Tighe, P. (2021). Accessing AI for clinical decision-making. *Frontiers in Digital Health*, 3. https://doi.org/10.3389/fdgth.2021.645232

Goralski, M. A., & Tan, T. K. (2020). Artificial intelligence and sustainable development. *The International Journal of Management Education*, 18(1), 100330. https://doi.org/10.1016/j.ijme.2019.100330

Gunn, V., Eappen, P., Brar, H. S., Brulin, E., & Muntaner, C. (2025). Integration of wearable devices in healthcare: The need to examine their implications for health workers. In P. Eappen, N. R. Vajjhala, D. Zikos, & K. P. Davidson (Eds.), *Remote Monitoring and Wearable Devices in Healthcare. Information Systems Engineering and Management*, vol. 63. Springer, Cham. https://doi.org/10.1007/978-3-031-98897-4_6

Harerimana, G., Kim, J., Yoo, H., & Jang, B. (2019). Deep learning for electronic health records analytics. *IEEE Access*, 7, 101245–101259. https://doi.org/10.1109/access.2019.2928363

Healthcare IT News. (2024). How IoT is transforming remote patient monitoring. https://www.healthcareitnews.com/news/how-iot-transforming-remote-patient-monitoring

Hilling, D., Ihaddouchen, I., Buijsman, S., Townsend, R., Gommers, D., & Genderen, M. (2025). The imperative of diversity and equity for the adoption of responsible AI in healthcare. *Frontiers in Artificial Intelligence*, 8. https://doi.org/10.3389/frai.2025.1577529

Holland & Hart LLP. (2024). Algorithmic accountability: The next frontier in employment law? Employers' Lawyers Blog. https://www.employerslawyersblog.com/2024/08/algorithmic-accountability-the-next-frontier-in-employment-law.html

Hossain, M., Muhammad, G., & Guizani, N. (2020). Explainable AI and mass surveillance system-based healthcare framework to combat covid-i9 like pandemics. *IEEE Network*, 34(4), 126–132. https://doi.org/10.1109/mnet.011.2000458

Howington, J., & Andrade, M. (2022). Preventing the next pandemic: A critical analysis of the utilization of AI in the U.S. healthcare system. https://doi.org/10.21203/rs.3.rs-1721483/v1

Hu, S. (2023). Deep learning in healthcare. *Highlights in Science Engineering and Technology*, 57, 279–285. https://doi.org/10.54097/hset.v57i.10014

Jain, V., Singh, N., Pradhan, S., & Gupta, P. (2020). Factors influencing AI implementation decision in Indian healthcare industry: A qualitative inquiry. In *International Conference on Transfer and Diffusion of IT (TDIT 2020), Tiruchirappalli, India, December 18–19, 2020* (pp. 635–640). Springer. https://doi.org/10.1007/978-3-030-64849-7_56

Janssen, A., Kavisha, S., Johnson, A., Marinic, A., Teede, H., & Shaw, T. (2024). Implementation of artificial intelligence applications in Australian healthcare organisations: Environmental scan findings. https://doi.org/10.3233/shti231142

Jeelani, O., Njie, M., & Korzhuk, V. (2024). Methods and algorithms of ensuring data privacy in AI-based healthcare systems and technologies. https://doi.org/10.3233/shti240640

Kaur, P., Mack, A., Patel, N., Pal, A., Singh, R., Michaud, A., & Mulflur, M. (2023). Unlocking the potential of artificial intelligence (AI) for healthcare. In S. P. Stawicki (Ed.), *Artificial Intelligence in Medicine and Surgery – An Exploration of Current Trends, Potential Opportunities, and Evolving Threats* (Vol. 1). IntechOpen. https://doi.org/10.5772/intechopen.111489

Koo, T., Zakaria, A., Ng, J., & Leong, X. (2024). Systematic review of the application of AI in healthcare and nursing care. *Malaysian Journal of Medical Sciences*, 31(5), 135–142. https://doi.org/10.21315/mjms2024.31.5.9

Kranthi, M., Sailaja, S., & Jyothi, E. (2024). Deep learning approaches for medical image processing in the big data era. *IJSMCSE*, 1(1), 24–31. https://doi.org/10.58599/ijsmcse.2024.1108

Krishnan, G., Singh, S., Pathania, M., Gosavi, S., Abhishek, S., Parchani, A., … & Dhar, M. (2023). AI in clinical medicine: Catalyzing a sustainable global healthcare paradigm. *Frontiers in Artificial Intelligence*, 6. https://doi.org/10.3389/frai.2023.1227091

Kumar, S., Singh, A., & Patel, R. (2024). The role of AI in hospitals and clinics: Transforming healthcare in the 21st century. *Healthcare Technology Letters*, 11(2), 45–52. https://doi.org/10.1049/htl2.12078

Lima, M. (2023). Computer vision: Anthropology of algorithmic bias in facial analysis tool. In A. Soofastaei (Ed.), *Numerical Simulation: Advanced Techniques for Science and Engineering*. IntechOpen. https://doi.org/10.5772/intechopen.110330

Malik, Y., Sircar, S., Bhat, S., Ansari, M., Pande, T., Kumar, P., … & Dhama, K. (2020). How AI may help the covid-19 pandemic: Pitfalls and lessons for the future. *Reviews in Medical Virology*, 31(5), 1–11. https://doi.org/10.1002/rmv.2205

Marinescu, Ş., Oncioiu, I., & Ghibanu, A. (2025). The digital transformation of healthcare through intelligent technologies: A path dependence-augmented-unified theory of acceptance and use of technology model for clinical decision support systems. *Healthcare*, 13(11), 1222. https://doi.org/10.3390/healthcare13111222

Meng, C., Trinh, L., Xu, N., Enouen, J., & Liu, Y. (2022). Interpretability and fairness evaluation of deep learning models on mimic-iv dataset. *Scientific Reports*, 12(1). https://doi.org/10.1038/s41598-022-11012-2

Morr, C., Singh, D., Sawhney, V., Fernandes, S., El-Lahib, Y., & Gorman, R. (2024). Exploring the intersection of AI and inclusive design for people with disabilities. *Studies in Health Technology and Informatics*, 316, 556–559. https://doi.org/10.3233/shti240475

Naik, N., Hameed, B., Shetty, D., Swain, D., Shah, M., Paul, R., … & Somani, B. (2022). Legal and ethical consideration in AI in healthcare: Who takes responsibility?. *Frontiers in Surgery*, 9. https://doi.org/10.3389/fsurg.2022.862322

Nguyen, D., Lan, C., & Chan, C. (2021). Deep ensemble learning approaches in healthcare to enhance the prediction and diagnosing performance: The workflows, deployments, and surveys on the statistical, image-based, and sequential datasets. *International Journal of Environmental Research and Public Health*, 18(20), 10811. https://doi.org/10.3390/ijerph182010811

Novelli, C., Taddeo, M. & Floridi, L. (2024). Accountability in artificial intelligence: What it is and how it works. *AI & Society*, 39, 1871–1882. https://doi.org/10.1007/s00146-023-01635-y

Purushotham, S., Meng, C., Che, Z., & Liu, Y. (2018). Benchmarking deep learning models on large healthcare datasets. *Journal of Biomedical Informatics*, 83, 112–134. https://doi.org/10.1016/j.jbi.2018.04.007

Radiological Society of North America. (2023). RSNA abdominal trauma detection AI challenge. https://www.rsna.org/rsnai/ai-image-challenge/abdominal-trauma-detection-ai-challenge

Rane, J., Kaya, Ö., Mallick, S., & Rane, N. (2024). Enhancing black-box models: Advances in explainable artificial intelligence for ethical decision-making. In J. Rane, S. K. Mallick, Ömer Kaya, & N. L. Rane, *Future Research Opportunities for Artificial Intelligence in Industry 4.0 and 5.0* (pp. 136–180). Deep Science Publishing. https://doi.org/10.70593/978-81-981271-0-5_4

Rehburg, F., Graefe, A., Hübner, M., & Thun, S. (2024). How interoperability can enable artificial intelligence in clinical applications. *Studies in Health Technology and Informatics*, 316, 596–600. https://doi.org/10.3233/shti240485

Rhem, A. (2023). Ethical use of data in AI applications. In M. Radenkovic (Ed.), *Ethics – Scientific Research, Ethical Issues, Artificial Intelligence and Education*. IntechOpen. https://doi.org/10.5772/intechopen.1001597

Samorani, M., & Blount, L. G. (2020). Machine learning and medical appointment scheduling: Creating and perpetuating inequalities in access to health care. *American Journal of Public Health*, 110(4), 440–441. https://doi.org/10.2105/AJPH.2020.305570

Shen, X., Zhou, Y., Shi, X. et al. (2024). The application of deep learning in abdominal trauma diagnosis by CT imaging. *World Journal of Emergency Surgery*, 19, 17. https://doi.org/10.1186/s13017-024-00546-7

Shimonski, R. (2020). *AI In Healthcare: How Artificial Intelligence is Changing IT Operations and Infrastructure Services*. John Wiley & Sons.

SoluteLabs. (2025). AI in healthcare: Building trust through accountability, responsibility & transparency. https://www.solutelabs.com/blog/ai-healthcare-accountability-responsibility-transparency

Steerling, E., Siira, E., Nilsén, P., Svedberg, P., & Nygren, J. (2023). Implementing AI in healthcare---the relevance of trust: A scoping review. *Frontiers in Health Services*, 3. https://doi.org/10.3389/frhs.2023.1211150

Stroud, A., Minteer, S., Zhu, X., Ridgeway, J., Miller, J., & Barry, B. (2024). Patient information needs for transparent and trustworthy AI in healthcare. *PLOS Digital Health*, 4, e0000826. https://doi.org/10.1371/journal.pdig.0000826

Subías-Beltrán, P., Pitarch, C., Migliorelli, C., Marte, L., Galofré, M., & Orte, S. (2024). In E. P. Dadios (Ed.), *Artificial Intelligence – Social, Ethical and Legal Issues*. IntechOpen. https://doi.org/10.5772/intechopen.1007444

Syrowatka, A., Kuznetsova, M., Alsubai, A., Beckman, A., Bain, P., Craig, K., … & Bates, D. (2021). Leveraging AI for pandemic preparedness and response: A scoping review to identify key use cases. *NPJ Digital Medicine*, 4(1). https://doi.org/10.1038/s41746-021-00459-8

Taherdoost, H. (2024). Wearable healthcare and continuous vital sign monitoring with IOT integration. *Computers, Materials & Continua,* 81(1), 79–104. https://doi.org/10.32604/cmc.2024.054378

Turchioe, M., Pepingco, C., Lytle, K., & Austin, R. (2024). Nurses' roles in artificial intelligence implementation: Results from a mixed-methods study. *Studies in Health Technology and Informatics*, 315, 223–227. https://doi.org/10.3233/shti240140

Varatharajan, R., Manogaran, G., Priyan, M. K., & Sundarasekar, R. (2018). Wearable sensor devices for early detection of Alzheimer disease using dynamic time warping algorithm. *Cluster Computing*, 21(1), 681–690. https://doi.org/10.1007/s10586-017-0977-2

Vayena, E., Blasimme, A., & Cohen, I. (2018). Machine learning in medicine: Addressing ethical challenges. *Plos Medicine*, 15(11), e1002689. https://doi.org/10.1371/journal.pmed.1002689

Wadden, J. J. (2023). Ethics and healthcare artificial intelligence: Some problems and solutions for advanced diagnostic systems (Doctoral dissertation, University of British Columbia). http://hdl.handle.net/2429/83850

Weiner, E., Dankwa-Mullan, I., Nelson, W., & Hassanpour, S. (2025). Ethical challenges and evolving strategies in the integration of AI into clinical practice. *Plos Digital Health*, 4(4), e0000810. https://doi.org/10.1371/journal.pdig.0000810

2 Algorithmic Scheduling Raises Questions of Transparency, Accountability, and the Future of Employment Conditions in Healthcare

Hilary Hall, Virginia Gunn, Karen Kennedy, Adam Elliott, Kelsey Morrison, and Matthew MacLeod

2.1 INTRODUCTION

Although antecedents and elements of algorithmic management (AM) have been percolating through healthcare for several decades, making the sector ripe for quick adoption of algorithmic management powered by recent advances in digital health technologies, the actual concept of AM has only recently been applied to healthcare research (Gunn, Eappen, Brar, ... & Muntaner, 2025; Rani et al., 2024; Staehelin et al., 2023; Yashnarbekov, 2025). In this chapter, we synthesize findings from an exploratory iterative review of available evidence regarding the application of algorithmic management in healthcare, with a focus on automated or algorithmic scheduling. Specifically, this chapter examines the use of algorithmic management in scheduling, addressing several transparency and accountability-related implications regarding staffing decisions. Additionally, the chapter discusses whether research on the application of algorithmic scheduling in healthcare incorporates considerations about its implications for health workers' employment and working conditions, work environment, health and well-being, or ethics. Several research gaps are highlighted, along with proposed directions for further study.

2.2 BACKGROUND

Healthcare systems across the world face constant change and evolution due to factors such as aging populations, new disease patterns, varying socioeconomic climates,

DOI: 10.1201/9781003624875-3

and novel technological developments, all with significant implications for the delivery of care. Swift technological advances in healthcare in recent decades have fundamentally changed the ways in which caring work is organized and directed (Cachata et al., 2024; Eappen, Stedman, & Gunn, 2025). While much attention has been paid to the economic or patient care impacts of digitalization, less focus has been directed toward the impact of informatics, health technologies, and digitization on the health labor force (Bronsoler et al., 2022; Eappen et al., 2025; Gunn, Eappen, Brar, ... & Muntaner, 2025). This lack of attention applies to algorithmic management, defined as the use of various digital technologies, ranging from simple to sophisticated, to automate or enhance managers' decision-making regarding work organization (e.g., planning work, surveillance, rewarding, disciplining, hiring, or firing workers) (Strauss Raats et al, 2024; Strauss Raats et al., 2025). Algorithmic management, first labeled by Lee et al. in 2015, is increasingly replacing, totally or partially, the work of human managers in organizations seeking to maximize efficiencies (Baiocco et al., 2022; Duggan et al., 2020; Fernández-Macías et al., 2023; Jarrahi et al., 2021; Lind et al., 2025; Milanez, 2025; Nilsson et al., 2025; Parent-Rocheleau & Parker, 2022; Rani et al., 2024; Williams & Khan, 2025; Wood, 2021). While algorithmic management is garnering increased attention from researchers across disciplines and economic sectors, to date most attention is directed to platform work, manufacturing, and logistics including warehousing and transportation, where these practices have been widely adopted (Baiocco et al., 2022; Duggan et al., 2020; Fernández-Macías et al., 2023; Jarrahi et al., 2021; Lind et al., 2025; Milanez, 2025; Nilsson et al., 2025; Rani et al., 2024; Wood, 2021).

Algorithmic management could have numerous implications for workers' employment and working conditions including intensified monitoring and surveillance, loss of professional autonomy, quantitative overload, increased pace and intensity, social isolation, lack of social support from co-workers and managers, reduced trust, lower job satisfaction, decreased engagement in work, increased power imbalances between workers and employers, and job insecurity (Baiocco et al., 2022; Duggan et al., 2020; Fernández-Macías et al., 2023; Jarrahi et al., 2021; Lind et al., 2025; Milanez, 2025; Nilsson et al., 2025; Parent-Rocheleau & Parker, 2022; Rani et al., 2024; Williams & Khan, 2025; Wood, 2021; Yashnarbekov, 2025). Despite an overwhelming array of negative implications, researchers contend that organizational choices and strategies regarding the mobilization and utilization of AM could moderate or alter its impact (Lee & Lee, 2023; Parent-Rocheleau & Parker, 2022). For example, algorithmic management could be used to maintain or improve the quality of work design (Parent-Rocheleau & Parker, 2022), or improve the accuracy of monitoring systems that facilitate proactive hazard identification and system maintenance, thus improving safety in mining or construction (Lee & Lee, 2023; Shevchenko & Slashchov, 2019). Unsurprisingly, given the numerous implications of algorithmic management for occupational health and safety, studying its range of manifestations across sectors and its impact on worker-related outcomes is a goal worth pursuing. This understanding would enable the development and implementation of interventions to reduce or mitigate the negative effects of algorithmic management on workers (Gunn, Quinlan, Lahti, … & Håkansta, 2025; Gunn, Strauss Raats, Lind, … & Håkansta, 2025).

2.3 METHODS

This study is based on an exploratory, iterative literature review of available evidence regarding the application of algorithmic management in healthcare conducted between January and November 2024. Since only a handful of healthcare-related studies used the concept of algorithmic management, a list of terms encompassing aspects of algorithmic management was created and refined through iterative searches. Search terms included: algorithmic supervision in healthcare, algorithms in healthcare, automation of managerial tasks in healthcare, algorithmic managerial control over medical authority, data-driven smart healthcare and workforce, digital workplace surveillance in healthcare, new public management in healthcare, automated workforce management, advanced management, algorithmic software, algorithmic scheduling systems, optimal scheduling, algorithmic scheduling, timesheet management, along with combinations of these terms and their synonyms.

To cover a multitude of databases, the search was done in Google Scholar, entering each key term separately and reviewing the first forty hits. Additionally, several nursing informatics or management-related journals (*Healthcare Management Science*; *Journal of Nursing Management*; *Nursing Management*; *Operations Research for Healthcare*; *Applied Clinical Informatics*; *Advanced Intelligent Systems*; *JMIR AI*; and *JMIR Medical Informatics*) were searched separately. The eligibility screening of titles and abstracts was done independently by two reviewers. Both the screening of full texts and data extraction were initially done by one reviewer for each study, followed by a second reviewer verifying the extraction and adding relevant information. Screening conflicts for both title/abstracts and full texts were resolved through discussions and with support from a third reviewer. Data extraction was completed using a tailored extraction form. For two extraction items, transparency and accountability in staffing decisions, the extraction was completed during the synthesis of findings stage, by one reviewer only. As this was an exploratory literature review, resources were neither screened for nor excluded based on quality.

While the larger literature review focused on a range of algorithmic management applications in healthcare, this chapter is limited to findings related to automated or algorithmic scheduling, commonly understood as the process of identifying the most advantageous way to assign health workers to shifts, often using several constraints to rank feasible solutions (Burke et al., 2010; Gutjahr & Rauner, 2007; Hadwan et al., 2013). The findings are presented in a narrative and tabular form.

2.3.1 Inclusion Criteria

To qualify for inclusion in the larger review, a study should have described—explicitly or implicitly—the use of algorithms to support decision-making made by human managers, or those working on their behalf (e.g., replace it totally or partially, or enhance it), regarding the organization of care work in healthcare settings. The focus was on decisions made to meet organizational goals, not clinician or professionally directed decisions made at the point of care and focused on patient outcomes. Studies covering digital tools that contribute to managerial decision-making processes by providing information that managers used to gather on their own to make work organization decisions were also considered. Eligible studies should have (i) clearly outlined the ways in which the algorithmic technology replaced, partially or totally, human decision-making and impacted the organization of work for health workers, including managers, (ii) be published in English before October 2024, and (iii) included an abstract or executive summary, and sufficient detail to allow data extraction for all included questions. Additionally, to be included in the analysis covered in this chapter, the publication should have addressed an automated scheduling system designed for healthcare workers, including managers. The review considered peer-reviewed journal articles, including conference papers.

2.3.2 Exclusion Criteria

In addition to excluding studies that did not meet the established inclusion criteria, we excluded those describing (i) the use of digital tools to meet the goals of clinicians, with no clear link made to the goals of the organization or management, or (ii) the ways in which digital health tools change the work of clinicians or other health workers without explicitly describing implications for work organization or management goals. Additionally, while algorithms designed to improve patient outcomes through clinical decision-making support might also influence the work of healthcare workers, supporting or, in some cases, replacing their care-related decision-making, studies examining such topics were outside the scope of this review and not considered for inclusion. Given that the term 'efficiency' can also relate to clinician time management, we excluded articles that mentioned efficiencies without situating the overall context of these efficiencies within organizational goals (e.g., use of digital tools to enable workers to complete more tasks, see more patients, etc.). We also excluded publications referring to clinician 'performance' in relation to standards of practice or evidence-informed practices to ensure a focus on employee performance in the context of work organization. Further, given this review was focused specifically on the use of algorithms for the replacement of human managers' work, we did not consider studies covering new ways in which digital tools can enable managerial control over previous aspects of work that were not under managerial control.

2.4 FINDINGS

Titles and abstracts of 285 relevant publications identified through Google Scholar and specific peer-reviewed journals were screened, with 55 relevant resources eligible for full article review across all eligible algorithmic management-related applications. One article was not accessible and of the remaining, 14 met the inclusion criteria. The 14 resources can be broadly characterized as related to compliance monitoring, automated scheduling, or workforce management systems. The latter are digital organizational systems that fully or partially replace managerial

TABLE 2.1
Characteristics of Included Studies

Number of Studies Included		10
Global Regions Represented*	Western Pacific	2
	Africa	1
	Europe	3
	Eastern Mediterranean	1
	Americas	1
Publication Date Range	Pre-2000	1
	2000–2010	3
	2011–2020	5
	2021–present	1
Status of Implementation	Implemented	5
	Planned	4
	Abstract future possibility	1
Definitions and Constructs Used	Explicitly referenced algorithmic management	0
	Did not explicitly use the term algorithmic management	10

* World Health Organization Regions (WHO, n.d.)

decision-making in the name of efficiency for allocation of resources, workforce planning, and/or staff scheduling (Krive, 2013). For this automated scheduling or health worker rostering-focused manuscript, we screened the titles and abstracts of these 14 studies, identifying ten relevant publications (Ahmed & Dalhem, 2019; Burke et al., 1999; Burke et al., 2010; Gutjahr & Rauner, 2007; Hadwan et al., 2013; Krive, 2013; Lartey & Akowuah, 2021; Legrain et al., 2020; Rönnberg & Larsson, 2010; Zhu et al., 2019).

Of the ten articles that use algorithmic management in the scheduling of healthcare staff, two include scheduling as part of a larger discussion about digital workforce management tools (Ahmed & Dalhem, 2019; Krive, 2013), while the remaining eight exclusively address the use of digital systems to fully or partially replace managerial decision-making about scheduling. Characteristics of the studies included are listed in Table 2.1.

2.4.1 Algorithmic or Automated Scheduling

The scheduling or rostering of staff refers to the assignment of a known quantity and skill mix of staff to a known demand for work (Burke et al., 1999; Rönnberg & Larsson, 2010). This managerial task is described as particularly complex and simultaneously important for its relation to safety (Ahmed & Dalhem, 2019), quality of care (Ahmed & Dalhem, 2019), and financial implications (Ahmed & Dalhem, 2019; Burke et al., 2010; Gutjahr & Rauner, 2007; Hadwan et al., 2013; Krive, 2013), including its impact on overtime and use of external staffing agencies (Krive, 2013;

Rönnberg & Larsson, 2010). Two studies indicate the use of automated scheduling for a variety of healthcare staff (Krive, 2013; Zhu et al., 2019) while the others focused specifically on the challenges of nurse rostering.

Rostering is described as distinct from, but related to, long-term planning decisions which include hiring and staff contract determinations such as part-time or full-time (Rönnberg & Larsson, 2010). For example, nursing shortages are described as leading to competition for workers, incentivizing organizations to find new ways to create quality schedules to improve recruitment and retention (Gutjahr & Rauner, 2007; Hadwan et al., 2013; Krive, 2013; Legrain et al., 2020; Rönnberg & Larsson, 2010; Zhu et al., 2019).

The international nature of the problem of healthcare scheduling is apparent as reported in Table 2.1. Implemented or planned automated scheduling included its use at specific hospitals, units, or associated clinics, as well as its use in regional care delivery networks. One article (Legrain et al., 2020) reported automated scheduling as an abstract future possibility in the form of an algorithm the authors submitted to the International Nurse Rostering Competition.

2.4.1.1 Brief Overview of the Use of Algorithms to Replace Managerial Decision-Making in Scheduling

Most scheduling-specific articles described replacing manual schedule generation with an algorithmic process guided by specific constraints (Burke et al., 1999; Burke et al., 2010; Gutjahr & Rauner, 2007; Hadwan et al., 2013; Lartey & Akowuah, 2021; Legrain et al., 2020; Rönnberg & Larsson, 2010; Zhu et al., 2019). Factors impacting the selection of constraints may include existing regulations and legal requirements of the country where the system has been implemented (Burke et al., 2010; Gutjahr & Rauner, 2007; Legrain et al., 2020), as well as varying organizational priorities such as maximizing nurses' working preferences or minimizing wage costs (Burke et al., 2010; Gutjahr & Rauner, 2007; Hadwan et al., 2013).

Hard constraints impose requirements the scheduling algorithm must meet in order to move forward with scheduling, such as a nurse being assigned to only one shift per day, ensuring the skill of the scheduled nurse meets the required demand, and the number of nurses being at least equal to the minimum staffing level set for the shift (Legrain et al., 2020). Soft constraints are aspirational goals for the algorithm, whose successful attainment is advisable to offer optimal service quality; however, meeting all of these is not required in order to move forward with scheduling (Legrain et al., 2020). Soft constraints may be violated in the development of the schedule, often referred to as costs, where each of the soft constraints can be weighted for different cost penalties (Burke et al., 1999; Burke et al., 2010; Gutjahr & Rauner, 2007; Hadwan et al., 2013; Lartey & Akowuah, 2021; Legrain et al., 2020).

Examples of soft constraints from Legrain et al. (2020) include the number of consecutive shifts a nurse works, the number of consecutive rest days the schedule creates, how many weekend shifts are scheduled, as well as nurses' personal preferences for one type of shift over another. As with hard constraints, these kinds of scheduling decisions would have been a responsibility of management before the use of algorithms.

2.4.1.2 Transparency in Algorithmic Decisions about Staffing

While a focus on transparency was not part of our initial data extraction, we noted a discrepancy in reports across included publications and extracted it as a secondary step. It was often difficult to ascertain how soft constraints were chosen or weighted in the identified resources. Only three scheduling-specific papers (Hadwan et al. 2013, Burke et al., 1999; Rönnberg & Larsson, 2010) included a specific discussion as to how soft constraints were determined or weighted. For example, Hadwan et al. (2013) report to have created their soft constraints in consultation with head nurses on different wards across the hospital, while Burke et al., (1999) indicate that some soft constraints in their system may be determined through agreement between the head nurse (or personnel manager) and the individual nurses.

Clarity as to how constraints are determined to be either hard or soft also varied across the scheduling-specific papers. Three papers (Burke et al., 1999; Gutjahr & Rauner, 2007; Rönnberg & Larsson, 2010) include some discussion of this distinction. For example, the minimum versus preferred number of personnel could be included as a hard or soft constraint by the system user in Burke et al. (1999). Furthermore, there is disparity across the articles where some may consider that, for example, working a day shift after a night shift is a hard constraint (Legrain et al., 2020), while others report this as a soft constraint (Lartey & Akowuah, 2021).

2.4.1.3 Workforce Management Tools

Krive (2013) describes the implementation of a specific workforce management platform whose goals were to reduce overtime, combine financial and scheduling reporting data, reduce the use of temporary staffing agencies, and increase productivity. Ahmed & Dalhem (2019) similarly implemented a specific workforce management system that included scheduling capacities as well as the capacity to (i) track and predict patient clinical status for staff allocation, (ii) base staffing levels on desired patient outcomes, and (iii) manage shortages and overtime through a given health unit's projected demand. In terms of operational specifics, these two resources do not describe hard or soft constraints of the systems deployed or the ways in which the system addresses competing demands in the execution of scheduling. Instead, these resources indicate that staff nurses can make duty requests through the system, as well as swap shifts with other nurses through the system (Ahmed & Dalhem, 2019; Krive, 2013).

2.4.1.4 Accountability in Algorithmic Decisions about Staffing

The degree of control retained by the manager or nurses in the use of automated scheduling was difficult to determine in most of the included publications. For example, the responsibility for approval of day on/off requests was not always clear. Burke et al. (2010) report these as soft constraints, which leave some ambiguity as to the autonomy of the manager in determining these requests). Rönnberg and Larsson (2010) meanwhile explain that leave requests become hard constraints in the deployment of the algorithm in their system; however, it is unclear in the article if these are pre-approved by the head nurse. Conversely, in Hadwan et al. (2013) there is no indication of the degree of control that would stay with hospital staff over the generated schedule. In Zhu et al. (2019) the manager is clearly positioned with the capacity to amend the schedule after its creation. Rönnberg and Larsson (2010), who are replacing a manual self-scheduling practice, indicate that because there will always be minor exceptions to the stated rules, the schedule produced should be considered a suggestion that can be amended by the nurses; this reflects a vocalized concern of the nurses in the study about their loss of influence in the scheduling process (Rönnberg & Larsson, 2010).

In an automatic scheduling experiment focused on the use of an institutionally created regional pool of nurses used to fill nurse needs (when individual hospitals cannot cover them), the specifications made by individuals deploying the scheduling algorithm may allow the posting of demands for open shifts very close to the day/time of the shift (e.g., minimum two days before) (Gutjahr & Rauner, 2007). Similarly, the scheduling algorithm may also finalize decisions on the nurse to be assigned to an open shift very close to the beginning of the shift (e.g., minimum two days before) (Gutjahr & Rauner, 2007). While it was not apparent that the experimental scenarios described used the minimum notice requirements, the possibility of using a scheduling system that posts and assigns shifts with such short notice could have implications for the working conditions, health, and well-being of the nurses who are assigned such shifts.

In Krive (2013), management decisions on scheduling are described as being replaced by the system's capacity to allow for self-scheduling; however, the means by which minimum staffing levels are maintained and the degree of control remaining with the manager are unclear from the description.

2.4.1.5 Possible Implications on Employment and Working Conditions, the Work Environment, Health and Well-Being, or Ethics

As reported in Table 2.2, seven of the ten publications included a specific discussion of the ways in which the digital system would impact employment and working conditions, for example in the form of a parameter to address over or under staffing in the scheduling system (Ahmed & Dalhem, 2019; Burke et al., 1999; Burke et al., 2010; Hadwan et al., 2013; Krive, 2013; Legrain et al., 2020; Rönnberg & Larsson, 2010). Fewer publications included a specific discussion about the impact of automated scheduling on the work environment, which captured less tangible questions about the technology's impact (Krive, 2013; Rönnberg & Larsson, 2010). None of the ten publications included a specific discussion about the impact of the technology on the health and well-being of workers. Several publications discussed worker satisfaction with the technology, but there was no discussion about the ways in which satisfaction with automatic scheduling would impact worker health or well-being. Several publications included parameters in the design of the scheduling program that may impact worker well-being, for example by restricting the number of consecutive shifts (Burke et al., 2010), but they did not include a specific discussion on the

TABLE 2.2
Possible Implications of Algorithmic Scheduling

Worker's Employment and Working Conditions	Does the publication describe how AM would impact employment or working conditions?	YES	7	Ahmed & Dalhem, 2019; Burke et al., 1999; Burke et al., 2010; Hadwan et al., 2013; Krive, 2013; Legrain et al., 2020; Rönnberg & Larsson, 2010
		NO	3	Gutjahr & Rauner, 2007; Lartey & Akowuah, 2021; Zhu et al., 2019
Work Environment	Does the publication describe how AM would impact the work environment?	YES	2	Krive, 2013; Rönnberg & Larsson, 2010
		NO	8	Ahmed & Dalhem, 2019; Burke et al., 1999; Burke et al., 2010; Gutjahr & Rauner, 2007; Hadwan et al., 2013; Lartey & Akowuah, 2021; Legrain et al., 2020; Zhu et al., 2019
Health & Well-Being	Does the publication specifically isolate the impact of the technology on worker health and well-being? (excluding worker satisfaction)	YES	0	
		NO	10	Ahmed & Dalhem, 2019; Burke et al., 1999; Burke et al., 2010; Gutjahr & Rauner, 2007; Hadwan et al., 2013; Krive, 2013; Lartey & Akowuah, 2021; Legrain et al., 2020; Rönnberg & Larsson, 2010; Zhu et al., 2019
Ethics	Does the publication discuss the ethics/ethical implications of changes to the organization of work through digital technology for the goals of managers or organizations?	YES	2	Gutjahr & Rauner, 2007; Rönnberg & Larsson, 2010
		NO	8	Ahmed & Dalhem, 2019; Burke et al., 1999; Burke et al., 2010; Hadwan et al., 2013; Krive, 2013; Lartey & Akowuah, 2021; Legrain et al., 2020; Zhu et al., 2019

impact of automated scheduling on the workers' health and well-being. Similarly, only two publications addressed ethical components of the automated scheduling systems, and this took the form of a discussion specific to the algorithm's attention to fairness in scheduling (Gutjahr & Rauner, 2007; Rönnberg & Larsson, 2010).

2.5 DISCUSSION

Advanced digital technologies can provide decision-support to complex organizations with multiple, large data streams and a large variety of actors in the system. This capacity helps explain the rise of AM in healthcare. By narrowing the findings of our broader literature review to the particular application of such technologies in scheduling, several prominent features about the impact of algorithmic management on healthcare practice arise.

2.5.1 Transparency in Algorithmic Staffing Decisions: Opportunity and Risk

2.5.1.1 Implicit Decisions Made Explicit

Most scheduling-specific publications included the identification of constraints, often labeled as hard or soft, which illustrates how implicit features of work organization become explicit with the introduction of managerial support technologies. Implicit values that a manager, a unit, a department, or healthcare organization may have that inform scheduling decisions are formalized and standardized with the introduction of these types of digital systems. Algorithms are coded to decide which aspects are more important, for example, to fulfill as many staff requests as possible with respect to scheduling or to fulfill them in a fair way (Rönnberg & Larsson, 2010). Explicit rules may have a positive impact by promoting fairness, for example by ensuring the burden of weekend or night shifts is equally distributed (Rönnberg & Larsson, 2010), though it should be noted that fairness itself is a slippery concept in the practice of healthcare scheduling. With adequate transparency, algorithmic management may also provide some surprising results. For example, in Legrain et al. (2020), where the authors are using established benchmarks from the 2015 International Nurse Rostering Competition, the authors note that the largest violation in their scheduling solution is related to the soft constraint restricting the number of days worked in a given schedule. They conclude: "This seems to indicate that the minimum demands are just too large to be covered by the nurses without extra work and that the units are understaffed" (Legrain et al., 2020, p. 208).

However, the use of algorithmic management in scheduling also brings the risk of *less* transparency regarding the ways in which competing values in relation to scheduling—for example in the form of constraints—are determined. For example, neither Ahmed & Dalhem (2019) nor Krive (2013) describe how the scheduling component of their workforce management system operates in this respect. Once scheduling-specific systems are embedded in larger, patented digital tools to support the organization of work, it is unclear from the publications identified in our search if a description of the ways in which decisions are made is available to workers, managers, or administrators. This is an important area for further study. Gutjahr and Rauner (2007) also note that artificial intelligence systems are being introduced to solve healthcare scheduling challenges, which raises further questions about the capacity to assess how these systems balance competing values given the well-known *black box* problem (Wadden, 2022) of many artificial intelligence systems. The behind-the-scenes operation of scheduling systems within workforce management systems and the degree of their transparency is an important area for further study.

2.5.1.2 Establishing the Evidence Behind Automated Decision-Support Systems

Automated scheduling may obscure questions about the ways in which minimum and desirable patient/nurse ratios are determined. Setting fixed nurse/patient ratios has long been a point of discussion in healthcare planning given its contested relation to cost, working conditions, and patient outcomes, as well as disagreements about how to evaluate these (Wynendaele et al., 2019). Using algorithms in scheduling decision-making bypasses this ongoing discussion by positioning minimum staffing ratios as fixed and preset *before* the execution of scheduling. The publications included in our study did not indicate the rationale, evidence, or process used to determine minimum or preferred staffing levels. These questions risk fading into the background of automated scheduling operations.

The way in which scheduling algorithms balance the cost of either adding an agency nurse, paying overtime to hospital nurses, or running below preferred staffing levels is also an important area for increased scrutiny. The development of algorithms based on calculation foregrounds this difficult negotiation by attaching a particular importance to each possibility (hard or soft constraint) and value (weighting the soft constraints). The implications of this kind of explicit, codified calculation in healthcare are yet to be seen. The capacity to assess this decision-making process is critical given the range of possible negative implications for care quality, as seen in numerous analyses linking inadequate nurse/patient staffing ratios to patient outcomes (Aiken et al., 2018; McHugh et al., 2021).

2.5.2 Accountability in Algorithmic Staffing Decisions

Accountability in the use of algorithms for scheduling decisions was highly variable in our findings. There are multiple facets of accountability with the use of these types of systems: to patients, funders, the public, and health workers. For the purposes of this study, we focused on the possible impacts of these systems on the worker. For example, to whom would a worker direct complaints about their schedule if the manager's capacity to control or adjust the output is often unclear, as determined in this study? The technology can leave the worker, including the manager, without meaningful recourse to challenge the operation of the algorithm or the outcome of the algorithm. For example, while unit managers may desire to adjust nurse/patient ratios based on changing patient acuity levels, the capacity of these systems to allow manager control of this was often unclear in our findings. This diffusion of responsibility in the creation of health worker schedules (between the software creators, the administrators who purchase it, and the managers who use it) parallels pertinent liability questions about the use of artificial intelligence more broadly in healthcare (Davidson et al., 2023; Eappen et al., 2025). This an important area for further research.

2.5.3 Implications of Algorithmic Scheduling for Employment and Working Conditions

Maximization of profit, improving productivity, and increasing efficiency are common drivers of AM in healthcare (Rani et al., 2024). All three of these drivers relate to the scheduling systems described in our study, which often sought to maximize use of the existing labor pool and decrease the use of agency staff. The approach described by Gutjahr and Rauner (2007) is of particular interest for its potential future implications for health workers' employment and working conditions. For instance, parameters on shift notification for non-full-time staff were to be set by the organization in Gutjahr and Rauner's (2007) proposal, with the example provided of the system deciding on the nurse to be assigned as late as two days before the shift starts. The approach of this system, where staff post offers of availability and organizations post demands which an automated system then coordinates for shift assignment, bears some similarity to other economic sectors where *just in time* scheduling has been implemented (Maffie & Hurtado, 2025; Rani et al., 2024). This type of scheduling could have negative implications for workers' employment and working conditions since the willingness of organizations to provide full-time work or contracts with guaranteed hours is decreasing (Andrijasevic, 2021) and the demands on workers to be available for shifts on short notice is increasing (Maffie & Hurtado, 2025). Further, *just in time* scheduling could pave the way for the *gigification* of healthcare work. Gigification is a complex process referring to a decrease in job quality and an intensification of work enabled by digital platforms, often characterized by short-time or temporary contract-based work that gradually replaces standard, full-time employment with contracts that are not time-bound (Au-Yeung et al., 2025; Veen et al., 2020). Glaser (2021) describes how the *uber-like nurse* marketing campaign of major United States Healthcare Management Organizations creates precarious working conditions, heightened worker surveillance, and increases codification of care practices. These flexible employment arrangements have spurred ongoing legal battles in the United States as to whether home care workers are to be classified as independent contractors even when they work for the same agency and sometimes even the same family for years or months, and, in most cases, the ways in which they organize and deliver their work is controlled by the agency. While the papers in our review did not suggest that staff utilizing self-scheduling practices in their organization have become or were independent contractors, in the milieu of cost containment efforts and an ongoing drive for labor optimization in healthcare (Crist-Gundman & Mulroney, 2011; Gunn et al., 2023) careful attention to this prospect is warranted given strong evidence linking gig or platform work to numerous negative outcomes for workers' physical and mental health (Matilla-Santander al., 2025).

2.5.4 Challenges Related to Studying Algorithmic Management in Healthcare

Examining the manifestations of algorithmic management or capturing workers' exposure to it is challenging in healthcare as compared to other industries for several reasons (Gunn, Eappen, Brar, ... & Muntaner, 2025). First, while algorithmic management refers to the use of algorithms to support human managers' decision-making regarding work organization, in healthcare numerous decisions regarding the organization of work, especially the delivery of care, are made by clinicians. Thus, nurses, doctors, and several other categories of allied health workers are self-regulated professionals educated and trained to make point of care decisions related to patient needs or outcomes without direction from a manager, which distinguishes them from workers in other sectors. Second, and closely related, managers and those working on their behalf (e.g., nurse in charge, shift lead, etc.) make decisions regarding the organization of work, including the delivery of care with the purpose of meeting organizational goals. Organizational goals may often overlap with clinician-specific goals related to patient care and improved outcomes; however, in many instances such goals compete with drives for organizational efficiency and cost savings. As a result, disentangling decision-making initiated by managers from that initiated by clinicians and analyzing which of these decisions are now supported by algorithms through digital technologies is not straightforward. Additionally, the lack of commonly agreed definitions of algorithmic management and the use of diverse terms or concepts to refer to this phenomenon makes the finding of existing studies examining its manifestations across economic sectors (Strauss Raats et al., 2024; Strauss Raats et al., 2025), including healthcare (Gunn, Bowdler, van Guijk, ... & Håkansta, 2024), difficult. While a wide range of terminologies are used to refer to algorithmic management across disciplines, in healthcare research we came across several concepts that bear resemblance to AM, especially when discussed in the context of digital surveillance, including managerialism, managerial domination, the rise of new public management, or managerial control over medical authority. Unsurprisingly, the complexity of algorithmic management in healthcare contributes to it being a poorly understood and understudied phenomenon in healthcare, with many of its less obvious applications remaining hidden within the intricacies of healthcare delivery (Gunn, Bowdler, van Guijk, ... & Håkansta, 2024; Gunn, Elliott, MacLeod, Morrison, & Kennedy, 2024). Further research into this topic is therefore warranted.

2.5.5 Strengths and Limitations

To the best of our knowledge, this review is one of only a few studies examining the application of algorithmic management to healthcare that pays close attention to its potential implications for the health workforce, thus moving this field of research forward. Conducting this literature review is a significant and timely endeavor given the increasing use of algorithmic management in healthcare (Rani et al., 2024; Staehelin et al., 2023), mirroring trends from other economic sectors (Baiocco et al., 2022; Duggan et al., 2020; Fernández-Macías et al., 2023; Jarrahi et al., 2021; Lind et al., 2025; Milanez, 2025; Nilsson et al., 2025; Rani et al., 2024; Wood, 2021). The expanded use of new technologies, such as algorithmic management, along with persisting health worker shortages (Rani et al., 2024; World Health Organization, 2025), including nursing professionals (Gunn et al., 2023), emphasize the need for new perspectives in identifying factors impacting health workforce sustainability (Darzi & Evans, 2016; Gunn et al., 2023). A key limitation of our study is that the literature review conducted was exploratory, not exhaustive. As a result, relevant studies covering the topics of focus for this manuscript may have been missed. Although the list of included studies is not exhaustive, this chapter is meant to spearhead discussions on issues related to the use of algorithmic scheduling in healthcare and its potential implications for employment and working conditions, worker health and well-being, staffing optimization, transparency, and accountability in decision-making.

2.6 CONCLUSION

Algorithmic management is gradually replacing, totally or partially, the work of human managers in organizations seeking to maximize efficiencies across a range of economic sectors and occupations. While the concept of algorithmic management has only recently found its way into healthcare research, we believe enabling structures and elements of it have been in existence in healthcare for several decades. In this chapter, we synthesize findings from an exploratory iterative review of available evidence regarding the application of algorithmic management in healthcare, with a focus on algorithmic scheduling. We discuss several transparency and accountability-related implications regarding staffing decisions and assess whether research on the application of algorithmic scheduling in healthcare incorporates considerations about its possible implications for health workers' employment and working conditions, work environment, health and well-being, or ethics. We assess there is international interest in the automation of health worker scheduling and that increased transparency about algorithmic scheduling decisions presents a potential opportunity to increase fairness. Notwithstanding its possible benefits, algorithmic scheduling may contribute to a worsening of job quality for health workers, especially if the process is not transparent, accountabilities are unclear, and if it contributes to an increase in precarious, low-quality employment in healthcare work. Despite the challenge of studying algorithmic management in healthcare, advancing this field of research forward is well warranted. The work of disentangling decision-making initiated by managers from that initiated by clinicians, who are self-regulated professionals educated and trained to make point of care decisions related to patient needs or outcomes without direction from a manager, needs further research attention in algorithmic management research. Research evidence from several economic fields highlights various links between algorithmic management and negative worker outcomes such as intensified monitoring and surveillance, loss of professional autonomy, quantitative overload, increased pace and intensity, social isolation, lack of social support from workers and managers, reduced trust, lower job satisfaction, decreased engagement in work, increased power imbalances between workers and employers, and job insecurity, marking the importance of its study within healthcare.

2.7 FUNDING

This work was supported by a 2024 50th Anniversary Scholar Award issued by Cape Breton University, NS, Canada to Virginia Gunn, Karen Kennedy, Adam Elliott, and Kelsey Morrison. The funder had no input in the development of this work.

REFERENCES

Ahmed, N., & Dalhem, W. (2019). The impact of implementing electronic workforce management system in Hamad Medical Corporation on nursing staff management. *Journal of Epidemiology and Public Health Reviews*, *4*(3). https://doi.org/10.16966/2471-8211.175

Aiken, L. H., Ceron, C., Simonetti, M., Lake, E. T., Galiano, A., Garbarini, A., ... & Smith, H. L. (2018). Hospital nurse staffing and patient outcomes. *Revista Médica Clínica Las Condes*, *29*(3), 322–327.

Andrijasevic, R. (2021). Just-in-time labour': Time-based management in the age of on-demand manufacturing. *Media and Management*, 31–63.

Au-Yeung, T. C., Chan, C. K. C., Ming, C. K. K., & Tsui, W. Y. A. (2025). The gig economy, platform work, and social policy: Food delivery workers' occupational welfare dilemma in Hong Kong. *Journal of Social Policy*, *54*(2), 673–691.

Baiocco, S., Fernández-Macías, E., Rani, U., & Pesole, A. (2022). The AM of work and its implications in different contexts. St. Louis: Federal Reserve Bank of St. Louis.

Bronsoler, A., Doyle, J., & Van Reenen, J. (2022). The impact of health information and communication technology on clinical quality, productivity, and workers. *Annual Review of Economics*, *14*(1), 23–46. https://doi.org/https:/doi.org/10.1146/annurev-economics-080921-101909

Burke, E., De Causmaecker, P., & Vanden Berghe, G. (1999). A hybrid tabu search algorithm for the nurse rostering problem. In B. McKay, X. Yao, C. S. Newton, J.-H. Kim, & T. Furuhashi (Eds.), *Simulated Evolution and Learning* (Vol. 1585, pp. 187–194). Springer Berlin Heidelberg. https://doi.org/10.1007/3-540-48873-1_25

Burke, E. K., Curtois, T., Qu, R., & Vanden Berghe, G. (2010). A scatter search methodology for the nurse rostering problem. *Journal of the Operational Research Society*, *61*(11), 1667–1679. https://doi.org/10.1057/jors.2009.118

Cachata, D., Costa, M., Magalhães, T., & Gaspar, F. (2024). The integration of information technology in the management and organization of nursing care in a hospital environment: A scoping review. *International Journal of Environmental Research and Public Health*, *21*(8), 968. https://doi.org/10.3390/ijerph21080968

Crist-Grundman, D., & Mulrooney, G. (2011). Effective workforce management starts with leveraging technology, while staffing optimization requires true collaboration. *Nursing Economics*, *29*(4), 195–200.

Darzi, A., & Evans, T. (2016). The global shortage of health workers—an opportunity to transform care. *The Lancet*, *388*(10060), 2576–2577.

Davidson, N., Nunnelley, S., Goldenberg, A., Régis, C., Flood, C. M., Scassa, T., Rudzicz, F., Cortez, N., Stedman, I., Martin-Bariteau F., and the workshop participants. (2023). *Machine MD: Law and Ethics of Health-Related A.I. Case Study 1: The OR Black Box*. Toronto: CIFAR.

DePillis, L., & Zhang, C. (2023, July 3). How health care remade the U.S. economy. *The New York Times*. https://www.nytimes.com/interactive/2025/07/03/business/economy/healthcare-jobs.html

Duggan, J., Sherman, U., Carbery, R., & McDonnell, A. (2020). Algorithmic management and app-work in the gig economy: A research agenda for employment relations and HRM. *Human Resource Management Journal*, *30*(1), 114–132.

Eappen, P., Davidson, K. P., MacLeod, M., Cousins, A., & Gunn, V. (2025). Global healthcare informatics: Structural considerations and workforce training challenges and solutions. In *Healthcare Informatics Innovation Post COVID-19 Pandemic* (pp. 160–179). Auerbach Publications.

Eappen, P., Stedman, I., & Gunn, V. (2025). Transforming healthcare: The role of health informatics and provider perspectives. In *Artificial Intelligence in Healthcare Information Systems—Security and Privacy Challenges* (pp. 203–216). Springer.

Fernández-Macías, E., Urzì Brancati, C., Wright, S., & Pesole, A. (2023). *The platformization of work. Evidence from the JRC AM and Platform Work Survey (AMPWork).* Publications Office of the European Union.

Glaser, A. L. (2021). Uberized care: Employment status, surveillance, and technological erasure in the home health care sector. *Anthropology of Work Review*, 42(1), 24–34. https://doi.org/10.1111/awr.12215

Gunn, V., Bowdler, M., van Guijk, C., Hernando, J., Kalakoski, V., Strauss Raats, P., Williams, P., Håkansta, K. (2024, November). Measuring workers' exposure to algorithmic management within the healthcare system: Examining barriers and possible solutions. Oral presentation at the EPICOH Early conference 2024, Barcelona, Spain. Published in Occupational and Environmental Medicine 2025; 82: A30–A31. https://doi.org/10.1136/oemed-2024-EPICOHabstracts.67

Gunn, V., Eappen, P., Brar, H. S., Brulin, E., & Muntaner, C. (2025). Integration of wearable devices in healthcare: The need to examine their implications for health workers. In *Remote Monitoring and Wearable Devices in Healthcare* (pp. 103–121). Cham: Springer Nature Switzerland. https://doi.org/10.1007/978-3-031-98897-4_6

Gunn, V., Elliott, A., Hall, H., MacLeod, M., Morrison, K., & Kennedy, K. (2024, December). Mapping the use of algorithmic management in healthcare and its possible implications for the health workforce: A scoping review. Invited presentation part of CBU Celebrating 50 Years of Academic Excellence Series events. CBU, Sydney, NS.

Gunn, V., Quinlan, M., Lahti H., Williams, P., Holm, J., Kalakoski, V., Strauss Raats, P., Lind, R., Lisen Löwstedt, L., MacLeod, M., & Håkansta, K. (2025, May). Interventions to enhance worker engagement in the design of algorithmic management applications in healthcare. Oral presentation at the 22nd European Congress of Work and Organizational Psychology 2025, Prague, Czech Republic.

Gunn, V., Strauss Raats, P., Lind, R., Holm, J., Elling, D., Lee Kyung, M., MacLeod, M., Quinlan, M., Williams, P., & Håkansta, C. (2025, May). What could be learned from a review of interventions addressing algorithmic management? Poster presentation at the Creating Sustainable Work Conference 2025, Stockholm, Sweden.

Gunn, V., Villeneuve, M., O'Campo, P., & Muntaner, C. (2023). Underfunding of nursing education and the precarious employment conditions of nurses: An exploration of contributing factors, Covid-19 pandemic implications, and structural solutions. In *Handbook on Gender and Public Sector Employment* (pp. 321–335). Edward Elgar Publishing.

Gutjahr, W. J., & Rauner, M. S. (2007). An ACO algorithm for a dynamic regional nurse-scheduling problem in Austria. *Computers & Operations Research*, *34*(3), 642–666. https://doi.org/10.1016/j.cor.2005.03.018

Hadwan, M., Ayob, M., Sabar, N. R., & Qu, R. (2013). A harmony search algorithm for nurse rostering problems. *Information Sciences*, *233*, 126–140. https://doi.org/10.1016/j.ins.2012.12.025

Jarrahi, M. H., Newlands, G., Lee, M. K., Wolf, C. T., Kinder, E., & Sutherland, W. (2021). AM in a work context. *Big Data & Society*, 8(2), 20539517211020332. https://doi.org/10.1177/20539517211020332

Krive, J. (2013). Building effective workforce management practices through shared governance and technology systems integration. *Nursing Economics, 31*(5), 231–236, 249.

Lartey, K., & Akowuah, E. K. (2021). An analysis of the application of the harmony search algorithm to solving the nurse rostering problem. *CIN: Computers, Informatics, Nursing*, *39*(5), 281–288. https://doi.org/10.1097/CIN.0000000000000689

Lee, M. K., Kusbit, D., Metsky, E., & Dabbish, L. (2015, April). Working with machines: The impact of algorithmic and data-driven management on human workers. In *Proceedings of the 33rd Annual ACM Conference on Human Factors in Computing Systems* (pp. 1603–1612).

Lee, J., & Lee, S. (2023). Construction site safety management: A computer vision and deep learning approach. *Sensors*, *23*(2), 944.

Legrain, A., Omer, J., & Rosat, S. (2020). An online stochastic algorithm for a dynamic nurse scheduling problem. *European Journal of Operational Research*, *285*(1), 196–210. https://doi.org/10.1016/j.ejor.2018.09.027

Lind, R., Raats, P. S., Nilsson, K., Håkansta, C., Gunn, V., Mangot-Sala, L., ... & Bodin, T. (2025). 66 effects of AM on occupational safety and health: A case study of a Swedish logistics company. https://oem.bmj.com/content/82/Suppl_1/A30.2

Lind, R., Strauss Raats, P., Nilsson, K., Hakansta, K., Gunn, V., Mangot-Sala, L., Matilla Santander, N., & Bodin, T. (2024, November). Effects of algorithmic management on occupational safety and health: A case study of a Swedish logistics company. Oral presentation at the EPICOH Early conference 2024, Barcelona, Spain. Published in Occupational and Environmental Medicine 2025; 82: A30. https://doi.org/10.1136/oemed-2024-EPICOHabstracts.66

Maffie, M. D., & Hurtado, H. (2025). The enshittification of work: Platform decay and labour conditions in the gig economy. *British Journal of Industrial Relations*, *64*(1), 5–20. https://onlinelibrary.wiley.com/doi/abs/10.1111/bjir.70004

Matilla-Santander, N., Lundh, F., Kvart, S., Baron, S. L., Bodin, T., Gevaert, J., ... & Kreshpaj, B. (2025). What is known about the health of location-based and online web-based digital labour platform workers? A scoping review of the literature. *BMC Public Health*, *25*(1), 2635.

McHugh, M. D., Aiken, L. H., Sloane, D. M., Windsor, C., Douglas, C., & Yates, P. (2021). Effects of nurse-to-patient ratio legislation on nurse staffing and patient mortality, readmissions, and length of stay: A prospective study in a panel of hospitals. *The Lancet*, *397*(10288), 1905–1913.

Milanez, A. (2025). Exploring win-win outcomes of AM: Lessons from a laboratory experiment on worker consultation. *OECD Artificial Intelligence Papers*, No. 43. https://www.oecd.org/en/publications/exploring-win-win-outcomes-of-algorithmic-management_84b59397-en.html

Nilsson, K. H., Matilla-Santander, N., Lee, M. K., Brulin, E., Bodin, T., & Håkansta, C. (2025). AM and occupational health: A comparative case study of organizational practices in logistics. *Safety Science*, *187*, 106863. https://doi.org/https://doi.org/10.1016/j.ssci.2025.106863

Parent-Rocheleau, X., & Parker, S. K. (2022). Algorithms as work designers: How algorithmic management influences the design of jobs. *Human Resource Management Review*, *32*(3), 100838. https://doi.org/10.1016/j.hrmr.2021.100838

Rani, U., Pesole, A., & Vazquez, G. (2024) Algorithmic management practices in regular workplaces – Case studies in logistics and healthcare. Publications Office of the European Union. https://data.europa.eu/doi/10.2760/712475

Rönnberg, E., & Larsson, T. (2010). Automating the self-scheduling process of nurses in Swedish healthcare: A pilot study. *Health Care Management Science*, *13*(1), 35–53. https://doi.org/10.1007/s10729-009-9107-x

Staehelin, D., Dolata, M., Peyer, N., Gerber, F., & Schwabe, G. (2023, August). Algorithmic management for community health worker in sub-Saharan Africa: Curse or blessing? In *IFIP Conference on Human-Computer Interaction* (pp. 94–114). Cham: Springer Nature Switzerland.

Strauss Raats, P., Gunn, V., Lind, R., Matilla-Santander, N., Holm, J., Boddler, M., Lee Kyung, M., Quinlan, M., van Gulijk, C., & Håkansta, K. (2025, May). Towards a standardized definition of AM: A modified Delphi approach. Oral presentation at the Creating Sustainable Work Conference 2025, Stockholm, Sweden.

Strauss Raats, P., Gunn, V., Håkansta, K., Lind, R., Hernando, J., & Quinlan, M. (2024, November). Using a modified Delphi approach to advance a common definition of AM Oral presentation at the EPICOH Early Career Conference 2024, Barcelona, Spain.

Veen, A., Kaine, S., Goods, C., & Barratt, T. (2020). The 'gigification' of work in the 21st Century. In *Contemporary Work and the Future of Employment in Developed Countries* (pp. 15–32). Routledge.

Wadden, J. J. (2022). Defining the undefinable: The black box problem in healthcare artificial intelligence. *Journal of Medical Ethics*, *48*(10), 764–768.

Williams, P., & Khan, M. H. (2025). Framing algorithmic management: Constructed antagonism on HR technology websites. *New Technology, Work and Employment*, *40*(1), 102–123.

Wood, A. J. (2021). AM: Consequences for work organisation and working conditions. St. Louis: Federal Reserve Bank of St. Louis.

World Health Organization. (n.d.). Where we work. https://www.who.int/about/structure

World Health Organization. (2025). *Health and Care Workforce Planning Tools: A Rapid Review* (9240106278). https://www.who.int/publications/i/item/9789240106277

Wynendaele, H., Willems, R., & Trybou, J. (2019). Systematic review: Association between the patient–nurse ratio and nurse outcomes in acute care hospitals. *Journal of Nursing Management*, *27*(5), 896–917. https://doi.org/10.1111/jonm.12764

Yashnarbekov, O. (2025). Algorithmic management and professional autonomy: The impact of digital performance monitoring on medical workers' contractual rights. *Elita. uz-Elektron Ilmiy Jurnal*, *3*(1), 30–49.

Zhu, L. R., Tong, J. H., Low, M. Y. H., Lau, B. H., Chen, M. X., & Wang, Z. (2019). An automated Staff Roster Planning System (SRPS) for healthcare industry. *2019 20th IEEE/ACIS International Conference on Software Engineering, Artificial Intelligence, Networking and Parallel/Distributed Computing (SNPD)*, 167–172. https://doi.org/10.1109/SNPD.2019.8935696

3 Ethical Implications of Artificial Intelligence in Healthcare

Christopher Partridge and Ruiling Guo

3.1 INTRODUCTION

The rapid integration of artificial intelligence (AI) in healthcare is transforming patient care, medical research, and healthcare administration. From predictive analytics to robotic-assisted surgery, AI-driven innovations are enhancing diagnostic accuracy, streamlining operations, and personalizing treatment plans. However, these advancements bring forth significant ethical concerns and challenges that must be addressed to ensure the responsible and equitable use of AI (Morley et al., 2020). The ethical implications of AI in healthcare encompass issues related to privacy, bias, transparency, accountability, patient autonomy, and more. As healthcare organizations increasingly rely on AI-powered systems, the ethical challenges require careful consideration, including the need for ethical guidelines and regulatory frameworks to ensure that AI enhances healthcare without compromising fundamental ethical principles (Davenport & Kalakota, 2019).

To identify existing research on ethical implications of AI in healthcare, a literature review was performed. The literature searches were conducted in professional databases of PubMed, CINAHL Complete, Academic Search Complete, Web of Science, Business Source Complete, Computers & Applied Sciences Complete, SocINDEX, and Google Scholar. The retrieved studies were reviewed and critically analyzed.

Literature review showed that one of the primary ethical concerns associated with AI in healthcare is patient privacy and data security (references). AI systems require vast amounts of patient data to function effectively, which raises concerns about data breaches, unauthorized access, and misuse of sensitive medical information. Ensuring compliance with regulations such as the Health Insurance Portability and Accountability Act (HIPAA) in the United States and the General Data Protection Regulation (GDPR) in Europe is crucial for maintaining patient trust (Mittelstadt et al., 2016). Ethical AI systems must incorporate robust data protection measures to safeguard patient information and prevent unintended harm.

Another pressing issue is algorithmic bias, which can lead to disparities in healthcare outcomes. AI models trained on biased datasets may inadvertently reinforce

DOI: 10.1201/9781003624875-4

existing inequalities in healthcare access and treatment. Studies have shown that AI-driven diagnostic tools may exhibit lower accuracy for certain demographic groups due to underrepresentation in training data (Obermeyer et al., 2019). Addressing bias in AI requires diverse and representative datasets, continuous model evaluation, and interdisciplinary collaboration to mitigate the risk of discriminatory outcomes.

Transparency and explainability, known as Explainable AI (XAI), are also critical ethical considerations in AI-driven healthcare. Many AI systems operate as "black boxes," making it difficult for healthcare professionals and patients to understand how decisions are made. This lack of interpretability can undermine trust in AI-driven recommendations and limit their clinical adoption (Samek et al., 2017). Developing AI systems that provide clear explanations for their outputs can enhance trust and facilitate informed decision-making. XAI aims to bridge this gap by providing human-readable insights into the decision-making process, thereby enhancing transparency and accountability (Adadi & Berrada, 2018). Furthermore, the use of AI raises questions about accountability and liability in medical decision-making. When an AI system makes an incorrect diagnosis or recommendation for treatment, determining responsibility can be complex. Traditional medical ethics principles place accountability on healthcare providers, but as AI becomes more autonomous, questions arise regarding liability and malpractice (Mittelstadt et al., 2016). Establishing clear accountability and legal frameworks is essential to address these ethical dilemmas and ensure that AI complements, rather than replaces, human expertise in healthcare settings (Gerke et al., 2020).

Lastly, AI's impact on patient autonomy and informed consent must be carefully considered. While AI has the potential to empower patients by providing personalized health insights, it also raises concerns about over-reliance on automated decision-making. Patients should have the right to understand and consent to AI-driven interventions, emphasizing the importance of ethical AI implementation that respects human dignity and decision-making capacity (Floridi et al., 2018).

The first aim of this chapter is to address the ethical concerns and implications of AI in healthcare, encompassing issues such as bias, fairness, privacy, accountability, equitable access, human-AI collaboration, and regulatory challenges. As AI continues to shape the future of healthcare, addressing these ethical challenges is crucial to ensuring its responsible and equitable use while minimizing potential harms (Elendu et al., 2023).

The second aim of this chapter is to provide recommended strategies and solutions such as fostering transparency, mitigating bias, and prioritizing patient-centered approaches. In order to protect individuals and communities, stakeholders can use AI's potential while upholding ethical principles and moral implications.

Despite these ethical concerns, AI has the potential to transform healthcare by improving efficiency, accuracy, and patient care outcomes. To fully realize these benefits while mitigating ethical risks, policymakers, developers, and healthcare professionals must collaborate to establish robust ethical guidelines. Ongoing research and interdisciplinary dialogue will be essential in ensuring that AI serves as a tool for equitable and ethical healthcare advancement.

3.2 CURRENT AI ETHICAL CONCERNS AND CHALLENGES

3.2.1 Patient Privacy and Data Security

The integration of AI into healthcare relies heavily on the collection and analysis of vast amounts of patient data. AI's ability to analyze vast datasets has revolutionized medical research and clinical decision-making. Machine learning algorithms can detect patterns in health records, imaging studies, and genomic data that would not be readily apparent otherwise, leading to earlier disease detection and more precise treatment recommendations. However, the ethical implications of AI in healthcare cannot be overlooked. While the use of AI enables improved diagnostics and personalized medicine, it also introduces significant patient privacy and data security concerns. Unauthorized data access, breaches, and unethical data usage can compromise patient trust and violate confidentiality. The examples suggest that AI-driven healthcare applications must balance innovation with the protection of patient privacy. Many AI models require continuous access to highly sensitive health information to improve performance, raising concerns about informed consent and data governance.

One of the central ethical dilemmas in AI-driven healthcare has evolved around data ownership of data (Leslie et al., 2021). As medical institutions, technology companies, and researchers collect and utilize patient data, questions continually arise about who holds the rights to this information and when and why it can be accessed. Should patients retain ownership of their health data, or do hospitals and AI developers have legitimate claims over it? At this point, this question is not fully or satisfactorily answered. The improper handling of such sensitive information raises concerns about data breaches, consent, and ownership (Leslie et al., 2021). Regulations such as the Health Insurance Portability and Accountability Act (HIPAA) in the United States and the General Data Protection Regulation (GDPR) in Europe attempt to mitigate these risks, but challenges persist in ensuring compliance across AI applications. Clear regulatory guidelines, contractual agreements with AI platforms and other systems, and ethical frameworks must address these concerns to prevent exploitation and ensure that patients maintain agency over their personal health information. Consent models should be structured in a way that grants individuals control over data-sharing agreements while still enabling scientific progress (Goktas & Grzybowski, 2025; Vo et al., 2023).

One notable example is Project Nightingale, a collaboration between Google and Ascension Health. This project involved the transfer and storage of vast amounts of patient data, including, but not limited to, names, test results, diagnoses, and various other personally identifiable protected hospitalization records, without explicit patient knowledge or consent. Google aimed to use AI to improve clinical decision-making, but the lack of transparency and failure to inform patients raised significant privacy concerns. The public backlash predictably ensued, leading to increased scrutiny of AI-driven healthcare collaborations. While Ascension and Google claimed compliance with HIPAA regulations, the case emphasized the need for stringent data governance, patient consent mechanisms, and ethical oversight in AI-driven healthcare initiatives. Ultimately, Project Nightingale serves as a cautionary tale about the risks of prioritizing technological advancement over patient rights and trust (Polevikov, 2023).

Another example is IBM Watson Health's AI-driven oncology project that was intended to provide personalized cancer treatment recommendations to assist treating clinicians, essentially acting as a clinical decision-support tool for oncology providers and their treatment teams. Initially, the project was hailed as a revolutionary approach to cancer treatment; however, Watson encountered significant challenges due to several key issues. The issues were primarily related to bias, poor data quality, overhyped/exaggerated marketing claims, a lack of robust clinical validation, and incomplete training data. The system provided recommendations that were sometimes unsafe or even, at times, wholly inconsistent with best clinical practices. All this highlighted the dangers of unchecked AI implementation in healthcare and led to concerns regarding autonomy, responsibility, fairness, and transparency in clinical decision-support systems. This case underscores the importance of rigorous validation, transparency, and ethical oversight in AI-driven medical applications (Debrabander & Mertes, 2022; Hantel et al., 2024; Zhang & Zhang, 2023; Deo, 2015).

3.2.2 Bias and Fairness in AI Algorithms

Bias and fairness in AI algorithms in healthcare are serious fundamental ethical concerns that can significantly impact patient outcomes and health equity. Bias in AI can stem from multiple sources, including historical inequalities in healthcare data, algorithmic design flaws, and systemic societal biases. AI systems rely on large datasets, including electronic health records (EHRs), imaging, genomic data, and a myriad of others to train models. If these datasets are biased, the resulting AI models will also be biased. This can lead to algorithmic discrimination, where the AI system systematically disadvantages certain populations. Moreover, biases may arise from how data is labeled, how AI models are trained, and the assumptions encoded in algorithms themselves. If an AI system is not carefully tested across diverse populations, it may amplify pre-existing disparities rather than mitigate them. Biases in AI decision-making can lead to significant consequences, such as disparities in disease diagnosis, inappropriate treatment recommendations, or unequal access to healthcare resources.

The impact of algorithmic bias on marginalized populations can be profound. Bias in AI algorithms can lead to disparities in healthcare access, quality, and outcomes. For instance, a widely cited case involved an algorithm used to prioritize care for Black patients, which was found to systematically underestimate their health needs compared to White patients, leading to unequal access to care. This pattern of underdiagnosis and unequal treatment can exacerbate existing health disparities for minority populations, women, and low-income patients (Ferryman et al., 2023; Chin et al., 2023; Cary et al., 2025). Therefore, healthcare organizations must proactively address bias through diverse and representative datasets, fairness-aware machine learning techniques, and rigorous validation testing. In addition, addressing bias and fairness in AI algorithms requires an interdisciplinary approach involving technologists, healthcare professionals, ethicists, and policymakers. By employing diverse data collection, bias detection and correction techniques, transparency, and continuous monitoring, healthcare systems can mitigate the risks of algorithmic bias and improve outcomes for all patients. Ongoing research and regulatory measures that are both forward-looking and readily adaptable in response to unforeseen developments are also necessary.

3.2.3 Transparency and Explainability

Transparency and explainability in AI refer to the ability of AI systems to provide clear, understandable, and interpretable, plain language explanations for their decisions and actions. In the practice of medicine, transparency and explainability are crucial for ensuring that healthcare providers and patients can trust and understand AI-driven recommendations. This is essential for informed decision-making, maintaining patient autonomy, and ensuring ethical clinical practice (Amann et al., 2020; Rasheed et al., 2022). There is a problem named "Black Box" which describes the challenge of the lack of transparency in many AI models, particularly deep learning systems. These models often do not provide clear explanations for their decisions, making it difficult for clinicians to understand how conclusions are reached. This opacity can hinder the adoption of AI in clinical settings, as healthcare providers may be reluctant to rely on systems they cannot fully comprehend (Rasheed et al., 2022; Sheu & Pardeshi, 2022).

There is a need for Explainable AI (XAI) in healthcare which refers to artificial intelligence systems designed to provide transparent, understandable, and interpretable decisions to healthcare professionals, patients, and other stakeholders. Unlike traditional "black-box" AI models, which provide outputs without explaining their reasoning, XAI ensures that users can comprehend the logic behind AI-driven predictions, classifications, and recommendations. XAI is ethically important because it allows AI systems to explain their reasoning, particularly in life-and-death decisions such as medical diagnoses. XAI also helps ensure that AI recommendations are transparent and interpretable, enabling clinicians to validate and trust the AI's conclusions. This is critical for maintaining patient safety and ensuring that AI systems are used responsibly in healthcare (Amann et al., 2020; Markus, Kors, & Rijnbeek, 2021).

In the case studies by Ferryman et al. (2023), Chin et al. (2023), and Cary et al. (2025), the lack of transparency and explainability in the problematic AI model contributed to the suboptimal outcomes as well as increased both risk and cost. For example, the radiologist was unable to understand the model's decision-making process, which limited their ability to identify and correct errors. This opacity or "black box" nature of AI prevented the radiologist from effectively collaborating with the AI system and ensuring accurate diagnoses (De-Giorgio et al., 2025). The case resulted in litigation, with the radiologist facing allegations of malpractice due to the reliance on the flawed AI model. The legal proceedings highlighted the need for XAI to ensure that clinicians can understand and trust AI recommendations.

XAI techniques, such as Local Interpretable Model-Agnostic Explanations (LIME) and SHapley Additive exPlanations (SHAP), can provide insights into how AI models make predictions, thereby improving transparency and accountability (Banja, Hollstein, & Bruno, 2022). Therefore, without transparency and explainability, the use of AI in healthcare may be met with skepticism, potentially leading to underutilization of beneficial technologies (Rasheed et al., 2022; An et al., 2025).

A relatively recent controversy involved the use of AI in pharmaceutical trials, where specific patient data usage raised significant ethical concerns. One such case occurred when an AI-driven drug development program used patient records without fully disclosing the methodology behind its decision-making. Trial participants were unaware of how their health data was being processed, and there was no clear explanation of how AI influenced trial outcomes. The lack of transparency in how AI analyzed patient data led to mistrust among patients and regulatory bodies, exacerbating ethical dilemmas surrounding informed consent and data protection.

As AI continues to reshape healthcare, robust privacy protections and ethical data governance remain critical. Healthcare organizations and policymakers must work collaboratively to establish guidelines that safeguard patient rights while fostering AI-driven innovation. Ethical AI practices should prioritize transparency, informed consent, and equitable access to technological advancements. Transparency in data usage policies, coupled with patient education, is necessary to maintain public confidence in AI-driven healthcare solutions (Elendu et al., 2023).

3.2.4 Accountability and Liability

The integration of AI in healthcare offers transformative potential but also raises significant ethical and legal challenges, particularly concerning accountability and liability. As AI systems become more autonomous, determining responsibility when errors or misadventures occur in diagnosis or treatment becomes increasingly complex.

The question of accountability when AI systems make errors in diagnosis or treatment is multifaceted. Responsibility can potentially lie with healthcare providers, software developers, or the institutions deploying the AI systems. The principal-agent relationship, where the physician is held responsible for AI decisions, risks reducing the adoption of AI tools due to potential liabilities. Alternatively, attributing liability to software developers or institutions may also be problematic due to the dynamic learning nature of AI, which complicates traditional definitions of product defects and responsibility (Bottomley & Thaldar, 2023; Maliha et al., 2021).

Regarding legal implications, generally speaking, the current legal frameworks are frequently inadequate to address the complexities of AI-related healthcare errors given that traditional malpractice laws focus on human error and device or pharmaceutical liability, making it more challenging to apply these principles to AI systems. The dynamic and evolving nature of AI further complicates liability determinations. There is an obvious need for updated legal frameworks that can accommodate the unique characteristics of AI, ensuring both accountability and the promotion of innovation (Maliha et al., 2021; Banja, Hollstein, & Bruno, 2022). A case that illustrated the accountability and liability issues using AI-assisted healthcare involved a radiologist who, at least partially, relied on an AI model for detecting cervical spine fractures in imaging. The AI model, which had received FDA approval, was used in clinical practice but performed poorly in real-world settings compared to its initial reported performance. The model's sensitivity and false positive rates were significantly influenced by patient age, fracture characteristics, and degenerative changes in the spine, resulting in missed diagnoses, incorrect referrals, and unnecessary additional care (Banja, Hollstein, & Bruno, 2022).

3.2.5 Autonomy and Informed Consent

Autonomy in medical ethics refers to the right of patients to make informed decisions about their own healthcare based on their perceptions regarding what is appropriate in the context of their overall health, beliefs, values, and desires. Informed consent is the process by which healthcare providers disclose relevant information to patients, ensuring they understand the risks, benefits, and alternatives of a proposed intervention and obtain their voluntary agreement to proceed. These principles are fundamental to respecting patient autonomy and ensuring ethical medical practice (Grady, 2015).

The integration of AI in healthcare has the potential to influence patient decision-making significantly at various points in the continuum of care. While AI can enhance decision-making by providing evidence-based recommendations, it also raises concerns about the potential for patients to feel pressured to follow AI-generated advice, potentially undermining their autonomy (Rose & Shapiro, 2024; Iserson, 2024). Patients may not fully understand how AI systems are involved in their care, which can complicate the consent process. There was a notable case involving an AI-driven diagnostic tool used in a large healthcare system. The platform was intended to assist in diagnosing various medical conditions by analyzing patient data and providing recommendations for further testing or treatment, specifically, decisions related to prioritizing care, identifying potential diagnoses, and suggesting treatment plans. Patients and families expressed concerns about the lack of transparency in how the AI made decisions, leading to mistrust and reluctance to accept AI-based recommendations. This case underscores the importance of clear communication and transparency in the use of AI to maintain patient trust and autonomy (Rose & Shapiro, 2024; Iserson, 2024).

It is essential for healthcare providers to explain the role of AI in diagnosis and treatment, including its limitations and potential biases, to ensure patients can make truly informed decisions (Rose & Shapiro, 2024; Iserson, 2024; Moulaei, Akhlaghpour, & Fatehi, 2025). Maintaining a balance between AI recommendations and human judgment is crucial for respecting patient autonomy. Shared decision-making involves collaboration between patients and healthcare providers and the integration of AI insights while considering patient preferences and values. This approach ensures that AI serves as a tool to support rather than replace human clinical judgment (Tarantini et al., 2025; Will, 2011).

3.2.6 Access and Equity in AI Adoption

Access and equity in AI adoption refer to the fair and inclusive distribution of AI-driven healthcare innovations, ensuring that all populations, regardless of socioeconomic status, geographic location, or demographic characteristics, benefit from these advancements. These principles are crucial for bridging the digital divide, preventing the exacerbation of existing health disparities, and promoting overall health equity. The digital divide indicates the gap between those who have access to modern information and communication technology and those who do not. In healthcare, this divide can lead to unequal access to AI-driven innovations, particularly affecting low-income and rural populations. These groups may lack the necessary infrastructure, such as high-speed internet and advanced medical facilities, to benefit from AI technologies, thereby widening health disparities (Kumar et al., 2024; Uche-Anya et al., 2021).

Concerning global health implications, AI has the potential to either widen or narrow health disparities on a global scale, depending on its implementation. In low- and middle-income countries (LMICs), the lack of resources and infrastructure can hinder the adoption of AI, potentially exacerbating health inequalities. Conversely, AI can also be leveraged to address specific health challenges in these regions, such as improving diagnostic accuracy and disease surveillance, provided that ethical and equitable practices are followed (Elendu et al., 2023; Dankwa-Mullan, 2024). An interesting example is the AIM-AHEAD program, which aims to increase access to AI-driven telemedicine in underserved areas. This initiative focuses on building infrastructure, training healthcare providers, and developing culturally competent AI tools to ensure equitable healthcare delivery. In order to promote access and equity, users of AI technology need to carefully implement and monitor its use to prevent unintended consequences (Kumar et al., 2024; Uche-Anya et al., 2021).

3.2.7 Ethical Use of AI in Research and Development

Medical ethics in research and development are also important for ensuring that innovations benefit patients while upholding ethical standards. AI's integration into healthcare research presents unique ethical challenges that must be addressed to maintain trust and integrity in medical practice. AI is increasingly being used in medical research such as drug development, clinical trials, and genomics. In drug development, AI can predict drug efficacy and safety, accelerating the discovery process. In genomics, AI can analyze large datasets to identify genetic markers for diseases. In clinical trials, AI can be used to enhance the design and management of the trials, including but not limited to improving participant selection and monitoring outcomes. However, ethical concerns arise regarding bias in participant selection and trial outcomes. Ensuring diverse and representative datasets, transparent algorithms, and continuous monitoring for bias are critical for ethical AI use in clinical trials (Goktas & Grzybowski, 2025).

Ethical considerations include ensuring data privacy, preventing algorithmic bias, and maintaining transparency in AI-driven decisions (Elendu et al., 2023; Goktas &

Grzybowski, 2025). In a controversial pharmaceutical trial, patient data was utilized by AI without the patients' consent. The lack of transparency in how AI analyzed patient data led to mistrust and ethical dilemmas. This case highlights the importance of clear communication, transparency, and ethical guidelines in AI-driven research (Elendu et al., 2023; Goktas & Grzybowski, 2025). Additionally, there were concerns about whether AI-based trial recommendations prioritized financial incentives over patient well-being. In that same case, alarming questions arose regarding the various selection criteria for inclusion and exclusion of trial participants, as the models may have accidentally excluded certain demographic groups, resulting in a lack of diversity in clinical trials. Ethical AI implementation in pharmaceutical trials must involve comprehensive patient consent procedures, independent audits of AI decision-making, and stringent oversight from regulatory agencies to ensure fairness and accountability (Elendu et al., 2023; Goktas & Grzybowski, 2025).

Another challenging issue involving the use of AI in medical research and development is to obtain informed consent, especially when algorithms analyze large, aggregated datasets. Patients may not fully understand how AI systems are involved in their care, which complicates the consent process. It is suggested that clear communication about the role of AI, its benefits, and its potential risks is essential for ethical informed consent (Elendu et al., 2023; Zhang & Zhang, 2023).

3.3 RECOMMENDED STRATEGIES AND SOLUTIONS

The integration of AI in healthcare promises significant advancements in diagnostics, treatment, and patient care. However, it also raises complex ethical challenges that must be addressed to ensure responsible and equitable use, as discussed above. This chapter offers key recommendations for mitigating potential ethical issues and dilemmas when using AI in healthcare.

1. **Patient Privacy and Data Security**
   - Prioritize patient-centric approaches that respect privacy while designing AI tools and fostering the development of improved datasets and technological advancements (Elendu et al., 2023; Morley et al., 2020).
   - Adhere to strict data security protocols among AI developers and healthcare providers, including advanced encryption, multi-factor authentication, and rigorous access controls.
   - Follow regulations such as the Health Insurance Portability and Accountability Act (HIPAA) and the General Data Protection Regulation (GDPR) to ensure that patient data is handled ethically.
   - Implement stringent policies on data anonymization and de-identification to reduce risks associated with unauthorized or unintended disclosures.
   - Ensure that patients have a clear understanding of how their information is being used, with the ability to opt out of certain AI-driven processes if they so choose.

- Emphasize ethical guidelines and ensure data diversity, fairness, and robust validation techniques.
- Adopt data collection methods that align with security and patient rights and societal norms/expectations (Morley et al., 2020).

2. **Bias and Fairness in AI Algorithms**
    - Collect diverse data to ensure that training datasets are representative of the entire population, including marginalized groups (Ferryman et al., 2023; Chin et al., 2023).
    - Implement techniques to detect and correct bias during the model development process, such as reweighting or resampling data (Rojas et al., 2022; Cary et al., 2025).
    - Regularly monitor AI models for bias and update them as needed in order to maintain fairness over time (Chin et al., 2023; Siddique et al., 2024).
    - Promote interdisciplinary collaboration among professionals such as data scientists, clinicians, and ethicists to ensure AI tools are designed to enhance equity rather than reinforce disparities (Ferryman, Mackintosh, & Ghassemi, 2023; Chin et al., 2023).
    - Implement proactive interventions, including diverse and representative training datasets, continuous bias audits, and the inclusion of ethical considerations in algorithm development.
    - Prioritize inclusivity to ensure equitable AI deployment across all populations.
3. **Transparency and Explainability**
    - Design AI algorithms that are transparent and explainable, which allows for better understanding and identification of potential biases (Ferryman et al., 2023; Sasseville et al., 2025).
    - Implement XAI techniques to improve trust, enhance clinical decision-making, and ensure equitable patient care.
    - Adopt ethical AI practices by prioritizing transparency, informed consent, and equitable access to technological advancements coupled with data usage policies and patient education (Elendu et al., 2023).
    - Establish guidelines that safeguard patient rights while fostering AI-driven innovation.
    - Understand the rapidly evolving technology and influence of AI in order to develop comprehensive, adaptable legal frameworks to promote transparency and explainability while safeguarding patient rights and maintaining public trust.
4. **Accountability and Liability**
    - Update the standard of care expectations to include AI recommendations that help clarify liability in different scenarios.
    - Develop novel/innovative insurance models that protect both healthcare providers and patients when AI-related errors occur.

- Implement special/no-fault adjudication systems that can help streamline compensation for patients without the need to prove medical liability or fault.
- Establish clear regulatory guidelines for AI development and deployment to ensure safety and accountability (Maliha et al., 2021; Banja, Hollstein, & Bruno, 2022).

5. **Autonomy and Informed Consent**
    - Ensure autonomy and informed consent in the context of AI in healthcare.
    - Provide clear explanations, maintain transparency, and foster shared decision-making.
    - Respect patient autonomy and uphold ethical standards in medical practice.
6. **Access and Equity in AI Adoption**
    - Create affordable tools and develop cost-effective AI solutions tailored to the needs of underserved populations and under-resourced areas.
    - Invest in the necessary infrastructure, such as internet connectivity and healthcare facilities, to support AI adoption.
    - Involve diverse populations in the design and testing of AI systems to ensure they meet the needs of all users and that AI technologies are accessible to all.
    - Develop and implement policy and regulations that promote equitable access to AI technologies and address potential biases (Kumar et al., 2024; Elendu et al., 2023; Yu & Zhai, 2024).
7. **Ethical Use of AI in Research and Development**
    - Adopt a multifaceted approach to address the ethical use of AI in research and development.
    - Ensure informed consent, prevent bias, and maintain transparency.
    - Harness AI's potential while upholding ethical standards.
    - Promote continuous collaboration and establish robust ethical frameworks for responsible AI integration in medical research and development.

3.4 FUTURE OF AI ETHICS IN HEALTHCARE

3.4.1 Evolving Ethical Challenges

As AI becomes more integrated into healthcare, new ethical issues emerge. One major concern is AI autonomy in decision-making, where AI systems may make clinical decisions with minimal human oversight. This raises questions about accountability, transparency, and the potential for errors. Ensuring that AI systems are designed with robust ethical frameworks is essential to address these challenges (Elendu et al., 2023; Goktas & Grzybowski, 2025).

3.4.2 Potential Future Ethical Dilemmas

Future ethical dilemmas may include fully automated surgeries and AI-based mental health interventions. These scenarios require careful consideration of patient autonomy, informed consent, and the potential for AI to replace human judgment. Developing clear ethical guidelines and regulatory frameworks will be essential to navigate these challenges responsibly (Elendu et al., 2023; Goktas & Grzybowski, 2025).

3.4.3 Building Ethical AI

Fostering collaboration between technologists, healthcare professionals, ethicists, and policymakers is crucial for developing responsible AI. This includes creating interdisciplinary teams to address ethical concerns, developing transparent algorithms, and ensuring diverse datasets to mitigate bias. Continuous monitoring and updating of ethical guidelines are necessary to keep pace with technological advancements (Elendu et al., 2023; Knopf, Frahm, & Pfotenhauer, 2023).

3.4.4 Regulatory Considerations

Different countries have varying regulations governing AI use in healthcare. In North America, the FDA classifies AI products as software as a medical device (SaMD) and has issued guidelines for good AI practice. In Europe, the EU AI Act has been introduced. The EU AI Act mandates that high-risk AI systems be designed for effective human oversight. Asian countries are also developing policies to regulate AI in healthcare. These regulations aim to ensure the safety, efficacy, and ethical use of AI technologies (Knopf, Frahm, & Pfotenhauer, 2023; Maynard, & Scragg, 2019).

Addressing the ethical use of AI in healthcare requires a comprehensive, multifaceted approach. By ensuring informed consent, preventing bias, and maintaining transparency, healthcare systems can harness AI's potential while upholding ethical standards. Continuous collaboration and robust ethical frameworks are essential for responsible AI integration in medical research and practice.

3.5 CONCLUSION

The integration of AI into healthcare presents numerous ethical challenges, including concerns about privacy, data security, bias, transparency, accountability, equitable access, and multiple others. In addition, AI systems must be designed to respect patient privacy, ensure informed consent, and maintain fairness across all demographic groups. Bias in AI algorithms can increase existing disparities in healthcare, making it crucial to implement fairness-aware machine learning and diverse datasets. Additionally, the "black box" problem raises concerns about transparency and the ability of clinicians and patients to understand AI-driven decisions. Ethical AI development must also address the overall accountability and liability in cases of errors or harm. Finally, the use of AI in medical research must uphold principles of autonomy, beneficence, and justice, ensuring that patients' rights and well-being remain central to innovation.

To develop AI ethically and responsibly in healthcare, an interdisciplinary approach is essential. Healthcare providers, technologists, policymakers, ethicists, and other stakeholders must collaborate to establish regulations and best practices that prioritize patient safety, privacy, and fairness. Ongoing research and transparency in AI development are critical for ensuring that AI-driven healthcare remains trustworthy and beneficial to all. Policymakers should work toward implementing comprehensive regulatory frameworks that balance innovation with ethical responsibility, and institutions must invest in bias mitigation strategies, fairness-aware AI development, and patient-centered policies. By fostering ethical AI adoption, the power of technology can be harnessed to improve healthcare outcomes while safeguarding fundamental human rights.

ACKNOWLEDGMENT

The authors would like to thank Mr Tyler Pratt for his assistance with the preliminary literature searches conducted prior to writing this chapter. His assistance is greatly appreciated.

REFERENCES

Adadi, A., & Berrada, M. (2018). Peeking inside the black-box: A survey on explainable artificial intelligence (XAI). *IEEE Access, 6*, 52138–52160. https://doi.org/10.1109/ACCESS.2018.2870052

Ali, S., Akhlaq, F., Imran, A. S., Kastrati, Z., Daudpota, S. M., & Moosa, M. (2023). The enlightening role of explainable artificial intelligence in medical & healthcare domains: A systematic literature review. *Computers in Biology and Medicine*, *166*, 107555. https://doi.org/10.1016/j.compbiomed.2023.107555

Amann, J., Blasimme, A., Vayena, E., Frey, D., Madai, V. I., & Precise4Q consortium. (2020). Explainability for artificial intelligence in healthcare: A multidisciplinary perspective. *BMC Medical Informatics and Decision Making*, *20*(1), 310. https://doi.org/10.1186/s12911-020-01332-6

An, S., Teo, K., McConnell, M. V., Marshall, J., Galloway, C., & Squirrell, D. (2025). AI explainability in oculomics: How it works, its role in establishing trust, and what still needs to be addressed. *Progress in Retinal and Eye Research*, *106*, 101352. Advance online publication. https://doi.org/10.1016/j.preteyeres.2025.101352

Banja, J. D., Hollstein, R. D., & Bruno, M. A. (2022). When artificial intelligence models surpass physician performance: Medical malpractice liability in an era of advanced artificial intelligence. *Journal of the American College of Radiology: JACR*, *19*(7), 816–820. https://doi.org/10.1016/j.jacr.2021.11.014

Bottomley, D., & Thaldar, D. (2023). Liability for harm caused by AI in healthcare: An overview of the core legal concepts. *Frontiers in Pharmacology*, *14*, 1297353. https://doi.org/10.3389/fphar.2023.1297353

Cary, M. P., Jr, Bessias, S., McCall, J., Pencina, M. J., Grady, S. D., Lytle, K., & Economou-Zavlanos, N. J. (2025). Empowering nurses to champion Health equity & BE FAIR: Bias elimination for fair and responsible AI in healthcare. *Journal of Nursing Scholarship: An Official Publication of Sigma Theta Tau International Honor Society of Nursing*, *57*(1), 130–139. https://doi.org/10.1111/jnu.13007

Chin, M. H., Afsar-Manesh, N., Bierman, A. S., Chang, C., Colón-Rodríguez, C. J., Dullabh, P., Duran, D. G., Fair, M., Hernandez-Boussard, T., Hightower, M., Jain, A., Jordan, W. B., Konya, S., Moore, R. H., Moore, T. T., Rodriguez, R., Shaheen, G., Snyder, L. P., Srinivasan, M., Umscheid, C. A., … Ohno-Machado, L. (2023). Guiding principles to address the impact of algorithm bias on racial and ethnic disparities in health and health care. *JAMA Network Open*, *6*(12), e2345050. https://doi.org/10.1001/jamanetworkopen.2023.45050

Dankwa-Mullan, I. (2024). Health equity and ethical considerations in using artificial intelligence in public health and medicine. *Preventing Chronic Disease*, *21*, E64. https://doi.org/10.5888/pcd21.240245

Davenport, T., & Kalakota, R. (2019). The potential for artificial intelligence in healthcare. *Future Healthcare Journal, 6*(2), 94–98. https://doi.org/10.7861/futurehosp.6-2-94

Debrabander, J., & Mertes, H. (2022). Watson, autonomy and value flexibility: Revisiting the debate. *Journal of Medical Ethics*, *48*(12), 1043–1047. https://doi.org/10.1136/medethics-2021-107513

De-Giorgio, F., Benedetti, B., Mancino, M., Sala, E., & Pascali, V. L. (2025). The need for balancing 'black box' systems and explainable artificial intelligence: A necessary implementation in radiology. *European Journal of Radiology*, *185*, 112014. https://doi.org/10.1016/j.ejrad.2025.112014

Deo, R. C. (2015). Machine learning in medicine. *Circulation*, *132*(20), 1920–1930. https://doi.org/10.1161/CIRCULATIONAHA.115.001593

Elendu, C., Amaechi, D. C., Elendu, T. C., Jingwa, K. A., Okoye, O. K., John Okah, M., Ladele, J. A., Farah, A. H., & Alimi, H. A. (2023). Ethical implications of AI and robotics in healthcare: A review. *Medicine*, *102*(50), e36671. https://doi.org/10.1097/MD.0000000000036671

Ferryman, K., Mackintosh, M., & Ghassemi, M. (2023). Considering biased data as informative artifacts in AI-assisted health care. *The New England Journal of Medicine*, *389*(9), 833–838. https://doi.org/10.1056/NEJMra2214964

Floridi, L., Cowls, J., Beltrametti, M., Chatila, R., Chazerand, P., Dignum, V., … & Vayena, E. (2018). AI4People—An ethical framework for a good AI society: Opportunities, risks, principles, and recommendations. *Minds and Machines, 28*, 689–707. https://doi.org/10.1007/s11023-018-9482-5

Gerke, S., Minssen, T., & Cohen, G. (2020). Ethical and legal challenges of artificial intelligence-driven healthcare. *Artificial Intelligence in Healthcare*, 295–336. https://doi.org/10.1016/B978-0-12-818438-7.00012-5

Goktas, P., & Grzybowski, A. (2025). Shaping the future of healthcare: Ethical clinical challenges and pathways to trustworthy AI. *Journal of Clinical Medicine*, *14*(5), 1605. https://doi.org/10.3390/jcm14051605

Grady, C. (2015). Enduring and emerging challenges of informed consent. *The New England Journal of Medicine*, *372*(9), 855–862. https://doi.org/10.1056/NEJMra1411250

Hantel, A., Walsh, T. P., Marron, J. M., Kehl, K. L., Sharp, R., Van Allen, E., & Abel, G. A. (2024). Perspectives of oncologists on the ethical implications of using artificial intelligence for cancer care. *JAMA Network Open*, *7*(3), e244077. https://doi.org/10.1001/jamanetworkopen.2024.4077

Iserson, K. V. (2024). Informed consent for artificial intelligence in emergency medicine: A practical guide. *The American Journal of Emergency Medicine*, *76*, 225–230. https://doi.org/10.1016/j.ajem.2023.11.022

Knopf, S., Frahm, N., & M Pfotenhauer, S. (2023). How neurotech start-ups envision ethical futures: Demarcation, deferral, delegation. *Science and Engineering Ethics*, *29*(1), 4. https://doi.org/10.1007/s11948-022-00421-1

Kumar, D., Malin, B. A., Vishwanatha, J. K., Wu, L., & Hedges, J. R. (2024). AI in biomedicine-a forward-looking perspective on health equity. *International Journal of Environmental Research and Public Health, 21*(12), 1642. https://doi.org/10.3390/ijerph21121642

Leslie, D., Mazumder, A., Peppin, A., Wolters, M. K., & Hagerty, A. (2021). Does "AI" stand for augmenting inequality in the era of COVID-19 healthcare? *BMJ, 372*, n304. https://doi.org/10.1136/bmj.n304

Maliha, G., Gerke, S., Cohen, I. G., & Parikh, R. B. (2021). Artificial intelligence and liability in medicine: Balancing safety and innovation. *The Milbank Quarterly, 99*(3), 629–647. https://doi.org/10.1111/1468-0009.12504

Markus, A. F., Kors, J. A., & Rijnbeek, P. R. (2021). The role of explainability in creating trustworthy artificial intelligence for health care: A comprehensive survey of the terminology, design choices, and evaluation strategies. *Journal of Biomedical Informatics, 113*, 103655. https://doi.org/10.1016/j.jbi.2020.103655

Maynard, A. D., & Scragg, M. (2019). The ethical and responsible development and application of advanced brain machine interfaces. *Journal of Medical Internet Research, 21*(10), e16321. https://doi.org/10.2196/16321

Mittelstadt, B. D., Allo, P., Taddeo, M., Wachter, S., & Floridi, L. (2016). The ethics of algorithms: Mapping the debate. *Big Data & Society, 3*(2), 1–21. https://doi.org/10.1177/2053951716679679

Morley, J., Machado, C. C. V., Burr, C., Cowls, J., Joshi, I., Taddeo, M., & Floridi, L. (2020). The ethics of AI in health care: A mapping review. *Social Science & Medicine (1982), 260*, 113172. https://doi.org/10.1016/j.socscimed.2020.113172

Moulaei, K., Akhlaghpour, S., & Fatehi, F. (2025). Patient consent for the secondary use of health data in artificial intelligence (AI) models: A scoping review. *International Journal of Medical Informatics, 198*, 105872. https://doi.org/10.1016/j.ijmedinf.2025.105872

Obermeyer, Z., Powers, B., Vogeli, C., & Mullainathan, S. (2019). Dissecting racial bias in an algorithm used to manage the health of populations. *Science, 366*(6464), 447–453. https://doi.org/10.1126/science.aax2342

Polevikov, S. (2023). Advancing AI in healthcare: A comprehensive review of best practices. *Clinica chimica acta; International Journal of Clinical Chemistry, 548*, 117519. https://doi.org/10.1016/j.cca.2023.117519

Rasheed, K., Qayyum, A., Ghaly, M., Al-Fuqaha, A., Razi, A., & Qadir, J. (2022). Explainable, trustworthy, and ethical machine learning for healthcare: A survey. *Computers in Biology and Medicine, 149*, 106043. https://doi.org/10.1016/j.compbiomed.2022.106043

Rojas, J. C., Fahrenbach, J., Makhni, S., Cook, S. C., Williams, J. S., Umscheid, C. A., & Chin, M. H. (2022). Framework for integrating equity into machine learning models: A case study. *Chest, 161*(6), 1621–1627. https://doi.org/10.1016/j.chest.2022.02.001

Rose, S. L., & Shapiro, D. (2024). An ethically supported framework for determining patient notification and informed consent practices when using artificial intelligence in health care. *Chest, 166*(3), 572–578. https://doi.org/10.1016/j.chest.2024.04.014

Samek, W., Wiegand, T., & Müller, K.-R. (2017). Explainable artificial intelligence: Understanding, visualizing, and interpreting deep learning models. *ITU Journal: ICT Discoveries, 1*(1), 39–48. https://doi.org/10.48550/arXiv.1708.08296

Sasseville, M., Ouellet, S., Rhéaume, C., Sahlia, M., Couture, V., Després, P., Paquette, J. S., Darmon, D., Bergeron, F., & Gagnon, M. P. (2025). Bias mitigation in primary health care artificial intelligence models: Scoping review. *Journal of Medical Internet Research, 27*, e60269. https://doi.org/10.2196/60269

Sheu, R. K., & Pardeshi, M. S. (2022). A survey on medical Explainable AI (XAI): Recent progress, explainability approach, human interaction and scoring system. *Sensors (Basel, Switzerland)*, *22*(20), 8068. https://doi.org/10.3390/s22208068

Siddique, S. M., Tipton, K., Leas, B., Jepson, C., Aysola, J., Cohen, J. B., Flores, E., Harhay, M. O., Schmidt, H., Weissman, G. E., Fricke, J., Treadwell, J. R., & Mull, N. K. (2024). The impact of health care algorithms on racial and ethnic disparities: A systematic review. *Annals of Internal Medicine*, *177*(4), 484–496. https://doi.org/10.7326/M23-2960

Tarantini, G., Fraccaro, C., Porzionato, A., Van Mieghem, N., Treede, H., Shammas, N., Szerlip, M., Thourani, V., Gerosa, G., Marchese, A., Speziale, G., Ludes, B., Pollak, S., Vanezis, P., & Ferrara, S. D. (2025). Informed consent and shared decision-making in modern medicine: Case-based approach, current gaps and practical proposal. *The American Journal of Cardiology*, *241*, 77–83. https://doi.org/10.1016/j.amjcard.2025.01.015

Uche-Anya, E., Anyane-Yeboa, A., Berzin, T. M., Ghassemi, M., & May, F. P. (2022). Artificial intelligence in gastroenterology and hepatology: How to advance clinical practice while ensuring health equity. *Gut*, *71*(9), 1909–1915. https://doi.org/10.1136/gutjnl-2021-326271

Vo, V., Chen, G., Aquino, Y. S. J., Carter, S. M., Do, Q. N., & Woode, M. E. (2023). Multi-stakeholder preferences for the use of artificial intelligence in healthcare: A systematic review and thematic analysis. *Social Science & Medicine (1982)*, *338*, 116357. https://doi.org/10.1016/j.socscimed.2023.116357

Will, J. F. (2011). A brief historical and theoretical perspective on patient autonomy and medical decision making: Part II: The autonomy model. *Chest*, *139*(6), 1491–1497. https://doi.org/10.1378/chest.11-0516

Yu, L., & Zhai, X. (2024). Use of artificial intelligence to address health disparities in low- and middle-income countries: A thematic analysis of ethical issues. *Public Health*, *234*, 77–83. https://doi.org/10.1016/j.puhe.2024.05.029

Zhang, J., & Zhang, Z. M. (2023). Ethics and governance of trustworthy medical artificial intelligence. *BMC Medical Informatics and Decision Making*, *23*(1), 7. https://doi.org/10.1186/s12911-023-02103-9

Part II

Transformative Technologies and Patient-Centered Care

4 Transformative Technology in Healthcare

The Role of Emerging Technologies in Patient-Centered Care

Zainab Almukhtar and Philip Eappen

4.1 INTRODUCTION TO PATIENT-CENTERED CARE

The National Institute of Medicine report *Crossing the Quality Chasm* (2001) emphasized that patient-centered care (PCC) is a priority goal in the 21st-century healthcare systems (*Institute of Medicine*, 2001). Despite the various definitions, they all agree on the basic concept of patient-centered care, that is, patient-centered care refers to the respect and the response to the individual patients' preferences, needs, and values. The values and needs of patients are to guide the decisions in healthcare (Constand et al., 2014; Lusk & Fater, 2013). Those needs, characteristics, and beliefs of patients are continuously incorporated into the healthcare decision-making to produce treatment plans that are tailored to individuals or groups of patients (Kane et al., 2015). Through PCC, the patient becomes an active participant in the healthcare decision-making rather than a passive recipient of their care (Chen et al., 2019). In other words, PCC transitions healthcare from a disease-centered to a patient-centered model (Miller et al., 2010). The core principles of PCC include respect for patient values, coordination of care, information provision, physical and emotional comfort, family involvement, and access to continuous care (Lusk & Fater, 2013). Patient-centered care has advantages for the patients, the staff, and the healthcare system. Some of the stated advantages are the enhancement of the quality and the outcomes of healthcare treatments (Edgman-Levitan & Schoenbaum, 2021) and the improvement in patient adherence. Evidence state that patient-centered care is associated with patient satisfaction with the healthcare process and with enhanced well-being (Tzelepis et al., 2015). It is indicated that patients are more compliant with the treatment when they feel that their needs are taken care of. PCC also supports the relationship between the patient and the caregiver and improves the utilization of resources in the healthcare system by directing resources to areas of need (Bertakis & Azari, 2011; Lusk & Fater, 2013).

DOI: 10.1201/9781003624875-6

Emergent and advanced technologies via their enhanced capabilities transformed PCC in healthcare. Those technologies enabled predictive, personalized, participatory, and preventive models of care (Sinha, 2024). They consist of artificial intelligence (AI), which is the tool used in the simulation of human intelligence by machines; the Internet of Things (IoT), which comprises connected devices that collect real-time health data; wearable devices that can be connected to IoT; and Blockchain, a decentralized technology that is applied to manage patient data, which are increasingly used in healthcare, and virtual reality. The adoption of those and other technologies (Soriano et al., 2022) has shifted the healthcare model from a traditional centralized model to a more decentralized patient-centered model (Sinha, 2024) and improved efficiency and outcomes of healthcare. One of the highly used technologies is artificial intelligence (AI), which often integrates with the other technologies and harnesses patients' data (Bjerring & Busch, 2021) to direct patient-centered healthcare decisions (Sauerbrei et al., 2023). The ability to analyze vast amounts of data and predict outcomes offered many opportunities in healthcare decision-making directed to the characteristics and needs of patient (Bjerring & Busch, 2021). Data that is collected from sensors and wearable devices provides a wide range of information about the characteristics and features of patients (Chiauzzi et al., 2015). When coupled with the predictive abilities of AI and technologies such as IoT and robotics, this data can inform optimized and personalized treatment plans (Kizer, 2002). For example, application of robotics in different contexts in healthcare enabled directing personalized treatment plans to different populations such as the elderly (Sabanovic et al., 2014). Despite the opportunities that emerging technologies, including AI, can offer to patient-centered care, there are several considerations and issues that need attention (Yadav, 2024). Those include concerns about privacy, regulations, interoperability, standardization, ethics, and the reliability of those emerging technologies (Shoghli et al., 2024). The cost and scalability of advanced technological devices are other concerns (Sabanovic et al., 2014). Importantly because the majority of those devices involve the use and collection of data, the security and privacy of data call for special attention (Karimian et al., 2022a).

It is expected that the application of advanced technologies in providing patient-centered and personalized healthcare solutions will continue to grow. The emerging state of healthcare is directed toward the integration of technologies like IoT-assisted wearable sensor devices, AI, and Blockchain (Reddy et al., 2020) to provide more accurate, personalized, and holistic solutions. However, to be able to reach the best outcomes of implementing those technologies, an understanding of areas of application as well as issues and obstacles is important. Special focus on AI is needed, as a tool that links many of those technologies (Sauerbrei et al., 2023). Within that, it is vital to identify issues and obstacles in using AI tools and how that interacts with different aspects of the communication between the patient and the medical provider, as well as issues related to the accuracy and regulations on the use of healthcare technologies. In the following, we investigate how emerging technologies with a focus on AI can be applied to patient-centered care, we review aspects of personalization and patient-centered approaches in healthcare, we discuss examples and areas of application, obstacles and issues, and then we propose directions to foster the application of emergent technologies in patient-centered care. Finally, we end the chapter with conclusions and future suggestions.

4.2 LITERATURE REVIEW

4.2.1 Personalization and Patient-Centered Care

Two important items of quality in healthcare are personalization and standardization of healthcare services (Ansmann & Pfaff, 2017). While standardization relates to following the medical and process standards in healthcare delivery, personalization is related to delivering healthcare that incorporates the personal needs, preferences, and characteristics of patients and populations (Bucher, 2023). Both personalization and standardization are important aspects in the delivery of healthcare (Ansmann & Pfaff, 2017). To deliver the needed services, healthcare should incorporate a balanced mixture of personalization and standardization based on the needs of patients and the medical conditions (Basu, 2011). In some literature, personalization is referred to as individualization (Bond et al., 2009; Pfaff et al., 2010). Personalization or individualization is a main correlate with patient-centered care. While following the general care standards, it is important that healthcare providers follow patient-centered and personalized care approaches. This is one of the essential points of the Quadratic Aim of Healthcare. The National Institute of Medicine in its Quadratic Aim emphasizes patient-centered care as a main aspect in healthcare delivery (Tzelepis et al., 2015). In the report *Crossing the Quality Chasm*, the National Institute of Medicine recognizes patient-centered care as a major aim in the new health system for the 21st century (Institute of Medicine, 2001). Despite the many definitions of patient-centered care, they all agree on a similar meaning. Patient-centered care is delivering healthcare that respects and responds to individual patient preferences, needs, and ensures that clinical and medical decisions are guided by those values (Edgman-Levitan & Schoenbaum, 2021; McCabe, 2004). At many times, patient-centered care and individualized or personalized care are used interchangeably as they are very closely related to healthcare tailored to the characteristics and needs of patients (Morgan & Yoder, 2012). Patient-centered care is also referred to as person-centered care (Chawla & Davis, 2013). Patient-centered care includes basic principles: respect for patient values; coordination and integration of care; information and education; physical comfort of the patient; emotional support; involvement of family and friends; and continuity and access to care (Heaton, 2014; Louis et al., 2019). By the adoption of patient-centered care approaches, healthcare is transformed from disease focus to patient focus where the patient becomes an active participant in healthcare decisions (Chiauzzi et al., 2015). Some of the stated benefits of patient-centered care approaches include, but are not limited to, the empowerment of patients, better outcome (Edgman-Levitan & Schoenbaum, 2021), more equitable healthcare delivery, better utilization of healthcare, enhanced adherence, empowerment, and satisfaction with healthcare providers (Al Muammar et al., 2018). Literature has indicated improved outcomes and health service utilization when patient-centered care was implemented. When patients are a part of healthcare decisions, they feel empowered (Miller et al., 2010). The outcomes of treatments are better when they incorporate the characteristics and needs of patients. Evidence indicates that patient-centered care improves the quality (Edgman-Levitan & Schoenbaum, 2021) and outcomes of healthcare and increases patient adherence to treatment, which results in positive impacts on patients' well-being (Robinson et al., 2008). By following patient-centered approaches in healthcare, resource utilization is enhanced as care is directed where and when it is needed (Pfaff et al., 2010). The proper application of patient-centered care requires a holistic understanding of the characteristics of patients and their experience with disease (Constand et al., 2014). As well as disease diagnosis, patient-centered care involves the education and awareness of patients and communities, as well as the prevention and treatment of disease (Morgan & Yoder, 2012).

An important backbone for patient-centered care is the collection and analysis of data to direct personalized and patient-centered treatment models (Chawla & Davis, 2013). Patient medical data provides pools of information about the conditions and preferences of patients, including biological, social, and environmental conditions (Edgman-Levitan & Schoenbaum, 2021) and data of patients and their families regarding the evaluation and preferences of healthcare. Advances in emerging technologies have transformed patient-centered care by enabling highly personalized and optimized treatments in different healthcare fields and enhancing timely data-driven decisions (Oyeniyi, 2024). The abilities of AI and technology applications have transformed healthcare from only diagnosis approaches to diagnosis and predictive approaches (van Veen et al., 2019). Technologies like the Internet of Things, telehealth, and robotics have enhanced patient-centered care in areas ranging from elderly care, personalized surgeries, mental health and others (Alharbi et al., 2023). From personalized treatment plans and predictive analytics to virtual assistants and remote monitoring, emerging healthcare technologies support a more proactive, accessible, and participatory model of care (Oyeniyi, 2024). Yet, as many AI technologies are expanding both in use and applications, it is vital to have a detailed understanding of the use and applications of those technologies, as well as the challenges and concerns related to the application of those technologies in patient-centered care. Matters like financial costs and benefits, privacy, standardization, and others need to be understood (Patel et al., 2008; Yadav, 2024). This understanding will enable setting guidelines on the use and adaptation of these technologies to advance patient-centered care. In the following section, we review areas of the applications of emergent technologies and AI in the delivery of patient-centered care.

4.2.2 Areas of Applications of Emerging Technologies in Patient-Centered Care

The developments in advanced technologies such as AI, mobile devices, 3G, 4G, and 5G networks and the decreasing price of sensors enabled the use of technology in different parts of healthcare (Bjerring & Busch, 2021). The main AI technologies include machine learning (ML), deep learning (DL), and natural language processing (NLP). Developments involving the integration of AI and personalized healthcare records and the use of telehealth enhanced communication with patients and provided advanced data collection and analyzing capabilities (Khoja et al., 2013). In the following, we explore different areas of the application of emerging technologies in the personalization of patient care or in patient-centered approaches.

4.2.1.1 Personalized Healthcare Records and E-Health in Patient-Centered Care

E-health enhances patient-centered care by improving access to health information, enabling patients to actively participate in decision-making, and fostering better communication with providers (Van Velthoven & Cordon, 2019). Tools such as telehealth, mobile apps, and electronic health records support personalized care that reflects patients' preferences and needs and promotes care continuity across healthcare settings (Ezeamii et al., 2024). Telehealth overcomes the barriers of distance in providing personalized care and improving access to patients living in rural areas. An example of the applications of telehealth is in chronic disease management such as diabetes where individualized care paths for patients are delivered (Du et al., 2025).

Health records play a crucial role in patient-centered medicine by consolidating patient information, which enables clinicians to tailor care to individual needs (Butler et al., 2021; Imison et al., 2016). Access to comprehensive longitudinal data supports accurate diagnoses and effective treatment planning incorporating the needs of patients, and continuity of care (Zhu et al., 2020). Furthermore, integrating patient preferences into health records ensures that clinical decisions are guided by the values and priorities of each patient (Institute of Medicine, 2001). As well as the benefits of EHR in directing treatment and medicine-related decisions, they are also important to improve access and streamline the processes of healthcare within the scope of patient-centeredness (Reisman, 2017). For examples, in primary care clinics, records can summarize the information of patients before the initial appointment, which helps care teams prepare outlines for personalized healthcare records. Some hospitals launched an application that uses patient portals via hospital-owned tablets (Kelly et al., 2019). Those portals give patients access to a range of medical information in real time, such as vital signs, problem lists, medication information (name, dose, route, frequency, side effects), test results, names and photographs of hospital providers, and links to a medical glossary and/or personalized education about their diagnoses decision (Kelly et al., 2018). When patients have access to their data and to healthcare information, they gain empowerment and feel more in charge of their health.

The large sets of healthcare records together with the abilities of AI and digital technologies facilitated the digital transformation and automated decision-making of modern healthcare (Miller et al., 2010; Negro-Calduch et al., 2021). Integrating healthcare data with the predictive abilities of AI offers solutions to the development and design of personalized treatment plans (Manne & Kantheti, 2021).

To create an integrated patient health record, data from different sources related to the patient should be integrated and communicated (Holt et al., 2020). Examples of data are data from healthcare providers, clinical data and data from wearables. Data such as the social determinants of health and patient behavioral preferences are important in designing patient-centered approaches (Holt et al., 2020). However, often much of this data is missing from electronic patients' records. As patients' records contain integrated data from different resources, there should be a connection between these records (Tak et al., 2024). This underscores the importance of interoperability and integration of data (Lehne et al., 2019). Interoperability refers to the ability of different digital applications and devices to seamlessly exchange, interpret, and use health information across organizational and technological boundaries, ensuring that data flows smoothly between healthcare providers. Applying AI tools to analyze and form models from EHR data can uncover patterns, clinical outcomes, and tailor healthcare plans according to individual patient characteristics (Esmaeilzadeh, 2020). The forms of healthcare data include structured data forms and unstructured data forms such as clinical notes, imaging, and genomics (G. Christopher et al., 2024). To integrate this data that is of different forms, there should be a right data infrastructure.

4.2.1.2 Application of Advanced Technologies in the Detection of Disease via Patient-Centered Approaches

The concept of patient-centeredness incorporates the needs and characteristics of patients to improve the health of individuals and populations (Edgman-Levitan & Schoenbaum, 2021). Patient-centered care approaches in healthcare span the prevention, diagnosis, and treatment of diseases (Donner-Banzhoff, 2018). Digital technologies and AI have enhanced the diagnosis of diseases in relation to genetic and biological features (Bourouis et al., 2014). Technologies such as pattern recognition, data analysis, and predictive modeling provide high-accuracy tools that predict the occurrence of complex diseases (Oyeniyi, 2024). An example is the AI tool and classifying algorithm used in the detection of early signs of skin cancer (Höhn et al., 2021). Using virtual care assistants, telehealth, remote patient monitoring, and image recognition technologies enables the detection of early symptoms of deterioration among patients (Du et al., 2025). This tool tracks patients' trajectories of daily blood sugar levels and helps design personalized health treatment plans. Another example is the AI tool developed by Google for the detection of diabetic retinopathy via digital images with very high accuracy (Jacoba et al., 2021). Digital twin technologies and predictive analytics allow clinicians to simulate treatment outcomes and optimize individualized interventions (M. Christopher, 2011; J. Liu et al., 2017).

An important area where AI has found potential is the prediction of disease outbreaks among patient groups, which has proven value during the spread of outbreaks and illnesses (Johnson et al., 2021). A noteworthy AI application is the detection of foodborne illness by using machine learning algorithms (Sadilek et al., 2018). The prediction of cardiovascular disease based on patient data is another example of AI application in patient-centered disease detection (Tibet et al., 2012). Deep learning

AI algorithms were applied in the analysis of results to direct interventional procedures for cardiovascular disease. Within community and population health, AI has been applied to analyze community-level data to track the spread of chronic and infectious conditions (Doan et al., n.d.; Villanueva-Miranda et al., 2025). Those tools support public health planning and policy decisions, contributing to more proactive and informed community health strategies (Rahimi et al., 2021). In the next section, we expand on personalized treatment plans by the application of emergent technologies.

4.2.1.3 Emerging Technologies and Personalized Treatment Plans

Personalized medicine approaches match the suitable medical care process for patients based on a range of patient characteristics such as contextual characteristics, genetics, and lifestyle (Alowais et al., 2023). As mentioned, combination of AI, wearables, and IoT introduces advanced capabilities in harnessing data to create healthcare plans based on the needs and values of patients (Liang et al., 2024; Sinha, 2024). Using patient data (genomics, lifestyle habits, comorbidities) and AI algorithms can generate highly customized treatment plans and recommendations (Patel et al., 2008). For instance, IBM Watson application in oncology can analyze vast clinical data to suggest cancer therapies tailored to the patient's profile (Chow et al., 2024). Using machine learning algorithms enabled the identification of needed medications based on patients' genomic information (Patel et al., 2008). Another example is applying neural networks in the prediction of the progression of Alzheimer's and Parkinson's disease by the integration of imaging data (MRI, fMRI) and genetic risk factors (M. Liu et al., 2018). Post operative care is another area where emerging technologies are applied to foster patient-centeredness (Wells et al., 2022). In post operative care, timely interventions and individualized rehabilitation plans can significantly impact recovery speed and outcomes.

Neural networks, especially recurrent models like LSTMs, have high capabilities in the analysis of data from wearable devices (heart rate monitors, movement trackers, temperature sensors) together with EHR data like medication history, comorbidities, and surgical details (Ballinger et al., 2018; Saadatnejad et al., 2019). An application to improve personalized post-operative care has been developed by coupling neural network technologies with wearable device sensor data and EHR (Kroll et al., 2017; Thompson et al., 2003). The tool continuously monitors patient metrics to detect patterns of abnormalities in recovery such as delayed wound healing and elevated pain levels. Remote patient monitoring devices have been used with AI in the detection of danger signs and assigning solutions during recovery (Liao et al., 2019). Another advanced healthcare technology used in patient-centered care is blockchain (H. S. Chen et al., 2019). Blockchain is a decentralized digital record that securely records and verifies transactions across a distributed network without the need for a central authority. In healthcare, it enables transparent, tamper-proof sharing of patient data while ensuring privacy and trust (Kasyapa & Vanmathi, 2024). By enabling, secure, decentralized storage of medical records, blockchain tools can grant patients ownership and control over their data while ensuring confidentiality. The patient-chain system, built on Hyperledger Fabric, allows controlled access to health records during emergencies, ensuring rapid care without compromising privacy (Le et al., 2022). Blockchain is also applied to remote monitoring tools to harness real-time data in monitoring home care patients and enhancing their well-being (H. S. Chen et al., 2019). Robotics have potential in enhancing patient-centered care by improving efficiency, precision, and access to services (Sabanovic et al., 2014). Robots can take on repetitive tasks, assist in rehabilitation, and aid in surgical procedures, allowing clinicians to spend more time with patients. In the following, we discuss the uses of advanced technology in patient-centered care within the mental and cognitive health context.

4.2.1.4 Emergent Technologies: Mental and Cognitive Health via Patient-Centeredness

Mental health is an important part of healthcare that includes high and complex interactions with personal and contextual factors (Duffy, 2010; Thornicroft et al., 2012). Patient-centered approaches and treatments are vital to mental health services as the mental health conditions of persons are highly related to personal, social, and environmental factors (Duffy, 2010).

Although emerging technologies have high potential in patient-centered design of mental health prevention and treatment services, there are several barriers (Coyle, avid, et al., 2009). Some of the barriers are the complex nature of mental health services and interactions, ethical requirements, restricted access to end users, and limited opportunities for experimentation and adaptation to individual needs. Despite this, the use of advanced technologies in mental health patient-centered care is witnessing continuous growth (Bucci et al., 2019; Coyle et al., 2009). One of the areas where AI technologies are used is in the design of mental health promotion and awareness initiatives (Chancellor & De Choudhury, 2020). Sentiment analysis technologies of social media posts have been used to detect views about mental health and accordingly design mental health awareness programs. AI technologies are used in the detection of mood fluctuations among patients with mental illness and in generating alerts for different patients based on the collected data (Injster et al., 2008). Within this, they analyze data that consist of voice, text, and facial expressions to assess mood, stress, or depression levels. An example of the use of advanced technology to provide personalized support for patients with mental health issues is the chatbot Woebot (Karkosz et al., 2024). This chatbot is based on cognitive-behavioral therapy (CBT), which engages users in supportive conversations and tracks emotional changes to direct mental awareness and well-being paths. Another AI-driven chatbot, Wysa, offers text-based, empathetic conversations to support users dealing with depression and anxiety (Joerin, 2018). AI tools have been applied in the detection of risk of developing mental health disorders based on certain patient-related characteristics (Graham et al., 2019), and designs personalized treatment methods. AI decision support systems (DSS) are used to support clinicians in the detection of mental health disorders (Trevedi et al., 2024). One example is the Texas Medication Algorithm Project that supports the diagnosis, treatment, and prevention of major depressive disorders.

Within community context, artificial intelligence offers powerful tools for analyzing mood through text, voice, and physiological data. By leveraging machine learning and neural networks, AI can detect emotional states and mental health risks with increasing accuracy. These technologies enable more personalized mental healthcare, though ethical and practical challenges remain (Zohuri & Zadeh, 2020). Also, a machine learning tool has been applied to design alternative treatments based on brain imaging and cognitive data (Dadi et al., 2021). The next section will review an important part in the application of emergent technologies in patient-centered care within elderly and home care.

4.2.1.5 Emerging Technologies in Home and Elderly Care via Patient-Centered Care

Care homes and elderly care are other avenues where advanced technologies and AI tools are used to provide patient-centered care. Those applications include scopes of detection and management of diseases and designing personalized interventions.

In long-term care environments, integrating AI with wearable IoT systems improves remote monitoring, enabling proactive interventions (Wang & Hsu, 2023). Research explores the convergence of emotional AI, IoT, and robotics to provide real-time, empathetic patient care (Shaik et al., 2023). Blockchain, alongside IoT and AI, supports secure, decentralized remote patient monitoring systems applied to elderly care with enhanced data privacy and responsiveness (Cheikhrouhou et al., 2023).

Wearables and sensors integrated with AI have been used to detect anomalies in real-time, supporting the management of chronic diseases such as diabetes or heart conditions among elderly patients (van Veen et al., 2019). An important application of advanced technologies for elderly care is in fall detection (Alharbi et al., 2023). This is done by the integration of AI with wearable sensors, computer vision, and IoT-based monitoring systems to analyze real-time motion, posture, and environmental data to distinguish between normal activity and dangerous falls. Another significant use of AI is in the prediction of health deterioration symptoms among elderly patients (Odell, 2015). The commercial platform Cera Care in the UK integrates patients' data on thousands of care records to predict health deterioration 7 days in advance, reducing hospital admissions by 52% and patient falls by 17%. The AlayaCare's AI integration enables homecare providers to automate personal clinical assessments and link them to recommended interventions, reducing planning time by over 60% (G. Christopher et al., 2024). Merging EHR data with the Fuzzy VIKOR method creates a tool to deliver personalized elderly care recommendations (Zohuri & Zadeh, 2020). This approach is based on categorizing five treatment options for the elderly population based on efficacy, safety, preferences, cost-effectiveness, and feasibility. Robotics are applied to provide personalized assistance to elderly patients (Sawik et al., 2023). Socially assistive robots are used to support independence, reduce caregiver burden, and improve well-being for home care patients. Despite the potential and promises of emerging technologies in patient-centered approaches, there are many considerations that should be taken into account in the applications. In the following section, we review and discuss the issues in the application of emerging technologies in healthcare.

4.2.3 Issues in the Application of AI in Healthcare

In this section, we categorize the major issues in the application of AI and emerging technologies in healthcare to bias, privacy, and adoption issues.

4.2.3.1 Biases in AI and Emerging Technologies

AI systems learn patterns and make decisions based on utilizing huge amounts of data and feeding this data into mathematical models (Bjerring & Busch, 2021). This data, and the outputs from the model, are used with devices such as robotics to guide personalized decisions. Some of the common mathematical algorithms in machine learning are supervised and unsupervised machine learning models (Olyanasab & Annabestani, 2024). In supervised machine learning, the model is trained on pre-labeled data, while in unsupervised machine learning, the model is used to predict patterns among unlabeled data (Vayena et al., 2018). In those and other models, the accuracy of outcomes or decisions highly relies on the quality and representativeness of the data as well as the accuracy of the model (Manne & Kantheti, 2021). A major issue in the application of data-based technologies is bias. The sources of biases can be data or inaccurate models, or misinterpretation of the models or results (Cross et al., 2024). Biases happen and accumulate throughout the AI life cycle, and if not dealt with, impact healthcare decisions negatively. In regard to data-based biases, the quality of the decisions from AI applications is related to the completeness and the quality of the used data (Manne & Kantheti, 2021). For example, data that is not representative of the population and of insufficient sample leads to wrong clinical predictions and fails to reflect patients' related factors (Cross et al., 2024). Discrimination in findings is one of the results of data bias. There have been many events of discrimination in relation to individual or group patients due to the inadequacy or misrepresentation of data (Obermeyer et al., 2019). Another source of bias in results is missing data (Mittermaier et al., 2023). Some kinds of data, like socioeconomic and personal data, may be hard to collect, causing many missing values in the data. This can result in bias in outcomes against underrepresented groups and increased healthcare disparities (Cross et al., 2024). A stated example of this bias is that patients with lower socioeconomic status often have less data on tests and diagnosis of certain diseases (Arpey et al., 2017). Many of those patients usually receive care from multiple institutions, which makes the collection of data via EHR more challenging. The reliability of the model and the data used for training are other sources of bias. Regarding model accuracy and representativeness, we know that AI models are trained on data (Cross et al., 2024). The model will lead to correct predictions if the used data is good and faulty predictions if the used data is bad. Sometimes, the choice of the model is not correct or not representative of the data. Another source of bias is the misunderstanding among healthcare workers regarding the outcomes and the results of the mathematical models in digital technologies and AI (Carey et al., 2024; Perry & Uuk, 2019).

4.2.3.2 Privacy and Ethics in Emerging Technologies

Medical and health data is a very critical and sensitive data source as it connects with the patient's personal characteristics and health (Banerjee et al., 2018). As stated advanced technological tools and AI models use this data to make personalized decisions in healthcare. Many times, healthcare organizations and bodies use this data for other purposes, such as for research and statistics, or share it without the knowledge of patients (Conger et al., 2013). To comply with privacy and ethical requirements, patients should be aware of the uses of their data and provide explicit consent regarding the sharing of that data. Patients should be fully made aware of how the data is used. The limitations of AI, including the possibility of breaches or malfunctions, should also be explained to the users. Proper safety control tools for AI should be put in place (Manne & Kantheti, 2021). A point of high importance is establishing privacy regulations for AI. There are still some concerns regarding this in both developed and developing countries, as many do not have clear regulations in place. In developing countries, safety regulations could be less scrutinized, which calls for attention (Mikava & Mamulaidze, 2023). Studies advise the use of regular monitoring and audits to track the safety, transparency, and quality of AI applications in healthcare (Cross et al., 2024; Esmaeilzadeh, 2020).

4.2.3.3 Adoption and Acceptance of AI in Healthcare

The acceptance and adoption of emerging technologies and AI in healthcare by patients, staff, and healthcare professionals is an area that calls for focus (Esmaeilzadeh, 2020). The trust in and readiness to use AI and other digital technologies among healthcare providers impacts the spread of those technologies. As healthcare is a very personalized field involving interaction between patients and professionals, some are cautious about the spread of AI. They fear that the use of AI might weaken the communication between patients and healthcare providers.

There is a caution among physicians and other healthcare professionals that AI and other smart technologies will undermine their role as sources of expertise and decision makers (Abdullah & Fakieh, 2020; Khan Rony et al., 2024). Many of the patient-centered approaches incorporate the communication between patients and healthcare staff as an important aspect of care. Relating to that, it is sometimes argued that although emerging healthcare technologies provide advanced solutions in patient-centered care, they can sometimes weaken the patient-physician direct communication (M. Chen et al., 2022; Rony et al., 2024).

Another area that impacts the use of advanced technologies in healthcare comes from the mistrust of both patients and healthcare professionals in the capabilities of those technologies in making correct personalized healthcare decisions (Aquino et al., 2023). Concerns about ethics and data privacy arise in patient-centered healthcare via advanced technologies, especially since those technologies involve the collection and usage of patient-related sensitive data (Silva et al., 2022). In addition to those issues, many healthcare providers are worried that the use of AI would overtake or replace their positions (Karimian et al., 2022a).

From the patients' side, one of the issues is the mistrust in AI tools. This is linked to factors of ambiguity about AI, worries about privacy, and autonomy in the choice of treatment (Scott et al., 2021). Mainly patients prefer to have an expert human opinion together with AI. A German study indicated that most patients have a positive view toward artificial intelligence, but most of those patients highly preferred that physicians supervise artificial intelligence tools (Fritsch et al., 2022). The usability of devices that collect data is a factor in the adoption of digital technologies. While a number of users of wearable devices indicate that those devices give them more autonomy and access to their personal data (Vayena et al., 2018). Others state that wearable devices restrict their movement and are not comfortable to put on (Jia et al., 2018). They also fear that those devices permit access to private data, which can be used in different ways by healthcare organizations. A point of argument is that AI tools should be more focused on the care and well-being of patients rather than making the work of the physicians easy (Lewin et al., 2024). This underscores the importance of incorporating the views and needs of users (patients) when designing digital technologies for personalized healthcare (Madanian et al., 2023). Concerns related to funding are that the focus on funding emergent technologies may take away from funding initiatives for bottom-up health services, like healthcare awareness and essential vaccine distribution (Lewin et al., 2024). Cost factors are compatibility with insurance policies, are other reasons that might limit the adoption of advanced technologies like IoT and Blockchain in patient's care (Yadav, 2024). Many of those technologies are expensive and are not supported by most insurance policies. By this, we stated the main issues and concerns in using emerging technologies in patient-centered healthcare. In the following part, we propose main directions to promote the use of AI and emergent technologies in personalized healthcare.

4.3 DIRECTIONS TO PROMOTE THE APPLICATION OF EMERGING TECHNOLOGIES IN PATIENT-CENTERED CARE

Based on the previous review and synthesis, we propose actions to leverage the applications of emergent technologies in providing patient-centered care. Those actions are divided into main categories of concern in AI and advanced technology applications.

4.3.1 Data Integration and Operability

To leverage the ability of emerging technologies to harness data and embed AI into clinical workflows toward personalized treatment (Patel et al., 2008; Alowais et al., 2023), the following paths are proposed:

- Create unified patient health records capable of integrating data from multiple sources such as behavioral, social, and environmental data (Holt et al., 2020; Tak et al., 2024). This data can be collected by wearable devices, telehealth platforms, and patients' data records.

- Incorporate social determinants of health data into EHR and patients' related data to better inform patient-centered decisions in healthcare.
- Put in place interoperability standards to enable seamless data exchange between systems and providers and ensure that the data used in patient-centered decisions in healthcare is accurate, complete, and up-to-date (Negro-Calduch et al., 2021).

4.3.2 Bias and Equity

- Enhancing patients' engagement and empowerment by expanding patient portals and mobile health applications that provide real-time access to health data (Kelly et al., 2018).
- Make sure that patients from different social groups and diverse demographics engage in using digital tools to better inform patient-centered decisions.
- Audit AI algorithms for bias to ensure that the training datasets are representative of diverse populations and incorporate data from underrepresented groups (Obermeyer et al., 2019; Cross et al., 2024).
- Establish focused KPIs focused on equity to track the ability of emerging technologies to reduce or exacerbate health disparities (Manne & Kantheti, 2021).
- Engage communities in the co-design of AI tools to ensure the incorporation of cultural, linguistic, and accessibility considerations in digital tools in healthcare (Ansmann & Pfaff, 2017).
- Conduct longitudinal studies to evaluate the long-term effects of emerging technologies on patient outcomes, equity, and cost-effectiveness (Oyeniyi, 2024).

4.3.3 Technology Advancements

- Foster predictive analytics tools in areas of detection of risk, progression of disease, post-surgical complications, and design of treatment trajectories (Liu et al., 2018; Christopher et al., 2024).
- Integrate AI into remote monitoring systems to allow better real time patient-centered healthcare plans with increased responsiveness (Shaik et al., 2023).
- Form integrated systems of emerging technologies such as integrating AI, IoT, wearables, and other technologies to form holistic patient-centered approaches throughout the awareness, detection, and treatment (Yadav, 2024).
- Collaborate with national and international stakeholders on the application of emerging technologies such as robotics and AI in mutual research and knowledge transfer (Elendu et al., 2023).
- Explore hybrid models that combine standardized protocols with flexible personalization powered by AI (Ansmann & Pfaff, 2017).

4.3.4 Privacy and Security

- Strengthen the informed consent process to enable patients to understand the activities of data collection, storing, analyzing, and sharing (Dankar et al., 2019).
- Put in place robust cybersecurity measures to protect against data breaches and unauthorized access, and make sure to update those measures with emerging security threats (Kruse et al., 2017).
- Maintain human oversight in AI decision-making, ensuring that physicians validate and contextualize algorithmic outputs (Fritsch et al., 2022; Lewin et al., 2024).
- Develop clear regulatory guidelines for AI in healthcare, including safety, efficacy, and accountability requirements (Mikava & Mamulaidze, 2023; Aquino et al., 2023).
- Establish clear accountability rules in using robotics and AI that describe possible errors and responsibilities (Mittelstadt et al., 2016).

4.3.5 Adoption of Emergent Technologies in Patient-Centered Care

- Encourage responsible adoption of advanced technologies in healthcare through funding, reimbursement models, stakeholder partnerships (Elendu et al., 2023; Reddy et al., 2020).
- Build trust and acceptance among healthcare professionals and patients by ensuring transparency in AI decision-making processes and clarifying that AI supports aims (Scott et al., 2021).
- Address patient and provider concerns regarding autonomy, job security, and changes in care delivery through open communication, participatory design, and demonstration projects (Abdullah & Fakieh, 2020).
- Promote gradual, phased adoption beginning with pilot programs in the application of healthcare technologies in patient-centered care, and utilize feedback to implement iterative developments (Laziz & Rachid, 2024).
- Provide AI literacy training for clinicians to improve confidence in using technology and interpreting AI-generated recommendations (Lambert et al., 2023).
- Redefine roles and workflows to integrate AI while preserving the human elements of patient-provider relationships (Karimian et al., 2022a).

4.4 CONCLUSION

This chapter reviewed the role of emerging technologies such as artificial intelligence, IoT, wearable sensors, blockchain, telehealth, and robotics in shaping patient-centered care across different healthcare contexts. It highlighted how these innovations improve personalization and enhance predictive and preventive capabilities. It investigates how data from variable sources is utilized to inform pathways for patient-centered healthcare plans. Applications in chronic disease management, elderly and home-based care, mental health, and acute interventions illustrate the applications and potential of advanced technologies in healthcare. New innovation designs that involve the integration of the stated technologies with large data from several resources are immigrating to direct holistic healthcare decision approaches. In the chapter, the potential of AI and predictive analysis to infer healthcare decisions based on the values and characteristics of patients in areas of diabetes management, after-surgery risk detection, and others is discussed.

The review also addresses key challenges such as equity, privacy and security concerns, interoperability gaps, algorithmic bias, regulatory uncertainties, and the need to balance personalization with standardization.

Looking ahead, the future landscape of emerging technologies in healthcare is likely to be characterized by deeper integration of AI with multi-source health data, enabling hyper-personalized care pathways that adapt dynamically to patient needs in real time (Bjerring & Busch, 2021). Innovation in emergent technologies in healthcare matures, patient-centered care through the creation of models incorporating predictive, participatory, and preventive approaches (Oyeniyi, 2024). Robotics enable personalized care for patients and more precise surgeries (Sabanovic et al., 2014; Soriano et al., 2022). Telehealth and mobile platforms are expected to reduce disparities by expanding access for underserved and rural populations (Grubaugh et al., 2008). Realizing this and other indicated advances in healthcare technologies toward patient-centeredness requires robust governance frameworks, ethical safeguards, and strategies that address interoperability, bias, and cost barriers (Obermeyer et al., 2019; Yadav, 2024). Collaborative partnerships between patients, providers, policymakers, and technology developers will be essential to ensure that these advancements are harnessed responsibly and inclusively. Ultimately, the thoughtful alignment of technological innovation with patient-centered values promises a healthcare system that is not only more efficient and responsive but also more humane, inclusive, and empowering. This chapter discussed aspects of patient-centered care and reviewed the application of advanced technology to incorporate patient-centered approaches in healthcare. Within that, it identified the main technologies and applications and issues in the application of those technologies. It provided strategic directions and pathways on how to advance healthcare technologies and overcome related issues. This will act as guidelines for designers and providers of healthcare technologies, and healthcare organizations.

REFERENCES

Abdullah, R., & Fakieh, B. (2020). Health care employees' perceptions of the use of artificial intelligence applications: Survey study. *Journal of Medical Internet Research, 22*(5), e17620. https://doi.org/10.2196/17620

Alharbi, H. A., Alharbi, K. K., & Hassan, C. A. U. (2023). Enhancing elderly fall detection through IoT-enabled smart flooring and AI for independent living sustainability. *Sustainability (Switzerland), 15*(22). https://doi.org/10.3390/su152215695

Alowais, S. A., Alghamdi, S. S., Alsuhebany, N., Alqahtani, T., Alshaya, A. I., Almohareb, S. N., Aldairem, A., Alrashed, M., Bin Saleh, K., Badreldin, H. A., Al Yami, M. S., Al Harbi, S., & Albekairy, A. M. (2023). Revolutionizing healthcare: The role of artificial intelligence in clinical practice. *BMC Medical Education, 23*(1). https://doi.org/10.1186/s12909-023-04698-z

Ansmann, L., & Pfaff, H. (2017). Providers and patients caught between standardization and individualization: Individualized standardization as a solution. *International Journal of Health Policy and Management*, *7*(4), 349–352. https://doi.org/10.15171/ijhpm.2017.95

Aquino, Y. S. J., Rogers, W. A., Braunack-Mayer, A., Frazer, H., Win, K. T., Houssami, N., Degeling, C., Semsarian, C., & Carter, S. M. (2023). Utopia versus dystopia: Professional perspectives on the impact of healthcare artificial intelligence on clinical roles and skills. *International Journal of Medical Informatics*, *169*. https://doi.org/10.1016/j.ijmedinf.2022.104903

Arpey, N. C., Gaglioti, A. H., & Rosenbaum, M. E. (2017). How socioeconomic status affects patient perceptions of health care: A qualitative study. *Journal of Primary Care and Community Health*, *8*(3), 169–175. https://doi.org/10.1177/2150131917697439

Ballinger, B., Hsieh, J., Singh, A., Sohoni, N., Wang, J., Tison, G., Marcus, G., Sanchez, J., Maguire, C., Olgin, J., & Pletcher, M. (2018). DeepHeart: Semi-supervised sequence learning for cardiovascular risk prediction. *Proceedings of the AAAI Conference on Artificial Intelligence*, *32*(1). https://doi.org/10.1609/aaai.v32i1.11891

Banerjee, S., Hemphill, T., & Longstreet, P. (2018). Wearable devices and healthcare: Data sharing and privacy. *Information Society*, *34*(1), 49–57. https://doi.org/10.1080/01972243.2017.1391912

Basu, A. (2011). Economics of individualization in comparative effectiveness research and a basis for a patient-centered health care. *Journal of Health Economics*, *30*(3), 549–559. https://doi.org/10.1016/j.jhealeco.2011.03.004

Bertakis, K. D., & Azari, R. (2011). Patient-centered care is associated with decreased health care utilization. *The Journal of the American Board of Family Medicine*, *24*(3), 229–239. https://doi.org/10.3122/jabfm.2011.03.100170

Bjerring, J. C., & Busch, J. (2021). Artificial intelligence and patient-centered decision-making. *Philosophy and Technology*, *34*(2), 349–371. https://doi.org/10.1007/s13347-019-00391-6

Bond, G. R., Drake, R. E., Rapp, C. A., McHugo, G. J., & Xie, H. (2009). Individualization and quality improvement: Two new scales to complement measurement of program fidelity. *Administration and Policy in Mental Health and Mental Health Services Research*, *36*(5), 349–357. https://doi.org/10.1007/s10488-009-0226-y

Bourouis, A., Feham, M., Hossain, M. A., & Zhang, L. (2014). An intelligent mobile based decision support system for retinal disease diagnosis. *Decision Support Systems*, *59*(1), 341–350. https://doi.org/10.1016/j.dss.2014.01.005

Bucci, S., Schwannauer, M., & Berry, N. (2019). The digital revolution and its impact on mental health care. *Psychology and Psychotherapy: Theory, Research and Practice*, *92*(2), 277–297. https://doi.org/10.1111/papt.12222

Bucher, A. (2023). The patient experience of the future is personalized: Using technology to scale an N of 1 approach. *Journal of Patient Experience*, *10*(4), 1–4. https://doi.org/10.1177/23743735231167975

Butler, J. M., Gibson, B., Lewis, L., Reiber, G., Kramer, H., Rupper, R., Herout, J., Long, B., Massaro, D., & Nebeker, J. (2021). Patient-centered care and the electronic health record: Exploring functionality and gaps. *JAMIA Open*, *3*(3), 360–368. https://doi.org/10.1093/JAMIAOPEN/OOAA044

Carey, S., Pang, A., & de Kamps, M. (2024). Fairness in AI for healthcare. *Future Healthcare Journal*, *11*(3), 100177. https://doi.org/10.1016/j.fhj.2024.100177

Chancellor, S., & De Choudhury, M. (2020). Methods in predictive techniques for mental health status on social media: A critical review. *NPJ Digital Medicine*, *3*(1). https://doi.org/10.1038/s41746-020-0233-7

Chawla, N. V., & Davis, D. A. (2013). Bringing big data to personalized healthcare: A patient-centered framework. *Journal of General Internal Medicine*, *28*(SUPPL.3). https://doi.org/10.1007/s11606-013-2455-8

Cheikhrouhou, O., Redowan Mahmud, M., Mershad, K., Jamil, F., Mahmud, R., Koubaa, A., & Rahimi Moosavi, S. (2023). A lightweight Blockchain and fog-enabled secure remote patient monitoring system. *arXiv:2301.03551*. https://doi.org/10.48550/arXiv.2301.03551

Chen, H. S., Jarrell, J. T., Carpenter, K. A., Cohen, D. S., & Huang, X. (2019). Blockchain in healthcare: A patient-centered model. *Biomedical Journal of Scientific & Technical Research, 20*(3), 15017–15022. https://pubmed.ncbi.nlm.nih.gov/31565696/

Chen, M., Zhang, B., Cai, Z., Seery, S., Gonzalez, M. J., Ali, N. M., Ren, R., Qiao, Y., Xue, P., & Jiang, Y. (2022). Acceptance of clinical artificial intelligence among physicians and medical students: A systematic review with cross-sectional survey. *Frontiers in Medicine*, *9*. https://doi.org/10.3389/fmed.2022.990604

Chiauzzi, E., Rodarte, C., & DasMahapatra, P. (2015). Patient-centered activity monitoring in the self-management of chronic health conditions. *BMC Medicine*, *13*(1). https://doi.org/10.1186/s12916-015-0319-2

Chow, R., Drkulec, H., Im, J. H. B., Tsai, J., Nafees, A., Kumar, S., Hou, T., Fazelzad, R., Leighl, N. B., Krzyzanowska, M., Wong, P., & Raman, S. (2024). The use of wearable devices in oncology patients: A systematic review. *Oncologist*, *29*(4), e419–e430. https://doi.org/10.1093/oncolo/oyad305

Christopher, G., Hertiage Samuel, A., Talati, D., & Brown, W. (2024). *AI-Based Personalized Healthcare: Tailoring Treatment and Transforming Patient Outcomes TITLE AI-Based Personalized Healthcare: Tailoring Treatment and Transforming Patient Outcomes Authors*. https://www.researchgate.net/publication/380465028

Christopher, M. (2011). Logistics and supply chain management. *International Commerce Review*, *7*(2), 144–150. https://doi.org/10.1007/s12146-007-0019-8

Conger, S., Pratt, J. H., & Loch, K. D. (2013). Personal information privacy and emerging technologies. *Information Systems Journal*, *23*(5), 401–417. https://doi.org/10.1111/j.1365-2575.2012.00402.x

Constand, M. K., MacDermid, J. C., Dal Bello-Haas, V., & Law, M. (2014). Scoping review of patient-centered care approaches in healthcare. *BMC Health Services Research*, *14*(1). https://doi.org/10.1186/1472-6963-14-271

Coyle, D., & Doherty, G. (2009). *Clinical Evaluation and Collaborative Design: Developing New Technologies for Mental Health*. https://dl.acm.org/doi/10.1145/1518701.1519013

Cross, J. L., Choma, M. A., & Onofrey, J. A. (2024). Bias in medical AI: Implications for clinical decision-making. *PLOS Digital Health*, *3*(11). https://doi.org/10.1371/journal.pdig.0000651

Dadi, K., Varoquaux, G., Houenou, J., Bzdok, D., Thirion, B., & Engemann, D. (2021). Population modeling with machine learning can enhance measures of mental health. *GigaScience*, *10*(10). https://doi.org/10.1093/gigascience/giab071

Dankar, F. K., Gergely, M., & Dankar, S. K. (2019). Informed consent in biomedical research. *Computational and Structural Biotechnology Journal*, *17*, 463–474. https://doi.org/10.1016/j.csbj.2019.03.010

Doan, S., Kawazoe, A., & Collier, N. (n.d.). *Global Health Monitor-A Web-based System for Detecting and Mapping Infectious Diseases*. http://chasen.org/~taku/software/TinySVM.

Donner-Banzhoff, N. (2018). Solving the diagnostic challenge: A patient-centered approach. *Annals of Family Medicine*, *16*(4), 353–358. https://doi.org/10.1370/afm.2264

Du, Z., Zhang, F., Ge, Y., Liu, Y., Yu, H., Wang, Y., Dalan, R., & Shen, X. (2025). Application of wearable devices in diabetes management. *Health and Metabolism*, *7*. https://doi.org/10.53941/hm.2025.100007

Duffy, S. (2010). *Personalisation in Mental Health.* http://www.centreforwelfarereform.org/library/by-az/personalisation-and-mental-health.html

Edgman-Levitan, S., & Schoenbaum, S. C. (2021). Patient-centered care: Achieving higher quality by designing care through the patient's eyes. *Israel Journal of Health Policy Research, 10*(1). https://doi.org/10.1186/s13584-021-00459-9

Elendu, C., Amaechi, D. C., Elendu, T. C., Jingwa, K. A., Okoye, O. K., John Okah, M., Ladele, J. A., Farah, A. H., & Alimi, H. A. (2023). Ethical implications of AI and robotics in healthcare: A review. *Medicine (United States), 102*(50), E36671. https://doi.org/10.1097/MD.0000000000036671

Esmaeilzadeh, P. (2020). Use of AI-based tools for healthcare purposes: A survey study from consumers' perspectives. *BMC Medical Informatics and Decision Making, 20*(1). https://doi.org/10.1186/s12911-020-01191-1

Ezeamii, V. C., Okobi, O. E., Wambai-Sani, H., Perera, G. S., Zaynieva, S., Okonkwo, C. C., Ohaiba, M. M., William-Enemali, P. C., Obodo, O. R., & Obiefuna, N. G. (2024). Revolutionizing healthcare: How telemedicine is improving patient outcomes and expanding access to care. *Cureus, 16*(7), e63881. https://doi.org/10.7759/cureus.63881

Fritsch, S. J., Blankenheim, A., Wahl, A., Hetfeld, P., Maassen, O., Deffge, S., Kunze, J., Rossaint, R., Riedel, M., Marx, G., & Bickenbach, J. (2022). Attitudes and perception of artificial intelligence in healthcare: A cross-sectional survey among patients. *Digital Health, 8*. https://doi.org/10.1177/20552076221116772

Graham, S., Depp, C., Lee, E. E., Nebeker, C., Tu, X., Kim, H. C., & Jeste, D. V. (2019). Artificial intelligence for mental health and mental illnesses: An overview. *Current Psychiatry Reports, 21*(11). https://doi.org/10.1007/s11920-019-1094-0

Grubaugh, A. L., Cain, G. D., Elhai, J. D., Patrick, S. L., & Frueh, B. C. (2008). Attitudes toward medical and mental health care delivered via telehealth applications among rural and urban primary care patients. *Journal of Nervous and Mental Disease, 196*(2), 166–170. https://doi.org/10.1097/NMD.0b013e318162aa2d

Heaton, C. J. (2014). *An Introduction to the Patient-Centered Medical Home.* http://www.choosingwisely.org/

Höhn, J., Hekler, A., Krieghoff-Henning, E., Kather, J. N., Utikal, J. S., Meier, F., Gellrich, F. F., Hauschild, A., French, L., Schlager, J. G., Ghoreschi, K., Wilhelm, T., Kutzner, H., Heppt, M., Haferkamp, S., Sondermann, W., Schadendorf, D., Schilling, B., Maron, R. C., … Brinker, T. J. (2021). Integrating patient data into skin cancer classification using convolutional neural networks: Systematic review. *Journal of Medical Internet Research, 23*(7). https://doi.org/10.2196/20708

Holt, J. M., Cusatis, R., Winn, A., Asan, O., Spanbauer, C., Williams, J. S., Flynn, K. E., Somai, M., Laud, P., & Crotty, B. H. (2020). The impact of previsit contextual data collection on patient-provider communication and patient activation: Study protocol for a randomized controlled trial. *JMIR Research Protocols, 9*(9). https://doi.org/10.2196/20309

Institute of Medicine. (2001). *Crossing the Quality Chasm: A New Health System for the 21st Century.* (2001). National Academies Press. https://doi.org/10.17226/10027

Imison, C., Castle-clarke, S., Watson, R., & Edwards, N. (2016). *Delivering the Benefits of Digital Health Care | The Nuffield Trust. February.* https://www.nuffieldtrust.org.uk/sites/default/files/2017-01/delivering-the-benefits-of-digital-technology-web-final.pdf

Jacoba, C. M. P., Celi, L. A., & Silva, P. S. (2021). Biomarkers for progression in diabetic retinopathy: Expanding personalized medicine through integration of AI with electronic health records. *Seminars in Ophthalmology, 36*(4), 250–257. https://doi.org/10.1080/08820538.2021.1893351

Jia, Y., Wang, W., Wen, D., Liang, L., Gao, L., & Lei, J. (2018). Perceived user preferences and usability evaluation of mainstream wearable devices for health monitoring. *PeerJ, 2018*(7). https://doi.org/10.7717/peerj.5350

Joerin, A. (2018). Using a mental health chatbot, Tess, to relieve symptoms of depression and anxiety. *JMIR Ment Health*. https://doi.org/10.1186/ISRCTN61214172

Johnson, K. B., Wei, W. Q., Weeraratne, D., Frisse, M. E., Misulis, K., Rhee, K., Zhao, J., & Snowdon, J. L. (2021). Precision medicine, AI, and the future of personalized health care. *Clinical and Translational Science*, *14*(1), 86–93. https://doi.org/10.1111/cts.12884

Kane, P. M., Murtagh, F. E. M., Ryan, K., Mahon, N. G., McAdam, B., McQuillan, R., Ellis-Smith, C., Tracey, C., Howley, C., Raleigh, C., O'Gara, G., Higginson, I. J., & Daveson, B. A. (2015). The gap between policy and practice: A systematic review of patient-centred care interventions in chronic heart failure. *Heart Failure Reviews*, *20*(6), 673–687. https://doi.org/10.1007/s10741-015-9508-5

Karimian, G., Petelos, E., & Evers, S. M. A. A. (2022). The ethical issues of the application of artificial intelligence in healthcare: A systematic scoping review. *AI and Ethics*, *2*(4), 539–551. https://doi.org/10.1007/s43681-021-00131-7

Karkosz, S., Szymański, R., Sanna, K., & Michałowski, J. (2024). Effectiveness of a web-based and mobile therapy chatbot on anxiety and depressive symptoms in subclinical young adults: Randomized controlled trial. *JMIR Formative Research*, *8*. https://doi.org/10.2196/47960

Kasyapa, M. S. B., & Vanmathi, C. (2024). Blockchain integration in healthcare: A comprehensive investigation of use cases, performance issues, and mitigation strategies. *Frontiers in Digital Health*, *6*. https://doi.org/10.3389/fdgth.2024.1359858

Kelly, M. M., Coller, R. J., & Hoonakker, P. L. T. (2018). Inpatient portals for hospitalized patients and caregivers: A systematic review. *Journal of Hospital Medicine*, *13*(6), 405–412. https://doi.org/10.12788/jhm.2894

Kelly, M. M., Hoonakker, P. L. T., & Coller, R. J. (2019). Inpatients sign on: An opportunity to engage hospitalized patients and caregivers using inpatient portals. *Medical Care*, *57*(2), 98–100. https://doi.org/10.1097/MLR.0000000000001043

Khan Rony, M. K., Akter, K., Nesa, L., Islam, M. T., Johra, F. T., Akter, F., Uddin, M. J., Begum, J., Noor, M. A., Ahmad, S., Tanha, S. M., Khatun, M. T., Bala, S. D., & Parvin, M. R. (2024). Healthcare workers' knowledge and attitudes regarding artificial intelligence adoption in healthcare: A cross-sectional study. *Heliyon*, *10*(23). https://doi.org/10.1016/j.heliyon.2024.e40775

Khoja, S., Durrani, H., Scott, R. E., Sajwani, A., & Piryani, U. (2013). Conceptual framework for development of comprehensive e-health evaluation tool. *Telemedicine Journal and E-Health: The Official Journal of the American Telemedicine Association*, *19*(1), 48–53. https://doi.org/10.1089/tmj.2012.0073

Kizer, K. W. (2002). The emerging imperative for health care quality improvement. *Academic Emergency Medicine*, *9*(11), 1078–1084. https://doi.org/10.1197/aemj.9.11.1078

Kroll, R. R., McKenzie, E. D., Boyd, J. G., Sheth, P., Howes, D., Wood, M., & Maslove, D. M. (2017). Use of wearable devices for post-discharge monitoring of ICU patients: A feasibility study. *Journal of Intensive Care*, *5*(1). https://doi.org/10.1186/s40560-017-0261-9

Kruse, C. S., Frederick, B., Jacobson, T., & Monticone, D. K. (2017). Cybersecurity in healthcare: A systematic review of modern threats and trends. *Technology and Health Care*, *25*(1), 1–10. https://doi.org/10.3233/THC-161263

Lambert, S. I., Madi, M., Sopka, S., Lenes, A., Stange, H., Buszello, C. P., & Stephan, A. (2023). An integrative review on the acceptance of artificial intelligence among healthcare professionals in hospitals. *NPJ Digital Medicine*, *6*(1). https://doi.org/10.1038/s41746-023-00852-5

Laziz, J., & Rachid, O. (2024). Investigating the influence of stakeholders' collaboration on open innovation in healthcare. *IJFMR*, *6*(2), 1–5. www.ijfmr.com

Le, H. T., Thanh, L. N. T., Vo, H. K., Luong, H. H., Tuan, K. N. H., Anh, T. D., Nguyen, T. A., Vuong, K. H. N., & Son, H. X. (2022). Patient-Chain: Patient-centered healthcare system a blockchain-based technology in dealing with emergencies. *Lecture Notes in Computer Science (Including Subseries Lecture Notes in Artificial Intelligence and Lecture Notes in Bioinformatics), 13148 LNCS*, 576–583. https://doi.org/10.1007/978-3-030-96772-7_54

Lehne, M., Sass, J., Essenwanger, A., Schepers, J., & Thun, S. (2019). Why digital medicine depends on interoperability. *NPJ Digital Medicine*, *2*(1). https://doi.org/10.1038/s41746-019-0158-1

Lewin, S., Chetty, R., Ihdayhid, A. R., & Dwivedi, G. (2024). Ethical challenges and opportunities in applying artificial intelligence to cardiovascular medicine. *Canadian Journal of Cardiology*, *40*(10), 1897–1906. https://doi.org/10.1016/j.cjca.2024.06.029

Liang, W. S., Beaulieu-Jones, B., Smalley, S., Snyder, M., Goetz, L. H., & Schork, N. J. (2024). Emerging therapeutic drug monitoring technologies: Considerations and opportunities in precision medicine. *Frontiers in Pharmacology*, *15*. https://doi.org/10.3389/fphar.2024.1348112

Liao, Y., Thompson, C., Peterson, S., Mandrola, J., & Beg, M. S. (2019). The future of wearable technologies and remote monitoring in health care. *American Society of Clinical Oncology Educational Book*, *39*, 115–121. https://doi.org/10.1200/edbk_238919

Liu, J., Wu, C., & Su, T. (2017). The reference effect in newsvendor model with strategic customers. *Management Decision*, *55*(5), 1006–1021. https://doi.org/10.1108/MD-09-2015-0419

Liu, M., Cheng, D., & Yan, W. (2018). Classification of alzheimer's disease by combination of convolutional and recurrent neural networks using FDG-PET images. *Frontiers in Neuroinformatics*, *12*. https://doi.org/10.3389/fninf.2018.00035

Louis, C. J., Clark, J. R., Gray, B., Brannon, D., & Parker, V. (2019). Service line structure and decision-maker attention in three health systems: Implications for patient-centered care. *Health Care Management Review*, *44*(1), 41–56. https://doi.org/10.1097/HMR.0000000000000172

Lusk, J. M., & Fater, K. (2013). A concept analysis of patient-centered care. *Nursing Forum*, *48*(2), 89–98. https://doi.org/10.1111/nuf.12019

Madanian, S., Nakarada-Kordic, I., Reay, S., & Chetty, T. (2023). Patients' perspectives on digital health tools. *PEC Innovation*, *2*. https://doi.org/10.1016/j.pecinn.2023.100171

Manne, R., & Kantheti, S. C. (2021). Application of artificial intelligence in healthcare: Chances and challenges. *Current Journal of Applied Science and Technology*, 78–89. https://doi.org/10.9734/cjast/2021/v40i631320

McCabe, C. (2004). Nurse-patient communication: An exploration of patients' experiences. *Journal of Clinical Nursing*, *13*(1), 41–49. https://doi.org/10.1111/j.1365–2702.2004.00817.x

Mikava, N., & Mamulaidze, T. (2023). Implications of artificial intelligence in healthcare in developing countries: Perspectives and challenges. *Agora International Journal of Economical Sciences*, *17*(2), 110–120. https://doi.org/10.15837/aijes.v17i2.6448

Miller, D., Rudick, R. A., & Hutchinson, M. (2010). Patient-centered outcomes translating clinical efficacy into benefits on health-related quality of life. *Neurology, 74*(Suppl 3), S24–S35. https://pubmed.ncbi.nlm.nih.gov/20421570/

Mittelstadt, B. D., Allo, P., Taddeo, M., Wachter, S., & Floridi, L. (2016). The ethics of algorithms: Mapping the debate. *Big Data and Society*, *3*(2). https://doi.org/10.1177/2053951716679679

Mittermaier, M., Raza, M. M., & Kvedar, J. C. (2023). Bias in AI-based models for medical applications: Challenges and mitigation strategies. *NPJ Digital Medicine*, *6*(1). Nature Research. https://doi.org/10.1038/s41746-023-00858-z

Morgan, S., & Yoder, L. H. (2012). A concept analysis of person-centered care. *Journal of Holistic Nursing*, *30*(1), 6–15. https://doi.org/10.1177/0898010111412189

Negro-Calduch, E., Azzopardi-Muscat, N., Krishnamurthy, R. S., & Novillo-Ortiz, D. (2021). Technological progress in electronic health record system optimization: Systematic review of systematic literature reviews. *International Journal of Medical Informatics*, *152*. https://doi.org/10.1016/j.ijmedinf.2021.104507

Obermeyer, Z., Powers, B., Vogeli, C., & Mullainathan, S. (2019). Dissecting racial bias in an algorithm used to manage the health of populations. *Science*, *366*(6464), 447–453. https://doi.org/10.1126/science.aax2342

Odell, M. (2015). Detection and management of the deteriorating ward patient: An evaluation of nursing practice. *Journal of Clinical Nursing*, *24*(1–2), 173–182. https://doi.org/10.1111/jocn.12655

Olyanasab, A., & Annabestani, M. (2024). Leveraging machine learning for personalized wearable biomedical devices: A review. *Journal of Personalized Medicine*, *14*(2). Multidisciplinary Digital Publishing Institute (MDPI). https://doi.org/10.3390/jpm14020203

Oyeniyi, J. (2024). The role of AI and mobile apps in patient-centric healthcare delivery. *World Journal of Advanced Research and Reviews*, *22*(1), 1897–1907. https://doi.org/10.30574/wjarr.2024.22.1.1331

Patel, V. L., Shortilffe, E., Stfanello, M., Szolovits, P., Berthold, M., Bellazzi, R., & Abu-Hanna, A. (2008). The role of emerging technologies in patient-centered care (3). *Artificial Intelligence in Medicine*, *1*(46), 5–17.

Perry, B., & Uuk, R. (2019). AI governance and the policymaking process: Key considerations for reducing ai risk. *Big Data and Cognitive Computing*, *3*(2), 1–17. https://doi.org/10.3390/bdcc3020026

Pfaff, H., Driller, E., Karbach, U., Kowalski, C., Scheibler, F., & Ommen, O. (2010). Standardization and individualization in care for the elderly: Proactive behavior through individualized standardization. *Open Longevity Science*, *4*(January 2015), 51–57. https://benthamopen.com/ABSTRACT/TOLSJ-4-51

Rahimi, S. A., Légaré, F., Sharma, G., Archambault, P., Zomahoun, H. T. V., Chandavong, S., Rheault, N., Wong, S. T., Langlois, L., Couturier, Y., Salmeron, J. L., Gagnon, M. P., & Légaré, J. (2021). Application of artificial intelligence in community-based primary health care: Systematic scoping review and critical appraisal. *Journal of Medical Internet Research*, *23*(9), e29839. https://doi.org/10.2196/29839

Reddy, S., Allan, S., Coghlan, S., & Cooper, P. (2020). A governance model for the application of AI in health care. *Journal of the American Medical Informatics Association*, *27*(3), 491–497. https://doi.org/10.1093/jamia/ocz192

Reisman, M. (2017). EHRs: The challenge of making electronic data usable and interoperable. *P&T: A Peer-Reviewed Journal for Formulary Management*, *42*(9), 572–575. https://pmc.ncbi.nlm.nih.gov/articles/PMC5565131/

Robinson, J. H., Callister, L. C., Berry, J. A., & Dearing, K. A. (2008). Patient-centered care and adherence: Definitions and applications to improve outcomes. *Journal of the American Academy of Nurse Practitioners*, *20*(12), 600–607. https://doi.org/10.1111/j.1745-7599.2008.00360.x

Rony, M. K. K., Parvin, M. R., Wahiduzzaman, M., Debnath, M., Bala, S. D., & Kayesh, I. (2024). "I Wonder if my Years of Training and Expertise Will be Devalued by Machines": Concerns about the replacement of medical professionals by artificial intelligence. *SAGE Open Nursing*, *10*. https://doi.org/10.1177/23779608241245220

Saadatnejad, S., Oveisi, M., & Hashemi, M. (2019). LSTM-based ECG classification for continuous monitoring on personal wearable devices. *IEEE Journal of Biomedical and Health Informatics*, *24*(2), 515–523. https://doi.org/10.1109/JBHI.2019.2911367

Sabanovic, S., Bennett, C. C., Piatt, J. A., Chang, W., Hakken, D., Kang, S., & Ayer, D. (2014). Participatory design of socially assistive robots for preventive patient-entered healthcare. *IEEE IROS Workshop on Assistive Robotics for Individuals with Disabilities*, 1–5. http://www.hummingbirdkit.com/

Sadilek, A., Caty, S., DiPrete, L., Mansour, R., Schenk, T., Bergtholdt, M., Jha, A., Ramaswami, P., & Gabrilovich, E. (2018). Machine-learned epidemiology: Real-time detection of foodborne illness at scale. *NPJ Digital Medicine*, *1*(1). https://doi.org/10.1038/s41746-018-0045-1

Sauerbrei, A., Kerasidou, A., Lucivero, F., & Hallowell, N. (2023). The impact of artificial intelligence on the person-centred, doctor-patient relationship: Some problems and solutions. *BMC Medical Informatics and Decision Making*, *23*(1) https://doi.org/10.1186/s12911-023-02162-y

Sawik, B., Tobis, S., Baum, E., Suwalska, A., Kropińska, S., Stachnik, K., Pérez-Bernabeu, E., Cildoz, M., Agustin, A., & Wieczorowska-Tobis, K. (2023). Robots for elderly care: Review, multi-criteria optimization model and qualitative case study. *Healthcare (Switzerland)*, *11*(9). https://doi.org/10.3390/healthcare11091286

Scott, I. A., Carter, S. M., & Coiera, E. (2021). Exploring stakeholder attitudes towards AI in clinical practice. *BMJ Health and Care Informatics*, *28*(1). https://doi.org/10.1136/bmjhci-2021-100450

Shaik, T., Tao, X., Higgins, N., Li, L., Gururajan, R., Zhou, X., & Acharya, U. R. (2023). Remote patient monitoring using artificial intelligence: Current state, applications, and challenges. *Wiley Interdisciplinary Reviews: Data Mining and Knowledge Discovery*, *13*(2). https://doi.org/10.1002/widm.1485

Shoghli, A., Darvish, M., & Sadeghian, Y. (2024). Balancing innovation and privacy: Ethical challenges in AI-Driven healthcare. *Journal of Reviews in Medical Sciences*, *4*(1), 31. https://doi.org/10.22034/jrms.2024.494112.1034

Silva, M. DA, Flood, C. M., Goldenberg, A., & Singh, D. N. (2022). Regulating the safety of health-related artificial intelligence (Réglementer la sécurité de l'intelligence artificielle dans les soins de santé). *Healthcare Policy*, *17*(4).

Sinha, R. (2024). The role and impact of new technologies on healthcare systems. *Discover Health Systems*, *3*(1). https://doi.org/10.1007/s44250-024-00163-w

Soriano, G. P., Yasuhara, Y., Ito, H., Matsumoto, K., Osaka, K., Kai, Y., Locsin, R., Schoenhofer, S., & Tanioka, T. (2022). Robots and robotics in nursing. *Healthcare (Switzerland)*, *10*(8). https://doi.org/10.3390/healthcare10081571

Tak, Y. W., Kim, J. H., Lee, J. H., & Lee, Y. (2024). Impact of encounters on patient app use: Results of a tethered mobile personal health record usage pattern analysis. *BMC Health Services Research*, *24*(1). https://doi.org/10.1186/s12913-024-11881-5

Thompson, J. S., Timothy Baxter, B., Allison, J. G., Johnson, F. E., Lee, K. K., & Young, W. (2003). Temporal patterns of postoperative complications. *Archives of Surgery*, *138*. http://archsurg.jamanetwork.com/

Thornicroft, G., Alem, A., Drake, R. E., Ito, H., Mari, J., McGeorge, P., Tara, R., & Semrau, M. (Eds.). (2012). *Community Mental Health: Putting Policy Into Practice Globally*. Wiley-Blackwell.

Tibet, M., Tian, M., Chen, J., Xu, L., Chen, H., Li, R., Cho, K., Wu, Y., & Yan, L. L. (2012). Electronic decision support for cardiovascular high-risk patients. *Journal of Mobile Technology in Medicine*, *1*(4), 2013. https://doi.org/10.7309/jmtm.44

Trevedi, M. H., Kern, J. K., Altshuler, K. Z., & Sunderajan, P. (2024). A computerized clinical decision support system as a means of implementing decision guidelines. *Psychiatric Services*, *55*(885), 879.

Tzelepis, F., Sanson-Fisher, R. W., Zucca, A. C., & Fradgley, E. A. (2015). Measuring the quality of patient-centered care: Why patient-reported measures are critical to reliable assessment. *Patient Preference and Adherence*, *9*, 831–835. https://doi.org/10.2147/PPA.S81975

van Veen, T., Binz, S., Muminovic, M., Chaudhry, K., Rose, K., Calo, S., Rammal, J. A., France, J., & Miller, J. B. (2019). Potential of mobile health technology to reduce health disparities in underserved communities. *Western Journal of Emergency Medicine*, *20*(5), 799–803. https://doi.org/10.5811/westjem.2019.6.41911

Van Velthoven, M. H., & Cordon, C. (2019). Sustainable adoption of digital health innovations: Perspectives from a stakeholder workshop. *Journal of Medical Internet Research*, *21*(3). https://doi.org/10.2196/11922

Vayena, E., Blasimme, A., & Cohen, I. G. (2018). Machine learning in medicine: Addressing ethical challenges. *PLoS Medicine*, *15*(11). https://doi.org/10.1371/journal.pmed.1002689

Villanueva-Miranda, I., Xiao, G., & Xie, Y. (2025). Artificial intelligence in early warning systems for infectious disease surveillance: A systematic review. *Frontiers in Public Health*, *13*. https://doi.org/10.3389/fpubh.2025.1609615

Wang, W. H., & Hsu, W. S. (2023). Integrating artificial intelligence and wearable IoT system in long-term care environments. *Sensors*, *23*(13). https://doi.org/10.3390/s23135913

Wells, C. I., Xu, W., Penfold, J. A., Keane, C., Gharibans, A. A., Bissett, I. P., & O'Grady, G. (2022). Wearable devices to monitor recovery after abdominal surgery: Scoping review. *BJS Open*, *6*(2). https://doi.org/10.1093/bjsopen/zrac031

Yadav, S. (2024). Transformative frontiers: A comprehensive review of emerging technologies in modern healthcare. *Cureus*, *16*(3), e56538. https://doi.org/10.7759/cureus.56538

Zhu, T., Liao, P., Luo, L., & Ye, H. Q. (2020). Data-driven models for capacity allocation of inpatient beds in a Chinese public hospital. *Computational and Mathematical Methods in Medicine*, *2020*. https://doi.org/10.1155/2020/8740457

Zohuri, B., & Zadeh, S. (2020). The utility of artificial intelligence for mood analysis, depression detection, and suicide risk management. *Journal of Health Science*, *8*(2). https://doi.org/10.17265/2328-7136/2020.02.003

5 The Impact of Adaptive Technologies on Strengthening Clinical Decision-Making Skills

Vismaya Annie Vinod and Philip Eappen

5.1 INTRODUCTION

Multiple adaptive technologies have been developed to aid healthcare settings in improving clinical decision-making skills. This paper aims to explore the impact of adaptive technologies such as AI and ML in strengthening clinical decision-making skills. Clinicians use AI in implementing guidelines where the information absorbed is employed to deliver recommendations in clinical decision-making processes (Alowais et al., 2023).

The term "clinical decision-making" refers to the ability of a practitioner to collect, analyze, and understand the diagnostic evidence to guide patients (Brügge et al., 2024). According to Miller et al. (2019), clinical decision-making is a detailed process that entails analyzing information, examining evidence obtained, and choosing the most suitable interventions to apply in healthcare, ensuring quality with minimal or no harm to the patient.

Chen et al. (2023) furnishes the importance of Artificial Intelligence (AI) and Machine Learning (ML) in clinical decision-making where clinicians receive support by obtaining evidence-based information at the point of care. The study supports the establishment of clinical decision-making support systems and the importance of facilitating patient care outcomes. Digital education is characterized by employing digital technologies to engage educational programs and promote efficient learning (Fontaine et al., 2019). Adaptive education is comprised of multiple components such as strategies, educational goals, timeframes, determinations, and classification. Addressing these components helps tailor the instructions according to the individual needs of healthcare learners (Fontaine et al., 2019).

5.2 OBJECTIVE

Examining the impact of adaptive technologies in enhancing decision-making skills.

 DOI: 10.1201/9781003624875-7

5.3 METHOD

This chapter is based on a narrative review of literature performed between January and April 2025. We conducted non-systematic searches across key literature databases like PubMed, PsycINFO, CINAHL, Scopus, and Google Scholar. We included peer-reviewed articles from multiple countries. Priority was given to peer-reviewed journals published within the last 5 years, considering their relevance to the subject of interest, but no filters were employed. The review is composed of the multiple aspects of clinical decision-making and the role of AI in facilitating clinical decision-making skills. The search strategy included keywords like clinical decision-making, virtual reality (VR), virtual triage (VT), clinical decision supporting systems (CDSS), deep learning technology, healthcare professionals, and adaptive education. We performed a detailed review of various studies, including systematic reviews, scoping reviews, survey analysis, and qualitative studies.

5.4 MAIN FOCUS OF THE CHAPTER

5.4.1 Outline of Clinical Decision-Making Skills

The process of making clinical decisions is crucial and requires multiple thoughts on the advantages and disadvantages of the decision made and the effect it will have on individual patients. Practitioners most times rely on intuitive judgments called heuristics to evaluate the pros and cons of the decision (Dobler et al., 2021).

Various types of decision-making in clinical settings are:

1. ***Analytic hierarchy process (AHP) in decision-making***: AHP is an identified clinical decision-making approach that involves collaborative participation of physicians and patients. It involves optimizing the selection criteria when multiple sets of criteria are available (Liberatore & Nydick, 2008).
2. ***Intuitive decision-making:*** Intuition is seen as a pertinent component in the decision-making process by nurses. Intuition here is supported by the clinical experience and knowledge gained (Melin-Johansson et al., 2017).
3. ***Participatory decision-making***: It relies on developing a supporting rapport during patient interaction and involves integrating the perspectives and opinions of patients (Elwyn et al., 2012).
4. ***Ethical decision-making***: This type of decision-making requires clinicians to have both legal and ethical accountability in delivering patient care. The ethical principles embodied within include diagnostic factors, patient priorities, personal values, and life satisfaction.

Clinical decision-making processes are experiencing heightened attention in response to rising concerns about healthcare costs and quality in medicine. Different practitioners have different strategies when it comes to clinical decision-making. This results in fluctuation in approaches for a single disease (Hlatky et al., 1990).

The inclination and willingness of patients to contribute to decision-making processes are influenced by their affective state and the strength of physician-patient interaction (Fisher et al., 2018). Proper utilization of available data sources is vital in decision-making processes. Perinatal and pediatric services are the key focus areas in service delivery, and their data require specific consideration. Superior and timely data can be achieved by enhancing the health information system (Zenebe et al., 2023).

5.4.2 Conceptual Framework of Adaptive Technologies in Clinical Settings

The introduction of technical support to clinical decision-making began in 1970 (Adams et al., 1986). Glasgow et al. (2019) emphasizes the importance of adaptive technology in developing an informed community of patients and healthcare providers. Adaptive technologies and interventions can play a significant role in revolutionizing the public health system where the normal interventions have failed (Naderbagi et al., 2024). Post COVID-19 pandemic period has witnessed the increased flow of digitalization in healthcare settings. The attempt to virtualize the treatment using virtual visits and AI-based interventions paved the way for advanced healthcare digitalization (Khosravi et al., 2024). In healthcare settings, clinical decision-making can be enhanced by adaptive technologies, which provide early alerts, support diagnosis, conduct tests and screenings through video technology, tailor treatment procedures to individual needs, and evaluate responses to subsequent treatments received (Adlung et al., 2021).

5.4.3 Artificial Intelligence–Driven Clinical Diagnosis

AI and ML aid clinical diagnosis by analyzing complex data and associated patterns, which in turn facilitate accuracy and precision in the reports. Multiple benefits are reported with the incorporation of AI in clinical decision-making, which comprises better antimicrobial stewardship, time management in obtaining the results, and improved therapeutic outcomes (Zumla et al., 2024). Levkovich (2025) explores the role of AI in diagnosing depression, where the initial signs and symptoms are mapped with the help of algorithms that detect patient information and separately analyze the past medical history and behavioral traits. The study mentions the instances where discrete symptoms are detected with the use of ML algorithms that process traits like verbal expressions and facial gestures. Tailoring to individual needs is a major advantage of AI. Similar customization is provided in the clinical decision-making process. AI algorithms identify individual characteristics that vary from person to person (Levkovich, 2025). AI-involved decision-making process seems to be less time-consuming compared to the traditional means of decision-making. Deep learning technology, which emerged with the advancement of AI, involves simulating intricate patterns and is useful in diagnosing neurological conditions at an early stage (AbuAlrob & Mesraoua, 2024). Integrating AI in CDSS is reported to improve accuracy and precision in diagnosing, along with decreasing the occurrence of clinical error (Ouanes & Farhah, 2024). Bodily activities can be observed, and irregular occurrences and events can be tracked with the help of AI. The AI's capacity to interpret electrocardiogram signals cannot be overlooked (Khosravi et al., 2024).

5.4.4 The Impact of Clinical Decision Support Systems (CDSS)

Niraula et al. (2023) explored the need for adaptive technologies to overcome barriers such as multiple factor engagement in clinical decision-making. The study demonstrates the implications of Adaptive Radiotherapy Clinical Decisions Support (ARCliDS), which is an adaptive technology solution employed in the oncology department. The respective software tool is comprised of an algorithm for analyzing and interpreting data, which enables the identification and selection of key variables, dealing with heterogeneity in patients, and ambiguities in response to treatments. There are multiple Clinical Decision Support Systems (CDSS) available to facilitate efficient decision-making processes in clinical settings. Digitalized clinical workflows and big data like electronic medical records are deployed to deliver such adaptive technologies (Sutton et al., 2020). The respective systems are found to be more effective as they support the healthcare providers by breaking down the complex tasks into a simpler style, along with the delivery of all required information, thereby improving overall efficiency and standard (Hak et al., 2022). Two different types of CDSS are i) Knowledge-based CDSS: they rely on the evidence collected from practice, studies, and clinical experience, and ii) Non-Knowledge-Based CDSS: These types of CDSS mostly function with the help of AI instead of working based on the data fed into the system (Sutton et al., 2020).

5.4.5 The Role of CDSS in Preventing Medical Errors

CDSS is found to be effective in minimizing the medical errors that happen in clinical settings with the release of warnings, prompts, proposals, and clinical guidelines (Chen et al., 2024). The error-diminishing trait of CDSS results in enhanced patient safety and efficacy in medical care. The Agency for Healthcare Research and Quality (AHRQ) supports the role of CDSS in delivering quality healthcare (Elhaddad & Hamam, 2024). Clinicians receive support from CDSS to identify the required dose for medications in accordance with the individual needs of patients, which in turn helps to avoid unwanted effects of the therapy administered (Shahmoradi et al., 2021).

5.4.6 Medical Imaging with the Help of Deep Learning Technology

In clinical settings, patients generally look forward to obtaining the best possible care services. AI helps facilitate the healthcare infrastructure with its optimal role in genomic medicine, diagnostic imaging, preventive medicine, and drug synthesis. The use of deep learning technology is mostly associated with computer-aided diagnosis (CAD), thereby supporting clinicians in decision-making processes. Machine learning algorithms are the backbone of CAD systems. Deep learning is comprised of a neural network structure that functions by absorbing the input and converting its complex form into a simple generalization (Tsuneki, 2022).

5.4.7 Predictive Models Guiding Clinical Decision-Making

Machine learning refers to the use of sophisticated computer systems that independently process data sets from multiple origins and detect patterns and connections to develop a model or algorithm through iterative learning (Scott et al., 2021). Through a wide spectrum of algorithms, machine learning attempts to streamline or mimic human cognition to perform tasks like prediction of outcomes and data analysis. Machine learning helps practitioners with its ability to draw insights from previously identified patterns from data and anticipate outcomes for new unfamiliar observations (Eloranta & Boman, 2022). It is the responsibility of the physician to verify if the data sets are of excellent quality, appropriately represent the intended population, and are comprehensive and reliable (Goldstein et al., 2017).

5.4.8 Cost-Effectiveness Associated with the AI-Driven Clinical Decision

Diagnostic devices driven by adaptive technology can be helpful in carrying out reiterative functions and in delivering results with precision and accuracy. This in turn prevents errors from the side of clinicians. These can be utilized in the case of mammograms and CT scans (Shaheen, 2021). The cost efficiency of AI-diagnostic machines can be attributed to their enhanced productivity and swiftness (Khalifa & Albadawy, 2024). AI-based diagnostics have proved to function without any discrimination or opinion-based bias. Directly and indirectly, adaptive technologies help patients save their time visiting the practitioner. In addition, adaptive technologies, apart from reducing health expenditure, support healthcare facilities with return on investment (Khanna et al., 2022). Ishii-Rousseau et al. (2022) demonstrated the importance of "Ecosystem as a Service (EaaS)" that helps develop the skills of healthcare professionals to deal with medical AI tools.

5.4.9 The Role of Adaptive Technology in Empowering Healthcare Professionals in Building Skills

The importance of digital skills among healthcare professionals can be categorized under the term "digitalized healthcare professional" (Brice & Almond, 2020). The healthcare settings are on their way to a complete transition from a totally labor-involved way to a digitalized setting. Healthcare professionals are expected to collaborate with modern technology. Studies have identified the pertinent role of adaptive technologies in helping healthcare professionals in developing skills. El Arab et al. (2025) emphasize the need for AI in facilitating nursing skills. Problem-solving skills, strategic thinking, interpersonal skills, and critical evaluation skills can be enhanced with the aid of adaptive technologies (El Arab et al., 2025). Morrow et al. (2023) studied the relation between adaptive technologies and emotional intelligence in healthcare settings. The study demonstrated how AI acts as a supportive mechanism in nurturing compassionate understanding and related response, the style of social connection, interpersonal skills, delivering clinical treatments, virtue-based education, medical expertise, and making therapeutic evaluations. AI-driven clinical practice brings forth some ethical dilemmas; therefore, learning ventures in healthcare curriculum must take required steps to avoid any such ethical issues (Civaner et al., 2022). AI-driven decision-support is found to boost the productivity of practitioners. The effectiveness and results of healthcare practices, along with patient experience, operational efficiency, and delivery of quality care, can be facilitated by AI and healthcare data. This in turn paves the way for leading techniques, monitoring of development, and delivery of constructive feedback with suggestions for betterment. By using AI, adaptive educational tools can be created to modify the learning material and its pacing (Khosravi et al., 2024).

5.4.10 Adaptive Education and Clinical Skills Development

Cook (2025) explores the application of the computer program "virtual patients (VP)" in tutoring and gauging clinical reasoning skills. VPs are configured to replicate real-life encounters with practitioners and patients and represent multiple scenarios as well. The higher costs of implementing limit the use of VPs. The problem can be resolved with a switch to a cheaper form of VPs developed utilizing AI large language models (Cook, 2025). AI-driven VPs act as a better training resource for emergency healthcare providers to evaluate a patient's health status and to deliver emergency care. Incorporating AI chatbots in VPs enhances cost efficiency in comparison to labor-intensive manual simulations (Gutiérrez Maquilón et al., 2024). VPs are an example of virtual reality (VR) that operate in 2-dimensional and 3-dimensional virtual environments and communicate directly with the users (Combs & Combs, 2019). Enabling medical students and trainees to work on diagnostic decision-support systems in a simulated environment fosters streamlined patient interaction, safer and more efficient triage, and optimized rapid response performance (Hamilton, 2024).

5.4.11 Clinical Decision-Making Simulation by Large Language Model (LLM)

Patient education in clinical environments can be facilitated with the use of LLMs, where they imitate patients with multiple medical conditions and behaviors. Likewise, LLMs facilitate student learning with the replication of real-world conversations with learners, which in turn serves as an affordable strategy for developing clinical decision skills (Brügge et al., 2024). Developing nonverbal communication among medical students facilitates efficient communication in situations involving uncertain prognosis (Piza et al., 2019). All these come into application when clinical decision-making is employed while clinical interviews are conducted with actual or mock patients (Brügge et al., 2024). Brügge et al. (2024) identified that the integration of systematic feedback into AI-driven patient interview sessions can strengthen the development of clinical decision-making skills.

5.4.12 Optimizing Workflow in Healthcare Employing AI

AI-driven workflow management is defined as the process that employs adaptive technologies to optimize the chain of tasks (Zayas-Cabán et al., 2021). Integration of AI in the healthcare system can manage the hurdles associated with the workforce demands (Bajwa et al., 2021). Automated workflow eases the work of the staff by collaborating multiple AI tools to perform multifaceted duties (Shahin et al., 2025). Integrating AI into the nursing profession facilitates proper management of time and improves decision-making skills. With the use of AI, nurses reported having better control of patient care. Automated operational tasks performed by AI allow more time for nurses to provide detailed care for patients. Moreover, AI-driven devices offer constant medical surveillance, thereby supporting the workflow with frontline care initiatives (Almagharbeh, 2024).

The electronic Canadian Triage and Acuity Scale (eCTAS) is an electronic clinical decision support system employed to enhance the well-being of patients along with the motive of raising care standards. ECTAS supports the work of clinicians and nurses by prioritizing the patients based on their subjective and objective details (Agnihotri et al., 2020). The incorporation of "patient-generated health data (PGHD)" into electronic health records (EHRs) offers multiple advantages to the healthcare system. Some of those include facilitation of shared decision-making, promotion of strong communication between practitioners and patients, and reduction in duration and expense of clinical encounters (Ye et al., 2024).

5.4.13 The Role of Real Time Analytics in Reducing Burden for Practitioners

When clinicians find it difficult to navigate technology in healthcare, it places a burden on them. Clinicians often experience exhaustion because of the demands raised by the EHR management and persistent inefficiencies in practice that hinder workflow and quality patient care (Craig et al., 2021). "Virtual triage (VT)" is an electronic tool that offers round-the-clock services that can be accessed by patients from anywhere with a stable internet connection, facilitating the assessment of symptoms and subsequent therapy. VT is designed to facilitate user satisfaction for both practitioners and patients (Gellert et al., 2023).

5.4.14 Barriers of Adaptive Technologies in Clinical Decision-Making

Multiple ethical considerations accompany the incorporation of AI in a healthcare facility. Confidentiality of the health-related and personal information of individuals is to be considered of the utmost importance (Dara & Azarpira, 2025). Ali et al. (2025) raise the need to upgrade the features of AI in response to new microbial threats. The chances of misprediction resulting from the deployment of adaptive technologies cannot be overlooked. Clinicians often find it challenging to comprehend the functions of multiple adaptive technologies, and it might result in medical errors. It is very important to consider the use of AI in the treatment and diagnosis of elevated-risk diseases. Therefore, the establishment of adaptive technologies in clinical settings correlates with the practitioners' task flow (Chustecki, 2024). Clinical AI tools have advanced to a point where they surpass human capabilities in clinical duties, particularly in diagnosing diseases (Dlugatch et al., 2024).

5.5 ETHICAL CONSIDERATIONS IN USING AI IN CLINICAL DECISION-MAKING

Racial prejudice: Obermeyer et al. (2019) revealed the racial bias identified in an AI algorithm where Black patients tended to have greater illness severity in comparison to White patients at the same risk score.

Clarity of reasoning: When clinical decision support excludes transparency, it challenges ethical values in healthcare and poses risks to both patients and communities (Amann et al., 2020).

Confidentiality: Price & Cohen (2019) describes two major ethical concerns regarding confidentiality with the use of AI in making predictions in healthcare. They are: i) Ethical concerns based on the outcomes and ii) Ethical concerns based on adherence to duty. The study adds that inadequate or excessive privacy measures can lead to tangible consequences for patients.

AI-associated bias: Biases that go unrecognized during the synthesis and deployment of medical tools that are driven by AI can result in increased health inequalities (Abràmoff et al., 2023).

5.6 RECOMMENDATIONS AND FUTURE DIRECTIONS

Hirosawa et al. (2024) emphasizes the impact of the incorporation of AI-powered hybrid intelligence into the healthcare system in enhancing the effectiveness of clinical decision-making. Elhaddad & Hamam (2024) support the need for user-focused design approaches for incorporating AI-based CDSS into the clinical workflow. The idea of human-in-the-loop machine learning helps construct systems that strengthen learning processes with input from a human expert (Bruckert et al., 2020). Shalabi et al. (2024) points to the vital need for sustained research with the goal of enhancing the utility of AI-driven technologies in clinical decision-making processes. The effective establishment of AI-driven CDSS in medical settings hinges on prioritizing key elements such as accessibility, credibility, and workflow alignment. This chapter encourages clinical schools to incorporate adaptive learning platforms in the curriculum as they can offer scenario-based simulations customized according to weaknesses and strengths exhibited by students. We look to the importance of hospitals and healthcare institutions being equipped with adaptive technologies that help healthcare providers refresh their decision-making skills. We emphasize the need for feedback-oriented adaptive tools to support clinicians in refining their clinical reasoning. Further research is needed to identify the long-term effects of the inclusion of adaptive technologies in clinical decision-making skills, healthcare outcomes, and patient safety.

REFERENCES

Abràmoff, M. D., Tarver, M. E., Loyo-Berrios, N., Trujillo, S., Char, D., Obermeyer, Z., Eydelman, M. B., Foundational Principles of Ophthalmic Imaging and Algorithmic Interpretation Working Group of the Collaborative Community for Ophthalmic Imaging Foundation, Washington, D.C., & Maisel, W. H. (2023). Considerations for addressing bias in artificial intelligence for health equity. *NPJ Digital Medicine*, 6(1), 170. https://doi.org/10.1038/s41746-023-00913-9

AbuAlrob, M. A., & Mesraoua, B. (2024). Harnessing artificial intelligence for the diagnosis and treatment of neurological emergencies: A comprehensive review of recent advances and future directions. *Frontiers in Neurology*, 15, 1485799. https://doi.org/10.3389/fneur.2024.1485799

Adams, I. D., Chan, M., Clifford, P. C., Cooke, W. M., Dallos, V., de Dombal, F. T., Edwards, M. H., Hancock, D. M., Hewett, D. J., & McIntyre, N. (1986). Computer aided diagnosis of acute abdominal pain: A multicentre study. *British Medical Journal* (Clinical research ed.), 293(6550), 800–804. https://doi.org/10.1136/bmj.293.6550.800

Adlung, L., Cohen, Y., Mor, U., & Elinav, E. (2021). Machine learning in clinical decision making. *Med* (New York, N.Y.), 2(6), 642–665. https://doi.org/10.1016/j.medj.2021.04.006

Agnihotri, Tanya, et al. (2020). Impact of an electronic decision-support system on nursing triage process: A usability and workflow analysis. *Canadian Journal of Nursing Research*, 53(2), 107–113. https://doi.org/10.1177/0844562119893514

Ali, H. H., Ali, H. M., Ali, H. M., Ali, M. A., Zaky, A. F., Touk, A. A., Darwiche, A. H., & Touk, A. A. (2025). The role and limitations of artificial intelligence in combating infectious disease outbreaks. *Cureus*, 17(1), e77070. https://doi.org/10.7759/cureus.77070

Almagharbeh, W. T. (2024). The impact of AI-based decision support systems on nursing workflows in critical care units. *International Nursing Review.* Advance online publication. https://doi.org/10.1111/inr.13011

Alowais, S. A., Alghamdi, S. S., Alsuhebany, N., Alqahtani, T., Alshaya, A. I., Almohareb, S. N., Aldairem, A., Alrashed, M., Bin Saleh, K., Badreldin, H. A., Al Yami, M. S., Al Harbi, S., & Albekairy, A. M. (2023). Revolutionizing healthcare: The role of artificial intelligence in clinical practice. *BMC Medical Education*, 23(1), 689. https://doi.org/10.1186/s12909-023-04698-z

Amann, J., Blasimme, A., Vayena, E., Frey, D., Madai, V. I., & Precise4Q consortium. (2020). Explainability for artificial intelligence in healthcare: A multidisciplinary perspective. *BMC Medical Informatics and Decision Making*, 20(1), 310. https://doi.org/10.1186/s12911-020-01332-6

Bajwa, J., Munir, U., Nori, A., & Williams, B. (2021). Artificial intelligence in healthcare: Transforming the practice of medicine. *Future Healthcare Journal*, 8(2), e188–e194. https://doi.org/10.7861/fhj.2021-0095

Brice, S., & Almond, H. (2020). Health professional digital capabilities frameworks: A scoping review. *Journal of Multidisciplinary Healthcare*, 13, 1375–1390. https://doi.org/10.2147/JMDH.S269412

Bruckert, S., Finzel, B., & Schmid, U. (2020). The next generation of medical decision support: A roadmap toward transparent expert companions. *Frontiers in Artificial Intelligence*, 3, 507973. https://doi.org/10.3389/frai.2020.507973

Brügge, E., Ricchizzi, S., Arenbeck, M., Keller, M. N., Schur, L., Stummer, W., Holling, M., Lu, M. H., & Darici, D. (2024). Large language models improve clinical decision making of medical students through patient simulation and structured feedback: A randomized controlled trial. *BMC Medical Education*, 24(1), 1391. https://doi.org/10.1186/s12909-024-06399-7

Chen, C. Y., Chen, Y. L., Scholl, J., Yang, H. C., & Li, Y. J. (2024). Ability of machine-learning based clinical decision support system to reduce alert fatigue, wrong-drug errors, and alert users about look alike, sound alike medication. *Computer Methods and Programs in Biomedicine*, 243, 107869. https://doi.org/10.1016/j.cmpb.2023.107869

Chen, Z., Liang, N., Zhang, H., Li, H., Yang, Y., Zong, X., Chen, Y., Wang, Y., & Shi, N. (2023). Harnessing the power of clinical decision support systems: Challenges and opportunities. *Open Heart*, 10(2), e002432. https://doi.org/10.1136/openhrt-2023-002432

Chustecki, M. (2024). Benefits and risks of AI in health care: Narrative review. *Interactive Journal of Medical Research*, 13, e53616. https://doi.org/10.2196/53616

Civaner, M. M., Uncu, Y., Bulut, F., Chalil, E. G., & Tatli, A. (2022). Artificial intelligence in medical education: A cross-sectional needs assessment. *BMC Medical Education*, 22(1), 772. https://doi.org/10.1186/s12909-022-03852-3

Combs, C. D., & Combs, P. F. (2019). Emerging roles of virtual patients in the age of AI. *AMA Journal of Ethics*, 21(2), E153–E159. https://doi.org/10.1001/amajethics.2019.153

Cook, D. A. (2025). Creating virtual patients using large language models: Scalable, global, and low cost. *Medical Teacher*, 47(1), 40–42. https://doi.org/10.1080/0142159X.2024.2376879

Dara, M., & Azarpira, N. (2025). Ethical considerations emerge from artificial intelligence (AI) in biotechnology. *Avicenna Journal of Medical Biotechnology*, 17(1), 80–81. https://doi.org/10.18502/ajmb.v17i1.17680

Dlugatch, R., Georgieva, A., & Kerasidou, A. (2024). AI-driven decision support systems and epistemic reliance: A qualitative study on obstetricians' and midwives' perspectives on integrating AI-driven CTG into clinical decision making. *BMC Medical Ethics*, 25(1), 6. https://doi.org/10.1186/s12910-023-00990-1

Dobler, C. C., Guyatt, G. H., Wang, Z., & Murad, M. H. (2021). Users' guide to medical decision analysis. *Mayo Clinic Proceedings*, 96(8), 2205–2217. https://doi.org/10.1016/j.mayocp.2021.02.003

El Arab, R. A., Al Moosa, O. A., Abuadas, F. H., & Somerville, J. (2025). The role of artificial intelligence in nursing education, and practice: An umbrella review. *Journal of Medical Internet Research*, 10.2196/69881. Advance online publication. https://doi.org/10.2196/69881

Elhaddad, M., & Hamam, S. (2024). AI-driven clinical decision support systems: An ongoing pursuit of potential. *Cureus*, 16(4), e57728. https://doi.org/10.7759/cureus.57728

Eloranta, S., & Boman, M. (2022). Predictive models for clinical decision making: Deep dives in practical machine learning. *Journal of Internal Medicine*, 292(2), 278–295. https://doi.org/10.1111/joim.13483

Elwyn, G., Frosch, D., Thomson, R., Joseph-Williams, N., Lloyd, A., Kinnersley, P., Cording, E., Tomson, D., Dodd, C., Rollnick, S., Edwards, A., & Barry, M. (2012). Shared decision making: A model for clinical practice. *Journal of General Internal Medicine*, 27(10), 1361–1367. https://doi.org/10.1007/s11606-012-2077-6

Enck, G. (2014). Six-step framework for ethical decision making. *Journal of Health Services Research & Policy*, 19(1), 62–64. https://doi.org/10.1177/1355819613511599

Fisher, K. A., Tan, A. S. L., Matlock, D. D., Saver, B., Mazor, K. M., & Pieterse, A. H. (2018). Keeping the patient in the center: Common challenges in the practice of shared decision making. *Patient Education and Counseling*, 101(12), 2195–2201. https://doi.org/10.1016/j.pec.2018.08.007

Fontaine, G., Cossette, S., Maheu-Cadotte, M. A., Mailhot, T., Deschênes, M. F., Mathieu-Dupuis, G., Côté, J., Gagnon, M. P., & Dubé, V. (2019). Efficacy of adaptive e-learning for health professionals and students: A systematic review and meta-analysis. *BMJ Open*, 9(8), e025252. https://doi.org/10.1136/bmjopen-2018-025252

Gellert, G. A., Rasławska-Socha, J., Marcjasz, N., Price, T., Heyduk, A., Mlodawska, A., Kuszczyński, K., Jędruch, A., & Orzechowski, P. (2023). The role of virtual triage in improving clinician experience and satisfaction: A narrative review. *Telemedicine Reports*, 4(1), 180–191. https://doi.org/10.1089/tmr.2023.0020

Glasgow, R. E., Huebschmann, A. G., Krist, A. H., & Degruy, F. V. (2019). An Adaptive, Contextual, Technology-Aided Support (ACTS) system for chronic illness self-management. *The Milbank Quarterly*, 97(3), 669–691. https://doi.org/10.1111/1468-0009.12412

Goldstein, B. A., Navar, A. M., Pencina, M. J., & Ioannidis, J. P. (2017). Opportunities and challenges in developing risk prediction models with electronic health records data: A systematic review. *Journal of the American Medical Informatics Association: JAMIA*, 24(1), 198–208. https://doi.org/10.1093/jamia/ocw042

Gutiérrez Maquilón, R., Uhl, J., Schrom-Feiertag, H., & Tscheligi, M. (2024). Integrating GPT-based AI into virtual patients to facilitate communication training among medical first responders: Usability study of mixed reality simulation. *JMIR Formative Research*, 8, e58623. https://doi.org/10.2196/58623

Hak, F., Guimarães, T., & Santos, M. (2022). Towards effective clinical decision support systems: A systematic review. *PloS One*, 17(8), e0272846. https://doi.org/10.1371/journal.pone.0272846

Hamilton, A. (2024). Artificial intelligence and healthcare simulation: The shifting landscape of medical education. *Cureus*, 16(5), e59747. https://doi.org/10.7759/cureus.59747

Hirosawa, T., Suzuki, T., Shiraishi, T., Hayashi, A., Fujii, Y., Harada, T., & Shimizu, T. (2024). Adapting artificial intelligence concepts to enhance clinical decision-making: A hybrid intelligence framework. *International Journal of General Medicine*, 17, 5417–5422. https://doi.org/10.2147/IJGM.S497753

Hlatky, M. A., Califf, R. M., Harrell, F. E., Jr, Lee, K. L., Mark, D. B., Muhlbaier, L. H., & Pryor, D. B. (1990). Clinical judgment and therapeutic decision making. *Journal of the American College of Cardiology*, 15(1), 1–14. https://doi.org/10.1016/0735-1097(90)90167-n

Ishii-Rousseau, J. E., Seino, S., Ebner, D. K., Vareth, M., Po, M. J., & Celi, L. A. (2022). The "Ecosystem as a Service (EaaS)" approach to advance clinical artificial intelligence (cAI). *PLOS Digital Health*, 1(2), e0000011. https://doi.org/10.1371/journal.pdig.0000011

Khalifa, M., & Albadawy, M. (2024). AI in diagnostic imaging: Revolutionising accuracy and efficiency. *Computer Methods and Programs in Biomedicine Update*, 5, 100146. https://doi.org/10.1016/j.cmpbup.2024.100146

Khanna, N. N., Maindarkar, M. A., Viswanathan, V., Fernandes, J. F. E., Paul, S., Bhagawati, M., Ahluwalia, P., Ruzsa, Z., Sharma, A., Kolluri, R., Singh, I. M., Laird, J. R., Fatemi, M., Alizad, A., Saba, L., Agarwal, V., Sharma, A., Teji, J. S., Al-Maini, M., Rathore, V., … Suri, J. S. (2022). Economics of artificial intelligence in healthcare: Diagnosis vs. treatment. *Healthcare* (Basel, Switzerland), 10(12), 2493. https://doi.org/10.3390/healthcare10122493

Khosravi, M., Zare, Z., Mojtabaeian, S. M., & Izadi, R. (2024). Artificial intelligence and decision-making in healthcare: A thematic analysis of a systematic review of reviews. *Health Services Research and Managerial Epidemiology*, 11, 23333928241234863. https://doi.org/10.1177/23333928241234863

Levkovich, I. (2025). Is artificial intelligence the next co-pilot for primary care in diagnosing and recommending treatments for depression?. *Medical Sciences* (Basel, Switzerland), 13(1), 8. https://doi.org/10.3390/medsci13010008

Liberatore, M. J., & Nydick, R. L. (2008). The analytic hierarchy process in medical and health care decision making: A literature review. *European Journal of Operational Research*, 189(1), 194–207. https://doi.org/10.1016/j.ejor.2007.05.001

Melin-Johansson, C., Palmqvist, R., & Rönnberg, L. (2017). Clinical intuition in the nursing process and decision-making—A mixed-studies review. *Journal of Clinical Nursing*, 26(23–24), 3936–3949. https://doi.org/10.1111/jocn.13814

Miller, K. E., Singh, H., Arnold, R., & Klein, G. (2019). Clinical decision-making in complex healthcare delivery systems. In Elsevier eBooks (pp. 858–864). https://doi.org/10.1016/b978-0-12-813467-2.00123-1

Morrow, E., Zidaru, T., Ross, F., Mason, C., Patel, K. D., Ream, M., & Stockley, R. (2023). Artificial intelligence technologies and compassion in healthcare: A systematic scoping review. *Frontiers in Psychology*, 13, 971044. https://doi.org/10.3389/fpsyg.2022.971044

Naderbagi, A., Loblay, V., Zahed, I. U. M., Ekambareshwar, M., Poulsen, A., Song, Y. J. C., Ospina-Pinillos, L., Krausz, M., Mamdouh Kamel, M., Hickie, I. B., & LaMonica, H. M. (2024). Cultural and contextual adaptation of digital health interventions: Narrative review. *Journal of Medical Internet Research*, 26, e55130. https://doi.org/10.2196/55130

Niraula, D., Sun, W., Jin, J., Dinov, I. D., Cuneo, K., Jamaluddin, J., Matuszak, M. M., Luo, Y., Lawrence, T. S., Jolly, S., Ten Haken, R. K., & El Naqa, I. (2023). A clinical decision support system for AI-assisted decision-making in response-adaptive radiotherapy (ARCliDS). *Scientific Reports*, 13(1), 5279–5279. https://doi.org/10.1038/s41598-023-32032-6

Obermeyer, Z., Powers, B., Vogeli, C., & Mullainathan, S. (2019). Dissecting racial bias in an algorithm used to manage the health of populations. *Science* (New York, N.Y.), 366(6464), 447–453. https://doi.org/10.1126/science.aax2342

Ouanes, K., & Farhah, N. (2024). Effectiveness of artificial intelligence (AI) in clinical decision support systems and care delivery. *Journal of Medical Systems*, 48(1), 74. https://doi.org/10.1007/s10916-024-02098-4

Piza, F., Piza, P., & Schwartzstein, R. M. (2019). The power of nonverbal communication in medical education. *Medical Teacher*, 41(4), 476–477. https://doi.org/10.1080/0142159X.2018.1454590

Price, W. N., 2nd, & Cohen, I. G. (2019). Privacy in the age of medical big data. *Nature Medicine*, 25(1), 37–43. https://doi.org/10.1038/s41591-018-0272-7

Scott, I., Carter, S., & Coiera, E. (2021). Clinician checklist for assessing suitability of machine learning applications in healthcare. *BMJ Health & Care Informatics*, 28(1), e100251. https://doi.org/10.1136/bmjhci-2020-100251

Shaheen, M. Y. (2021, September 28). AI in Healthcare: Medical and socio-economic benefits and challenges. https://doi.org/10.31219/osf.io/um38t

Shahmoradi, L., Safdari, R., Ahmadi, H., & Zahmatkeshan, M. (2021). Clinical decision support systems-based interventions to improve medication outcomes: A systematic literature review on features and effects. *Medical Journal of the Islamic Republic of Iran*, 35, 27. https://doi.org/10.47176/mjiri.35.27

Shahin, M. H., Goswami, S., Lobentanzer, S., & Corrigan, B. W. (2025). Agents for change: Artificial intelligent workflows for quantitative clinical pharmacology and translational sciences. *Clinical and Translational Science*, 18(3), e70188. https://doi.org/10.1111/cts.70188

Shalabi, K. M., Sayed, H. M., Pakkir Mohamed, S. H., Basuodan, R. M., Alahmari, W. S., & Shaik, S. A. (2024). A scoping review of the benefits and challenges of mHealth for clinical decision-making in neuro-physiotherapy. *European Review for Medical and Pharmacological Sciences*, 28(10), 3479–3492. https://doi.org/10.26355/eurrev_202405_36282

Sutton, R. T., Pincock, D., Baumgart, D. C., Sadowski, D. C., Fedorak, R. N., & Kroeker, K. I. (2020). An overview of clinical decision support systems: Benefits, risks, and strategies for success. *NPJ Digital Medicine*, 3, 17. https://doi.org/10.1038/s41746-020-0221-y

Thomas Craig, K. J., Willis, V. C., Gruen, D., Rhee, K., & Jackson, G. P. (2021). The burden of the digital environment: A systematic review on organization-directed workplace interventions to mitigate physician burnout. *Journal of the American Medical Informatics Association: JAMIA*, 28(5), 985–997. https://doi.org/10.1093/jamia/ocaa301

Tsuneki, M. (2022). Deep learning models in medical image analysis. *Journal of Oral Biosciences*, 64(3), 312–320. https://doi.org/10.1016/j.job.2022.03.003

Ye, J., Woods, D., Jordan, N., & Starren, J. (2024). The role of artificial intelligence for the application of integrating electronic health records and patient-generated data in clinical decision support. AMIA Joint Summits on Translational Science proceedings. *AMIA Joint Summits on Translational Science*, 2024, 459–467.

Zayas-Cabán, T., Haque, S. N., & Kemper, N. (2021). Identifying opportunities for workflow automation in health care: Lessons learned from other industries. *Applied Clinical Informatics*, 12(3), 686–697. https://doi.org/10.1055/s-0041-1731744

Zenebe, G. A., Alemu, W., Yehualashet, D., & Nakachew, M. (2023). Improving data use in decision-making and utilization of maternal healthcare services through a data-informed platform for health approaches in districts of the Gedeo Zone, southern Ethiopia, 2023: A cluster-randomized control trial. *Frontiers in Health Services*, 3, 1125399. https://doi.org/10.3389/frhs.2023.1125399

Zumla, A., Ahmed, R., & Bakhri, K. (2024). The role of artificial intelligence in the diagnosis, imaging, and treatment of thoracic empyema. *Current Opinion in Pulmonary Medicine*. Advance online publication. https://doi.org/10.1097/MCP.0000000000001150

6 AI-Enabled Bidirectional Healthcare

Advancing Patient Outcomes Through Intelligent Device-Provider Communication Systems

Ranney D.J. and Edward A.A.

6.1 FRAMING STATEMENT

In June 2006, a group of academics/professionals gathered in Addis Ababa, Ethiopia, to hear from then-Minister of Health, Dr Tedros Adhanom Ghebreyesus. He was accompanied by the CEO of Tikur Anbessa (aka Black Lion) Hospital, the largest facility in Addis Ababa. Dr Tedros' message was simple: go out into the field and work with administrators to help them run their facilities more effectively and efficiently. Breaking the current system was an expectation. The message from the Black Lion CEO was even simpler: If you're going to put together a report of what we don't have, just set it on my desk and I'll file it with all the others.

These words of wisdom help drive the purpose of this paper: we will not be spending unnecessary time pointing out the weaknesses or struggles of implementing Artificial Intelligence (AI) tools in developing or rural locations across the globe. Rather, the authors seek to address, "how can AI be used to improve patient outcomes in rural areas?"

The authors are not looking to minimize the hurdles faced by implementing any AI tool – there are many, and we will go through them. But the focus of this paper is not to provide more fodder for the naysayers who will always push back with, "they're not ready." Our simple response, "we have the ability to do something now and avoid unnecessary deaths."

DOI: 10.1201/9781003624875-8

6.2 ISN'T THIS A LOT OF WORK FOR MINIMAL IMPACT?

The proposed solution of connecting rural and urban care providers isn't new. The entire purpose of telemedicine – the idea of physically distanced healthcare staff communicating over the telephone, radio, the internet, etc., to care for a patient – has existed formally in some form since at least the time of Dr Einthoven's 1906 transmission of electrocardiograms over phone lines. To quote the good doctor, "Where there is a link, actual and figurative, between laboratory and hospital, and collaboration between physiologist and clinician, each remaining master in his territory, there one may fruitfully utilize these new electrical methods of research" (Strehle & Shabde, 2006, p. 956).

It's precisely this line of thought that brings these authors together to answer, "isn't this a lot of work for minimal impact?" with a resounding "no." There are no minimal steps when pursuing improvements to patient health and outcomes. Using AI to connect urban and rural care providers and ensure both have the best available information for treating the patient is a solid step in the evolution of AI, healthcare, and telemedicine.

With this intent in mind, let's turn our attention to developing an AI-driven rural healthcare solution.

6.3 INTRODUCTION

6.3.1 A Few Thoughts Before We Move On

We, the authors, fully acknowledge the capabilities and skills of medical staff throughout the developing world. If these individuals were unable to positively impact patients' lives, no one would survive even minor trauma. In no way are we suggesting incompetence on the part of these care providers. In fact, we have nothing but the deepest appreciation for everything these medical staff do to help their patients.

Secondly, the authors are proposing the integration of AI into current (or updated) national health infrastructure via a private/public partnership or a nonprofit initiative in which urban providers and specialists work with rural staff. Regardless of the ownership/structure, there is a single goal: use AI and associated tools to ensure those in resource-scarce locations receive positive, life-saving expertise and assistance in real time.

Finally, the authors are, in no way, suggesting governments replace qualified providers with AI and associated tools. These tools augment the expertise of both frontline providers and remote specialists, ensuring all have access to timely, relevant, and localized medical guidance. It is the combination of human expertise and AI assistance that will make a positive difference for all.

6.3.2 Why Does AI-Enabled Healthcare Matter in Developing Nations?

With a focus on bringing responsible AI and tools into the healthcare world, this paper argues that we have the ability, the know-how, and the expertise to do so. Further, we argue there's no time to waste; lives are at stake. But before we can progress, we need to ask the following questions:

1. Is there truly a provider shortage, and if so, why?
2. What's been done/being done to address the physician shortage?
3. What can be done to address the provider shortage?

6.3.3 How Bad Is the Physician Shortage?

Globally, we're facing a physician shortage, with the World Health Organization (WHO) estimating (in 2019) the shortage at 2.8 million (Saluja et al., 2020). When one considers the struggles faced by the developing world in retaining its healthcare workforce (Mohammadiaghdam et al., 2020), it's not a leap to say underdeveloped nations and their populations are the ones enduring the most pain.

6.3.4 But Why Is There a Provider Shortage and Why Are Providers in the Developing World Leaving for "Greener Pastures"?

This is a more complex question and has two main driving forces: First, why are providers unwilling to relocate within their own nation, and second, why are providers in developing nations leaving for the developed world? To be fair, upward mobility, seeking "greener pastures," a desire to have a better work/life balance, etc., aren't problems in the developing world. For the most part, people want to do well. They wish to be financially secure, safe from crime, etc., and to say migration is a problem would be wrong … migration is a result of an inability to achieve (or the perception thereof) a certain level of something – financial, safety, etc.

When we look deeper into the "why don't providers relocate internally" question, we hear the reasons for the situation are many: pay is low, the area is too remote, the family is too far away, the facility is too old, etc. These subjective observations are confirmed through studies which cite "the reasons as financial, career and professional, working conditions, personal, living conditions, and cultural" in nature (Mohammadiaghdam et al., 2020, Results section).

Looking at the question of migration outside one's home nation, we see a similar rationale, with a twist. Some see providers who leave their home nation, which so desperately needs their highly skilled help, as amounting to near-treasonous levels. It's somehow unethical for these individuals to leave the situation for personal reasons. It's this sense of treachery that has some (Runnels et al., 2011) questioning the recruitment of these professionals.

6.3.5 What Has Been Done or Is Beng Done or Proposed to Address the Provider Shortage?

For some organizations, the answer is, "find and train more physicians." This is naive, arrogant, and completely ignorant of the situation on the ground. Others (Al-Shamsi, 2017) argue for revamping the medical training to allow for more individuals to become providers. It hardly seems worthy of argument to say decreasing the knowledge base of providers is an answer to this issue. Still others suggest making it illegal for physicians to leave their home nation or be recruited by high-income nations, an argument the authors won't entertain.

6.3.6 What Can Be Done to Address the Physician Shortage?

If one stops and takes a breath at this point, the picture is as follows: there is a tremendous shortage of physicians across the globe, particularly in the developing world. The reasons cross the spectrum from personal and cultural to professional. The "train more physicians" mentality is not the answer. So where are we?

Government incentives (e.g., pay for school in return for practicing in a remote area) simply don't work. Many providers will tell you they're not going to go where the government tells them. Dragging these providers, kicking and screaming, to a remote location isn't likely to have a positive outcome for anyone. Unfortunately, many international organizations insist that all medical facilities, regardless of purpose, size, or location, be staffed by MDs. While the intent is to ensure high-quality care, this rigidity ignores the realities on the ground. Rather than adapting policies to better support life-saving interventions in remote areas, these organizations often create bureaucratic barriers that limit innovation. For the governments, there is no win here. And so, while others try to figure out how to work within this constrained system of carrot and stick, some are looking to develop creative and practical solutions that will help people.

One would be forgiven if, at this point, they were to ask, "if there are so many clear issues, what can be done and why is AI being touted as part of that solution?" The full answer, which is far more complex than "build it and they'll come," or make the education requirements easier or courses shorter. Governments have tried to tie education costs/reimbursement to public service with limited success – you can't expect a physician to perform their best if you demand they relocate to a place they wouldn't have chosen themselves. The demand by some that all medical facilities, regardless of location or size, be fully staffed by licensed physicians to ensure high-quality care is a pipe dream. But we can't throw our hands in the air and claim there's nothing we can do about it. There is, and that solution is at the heart of this paper.

6.3.7 How Can AI Help Developing Nations Meet the Needs of Their Populations?

Artificial Intelligence (AI) and associated tools such as machine learning (ML), data analysis and science (DA/DS), etc., allow providers (regardless of their location) to quickly find reliable, evidence-based information on a universe of topics. From "I have a patient exhibiting x-symptoms," to "the lab results for my patient show elevated x, what does this suggest?"

Rather than forcing traditional models into broken systems, AI offers an opportunity to develop creative and scalable solutions that complement existing healthcare infrastructure. AI-enabled bidirectional healthcare communication can provide real-time medical expertise to frontline workers, empower rural providers with decision-support tools, and ultimately improve patient outcomes by making healthcare guidance more accessible. By focusing on developing nations, we not only address an urgent global health challenge but also set a precedent for AI-driven healthcare solutions that can be adapted to rural and underserved communities worldwide.

AI is transforming healthcare globally, offering new ways to improve medical decision-making, patient engagement, and healthcare delivery. However, much of this progress is concentrated in high-resource settings, while low-resource regions—such as Africa, South America, and parts of Asia—face unique challenges that require tailored AI solutions. The intersection of AI and bidirectional healthcare communication presents an opportunity to bridge gaps in healthcare access, empower frontline health workers, and improve patient outcomes in underserved areas.

6.3.8 How Can Bidirectional AI Communication Improve Patient Outcomes?

Bidirectional AI, as used in this chapter, refers to the two-way super-communication between a provider (and their staff, office, or facility) and the patient (and their local provider, facility, and family). However, it extends beyond simple communication—it involves a system that "understands" the conversation and introduces evidence-based recommendations for providers to consider.

Imagine two healthcare professionals: one is a practicing trauma physician, while the other has received minimal trauma training from a local university or facility—functioning as a competent assistant. Currently, in many remote regions of Ethiopia, for example, a patient experiencing severe trauma faces a dire prognosis due to the lack of available medical expertise. The vast majority of remote regions lack hospitals, and only a handful have emergency care clinics. Even if a patient manages to reach a facility, the probability of a qualified trauma specialist being on-site is near zero.

Now, envision a small clinic staffed by a few care providers with various skills—trauma, pharmacy, and general care—located within minutes of the patient. The trauma staff assesses the patient and, using an app, connects with a pre-appointed physician. If bandwidth allows, video can be used; if not, lower-bandwidth methods, such as text-based updates, facilitate the exchange of critical information. While the local trauma staff administers basic life-saving measures, the trauma physician remotely evaluates the situation.

Here's where AI plays a crucial role. Suppose the physician requests a specific device or treatment that is unavailable at the remote location. AI steps in to suggest alternative options based on available resources. If the initial recommendation is not suitable, AI provides further alternatives in real time. This back-and-forth exchange ensures that an optimal, evidence-based treatment plan is created, even in areas with limited medical infrastructure. Once the physician finalizes the plan, the remote team receives and executes it. If sufficient bandwidth is available, the entire process occurs seamlessly in real time. If only SMS-level connectivity exists, the system still functions effectively, ensuring that critical medical decisions are communicated and executed efficiently.

The ability for remote healthcare workers to access, in real time, the expertise of accredited medical professionals is key to improving healthcare outcomes. International organizations, despite their well-intended policies, often express skepticism about the use of non-MD practitioners in remote locations, arguing that such practices put patients at risk. In an ideal world where every patient has immediate access to physicians and specialists, there would be no need for alternative healthcare models. However, the reality is that much of the world struggles to provide even basic healthcare access, let alone specialized care. General practitioners are scarce in many regions, and specialists are even rarer—often unwilling to relocate to remote areas due to lower salaries, isolation, and lack of professional opportunities.

Whether international organizations acknowledge it or not, alternative solutions to physician shortages are essential. With this in mind, the authors propose an approach where bidirectional AI and associated tools become an integral part of the healthcare system, empowering local providers and expanding access to medical expertise in real time. Crucially, AI's ability to near-instantly provide evidence-based recommendations to urban-based physicians is possible because it can assess and understand regional resource availability in real time. This dynamic intelligence ensures that even in the most resource-limited settings, providers can make informed decisions with actionable alternatives. While this naturally leads into broader discussions of AI-driven supply chain management, its immediate application in bridging healthcare access gaps cannot be overstated.

The authors believe addressing these challenges is the first step in developing a global AI-integrated healthcare solution.

6.4 BACKGROUND

6.4.1 How Long Have Humans Sought to Develop Intelligent Systems?

Being human, we seem to feel imperfect, incomplete, and insufficient. In a general way, we're amazing machines capable of incredible things. From our opposable thumbs allowing us to use tools to building telescopes capable of looking back to the birth of our universe, we continue to push the boundaries of what we can accomplish. However, we're somehow never satisfied. Unable to store and interpret all we see, we build structures for predicting the seasons (think Stonehenge), to understand the movement of the stars (think Antikythera mechanism), or structures current-day scientists don't fully understand (think Egyptian pyramids and their connection to harnessing natural forces). There's this general sense that we can do more or be better if we can just invent the "right" thing to help us get there.

Since the dawn of civilization, humans have sought to build tools that extend their abilities, automate labor, and encode knowledge. Ancient structures such as Stonehenge, the Mayan calendar, and the Great Pyramids of Egypt reflect early attempts to measure time, predict celestial events, and harness natural forces – systems that some argue were primitive forms of computational thinking. While these structures aren't computers in the modern sense, they demonstrate a fundamental human drive ... to develop intelligent systems that process information, solve problems, and reduce human burden. AI is simply the latest iteration of this effort – a tool designed to extend human expertise, not replace it.

This paper examines how the appropriate development and use of artificial intelligence (AI) and associated tools are the present-day "right" thing, and making use of these tools will further our demand for doing more and being better.

6.4.2 Why Is Bidirectional Healthcare Communication Essential?

No single provider has all the answers. Specialists at the world's most advanced research and teaching hospitals can't, for example, look at a patient and provide a full blood work-up. The laboratory and its skilled technicians and their resources provide that information to the specialist. Bidirectional communication, as used in this paper, is any communication taking place between two parties. There is no requirement for the two parties to be specialists, medical doctors, nurses, etc.

Effective healthcare delivery depends on seamless communication between patients and providers. In many developing nations, frontline healthcare workers operate in resource-limited environments, often with only basic training and limited access to specialist consultation. This communication gap delays treatment, increases medical errors, and negatively impacts patient outcomes.

AI-powered systems, such as chatbots, voice recognition tools, and predictive analytics, offer an opportunity to enhance bidirectional communication, ensuring that healthcare workers receive real-time, evidence-based guidance while patients get timely, understandable responses to health concerns.

6.4.3 Where Is AI Being Used in the Developing World? Who Is Doing the Work?

Go to Google (or preferred search engine) and type in AI in healthcare. Though results will vary based on your own history and past internet use, you'll see articles with titles mentioning AI and chatbots, the role of AI in decision-support systems, AI and predictive analytics, and AI wearables and their use in chronic care. Add "developing world" or "Africa" to that search and you're going to get a much different list. You'll now see such topics as AI in bridging the clinical gap, AI and data science are the keys to tomorrow's healthcare, etc. One can "feel" the difference, but it takes a moment to realize AI and its use/role in healthcare is very different in developed (or high-income) nations than in developing (or low-income) nations.

6.4.5 How Is AI Currently Used in Healthcare in the Developed World?

AI solutions typically leverage a combination of machine learning (ML), deep learning (DL), and more recently, explainable AI (XAI). ML algorithms support clinical decision support systems by identifying patterns in structured data like lab results or patient histories. DL extends this capability by analyzing complex data such as radiology images, voice, or video input – making it particularly useful for diagnostics and triage tools in both developed and developing regions. Explainable AI (XAI), a subfield focused on making algorithmic decision-making transparent and interpretable, is especially important in clinical environments where physicians must justify decisions based on AI suggestions. These forms of AI are becoming increasingly relevant as healthcare systems explore integration into diagnostic, administrative, and patient-facing workflows.

In high-income (developed) nations, AI is revolutionizing healthcare through:

- AI chatbots for patient triage and symptom checking (Tang et al., 2021)
- Clinical decision support systems (CDSS) that assist healthcare workers (Bajgain et al., 2023)
- Predictive analytics for disease forecasting and outbreak tracking (Garcia-Vidal et al., 2019)
- Remote monitoring and IoT-enabled wearables for chronic disease management (Alshamrani, 2022)

In contrast, in developing nations, AI is being positioned as a democratizing force – a tool capable of improving healthcare access and outcomes across entire populations. The primary goal is not market segmentation but medical inclusion. It's about using AI to ensure that all patients, regardless of location or income, receive the best care available. This contrast highlights not just a technological gap but a philosophical one: while one system seeks to refine an already robust structure, the other seeks to build and extend basic life-saving capabilities where they are most needed.

However, most AI solutions are designed for high-tech, high-bandwidth environments. Not only are the uses of AI different in developed and developing nations, but the narratives driving their adoption also diverge significantly. In developed nations, AI is often positioned as a tool to enhance patient engagement, streamline administrative workflows, and personalize care delivery – frequently serving the dual purpose of improving service quality and driving commercial outcomes. Increasingly, patient data is being used to inform marketing strategies and consumer behavior analytics.

Few models have been customized for developing nations, where challenges like poor internet connectivity, lack of digital infrastructure, and diverse linguistic and cultural contexts require specialized approaches.

6.4.6 Why Must AI Solutions Be Localized for Developing Nations?

Many nations create and maintain essential drug and therapeutics lists, and the WHO offers a model list that some argue should become the universal standard (Piggott et al., 2022). While such a list could streamline supply chain operations, it overlooks a critical truth: there is no such thing as "one disease, one drug."

The reality is far more complex. Drug choice varies by geography (due to regional pathogen strains or prescribing habits), by patient (due to allergies, comorbidities, or genetic factors), and by supply chain (due to availability or affordability). AI solutions must recognize these variables, not flatten them.

A universal AI-driven recommendation system – if based solely on a centralized drug list – risks encouraging inappropriate prescribing, undermining local protocols, and even accelerating problems like antimicrobial resistance. This author, among others, cautions against such oversimplification. Instead, AI must be trained on region-specific clinical guidelines, localized pharmacy inventories, and real-time infrastructure realities to ensure meaningful and ethical care delivery in diverse settings.

AI healthcare tools must be localized and adaptable to the unique healthcare landscapes of different developing regions. For instance, malaria diagnosis and treatment guidelines in rural Ethiopia may differ from those in remote areas of the Amazon. A one-size-fits-all AI approach will fail in such a dynamic setting. Instead, AI must be:

- Region-specific: Trained on local disease patterns
- Language-adaptive: Able to operate in multiple languages and dialects
- Infrastructure-aware: Functioning offline or with low-bandwidth updates

6.5 THE ROLE OF AI IN BIDIRECTIONAL HEALTHCARE COMMUNICATION

6.5.1 How Can AI Enhance Patient-Provider Interactions?

Hospitals, urgent care centers, emergency rooms, etc., are busy facilities. For patients, these places are also scary and cold … staff move quickly between patients, phones are continually ringing, sounds of machines beeping/alarms going off, people saying things to one another using medical jargon, etc. It's important to remember the reason everyone (aside from the patient) is on-site: caring for the patients. And a big part of that care is ensuring the patient and their best interests are heard. How can AI possibly assist in situations where so much is happening?

A few of the areas being touted as perfect for AI involvement:

Throughout the world, everyday consumers are running into AI-driven communication systems. Contact Absa through WhatsApp, and you're going to get a chatbot asking, "how can I help you?" Found a bed and breakfast in Cape St. Francis you'd like to book? Chances are, your first contact with the business will be a discussion with a chatbot to find open days.

6.5.1.1 But Can AI Chatbots Help With Healthcare Questions?

Yes, but ... unlike retail use of chatbots, the worst case is a less-than-happy experience. Perhaps the chatbot can't understand your speech, or doesn't have an answer to your question and tells you to call back during normal business hours. The outcome of the interaction isn't going to make you happy, and may even lead you to consider doing business elsewhere, but you're not likely to mistakenly hear, "Your lab results require immediate follow-up," or "the person you're calling about has passed on." Simply, the poor retail experience is, unfortunately, part of the overall experience we've all grown accustomed to; but a poor health-related experience due to a misinterpretation of a lab result or misreading of a patient status is something much worse. It's for that reason we must move slowly with AI integration into our health systems. Like retail, it would be wise for healthcare facilities to consider similar moves:

Use an AI chatbot as a triage tool for incoming patient and customer calls related to clinic hours or upcoming community events. Yes, these are important calls and questions, but people expect to interact with AI for the basics.

If your facility caters to a variety of backgrounds and languages, consider using AI as a translator (that is, for speech recognition). This is not a full recommendation to replace medical translators, but rather to serve as an assistant in situations where a translator is unavailable. Most patients would rather have the physician or other care provider slowly attempt to translate into something they can understand than leave the patient sitting silently, clearly wondering: what's going on?

Use AI in situations where specific steps must be taken in a specific order (that is, decision support). For example, if you're a laboratory technician and drawing blood for a rare condition requires the use of a specific blood tube, filled to a specific level, stored at a specific temperature, and spun for 35 seconds (this is a purely fictitious example). An AI assistant at your side, walking you through each step, one at a time, could prove beneficial and ensure the test was appropriately prepared.

There's much we can learn from the retail use of AI, the key being, "if a customer isn't happy with their interaction, they'll look elsewhere." This reality is hitting developed nations in the pocketbook and helps to explain why they're working so hard to gather as much patient data as possible for their marketing efforts. They know patients are paying more attention to their own care and are less inclined to stay at any facility if any part of that care isn't great. For the developing world, our key focus is to bridge the care availability gap. We're not looking to get all data on all patients to help our marketing team; we're looking to build libraries of knowledge our physicians and AI systems can access in order to ensure all patients get the best possible care, regardless of their location.

6.5.1.2 Retail AI vs. Healthcare AI: Why the Stakes Differ

The use of AI-powered chatbots in consumer services is now widespread. Whether booking a bed and breakfast, checking bank balances, or confirming a delivery, consumers have grown used to interacting with digital agents. A poor chatbot experience in these contexts might be frustrating – it may misunderstand a request, offer a generic response, or ask you to call back during office hours – but the worst outcome is typically inconvenience.

In healthcare, however, the stakes are dramatically higher. Imagine a chatbot misunderstanding a patient's request for help to interpret lab results, or incorrectly reporting a loved one's status. These aren't customer service failures – they're moments that could lead to harm, fear, or worse.

Because of this risk, healthcare must adopt a fundamentally different posture toward chatbot deployment. The question isn't just whether AI can help … but when, where, and with what safeguards?

That's why early integration of chatbots in healthcare should focus on areas where precision is less critical, but operational efficiency is still valuable: providing clinic hours, directions, event reminders, or general health literacy prompts. This matches user expectations – most people now expect some AI interaction at the front line of service – and keeps the (human) care provider central to care delivery.

If developed responsibly, AI can help restore the human element to clinical care – not replace it, but amplify it, especially in environments stretched thin by geography, staffing, or infrastructure.

6.5.2 How Can AI Improve Clinical Decision Support?

Building on AI's role in front-line patient communication, we now turn to its deeper integration within clinical workflows. Beyond those areas retail has deemed "safe" (e.g., scheduling and translation), AI's potential to guide medical decision-making – especially where specialists are scarce – represents one of the most promising avenues for strengthening care quality in low-resource settings.

Predictive Analytics for Disease Trends: AI is able to quickly review and analyze information in real-time. Not only are models able to look in the rearview mirror and make connections, AI can use real-time data and assist in predicting paths of least resistance for diseases such as malaria. By prediction, it must be noted, we're not talking (yet) of an AI model predicting individual infection, but are saying a model with information on such things as weather patterns, drug shortages, provider capability, etc., can suggest areas that are at higher risk than others (Andigema et al., 2024).

Machine Learning for Personalized Care: AI can analyze patient history and suggest customized treatment plans.

6.5.3 How Can AI-Powered Devices Improve Remote Healthcare?

Low-Cost IoT Monitoring Systems: We've briefly mentioned the role wearable AI (e.g., smartwatches) play in healthcare. We've further envisioned how these devices could become fully integrated into the healthcare information stream between patient and provider. This role as individual health information provider could, if equipment pricing, device longevity, and other item-specific issues (e.g., updates over slow internet, strength of equipment, battery life, etc.) grow much larger.

Offline AI-Assisted Health Record Systems: Not as glamorous as smartwatch introduction and use, AI has the ability to assist in the building and sustainability of hard copy health records. For many, having a standardized record system will go a long way in patient care.

6.6 AI'S CONTRIBUTION TO PATIENT OUTCOMES

6.6.1 How Does AI Improve Communication and Patient Engagement?

AI can, in near real-time, produce information (ranging from what supplies are on-site in the rural clinic, to the on-site staff knowledge levels, to which desired care options are available) to the urban specialist. With this information in hand, the urban physician has all the tools he or she needs to ensure the best treatment is given to the rural clinic's patient. This certainty has previously been unavailable, leaving rural clinics to fend for themselves and do their best.

A secondary and highly beneficial aspect of AI: patient communication. With few exceptions, businesses (healthcare or otherwise) employ people to answer customer questions. This initial (and ongoing) point of contact between customers (or patients) and business is oftentimes the maker or breaker of business sustainability and success (Wang et al., 2022).

6.6.2 How Does AI Enable Personalized Care and Predictive Insights?

The potential of AI can sometimes be best envisioned through practical questioning and examples. How do you know the "right time" to get a flu shot? How do you know you really need it (the flu shot)? Are you sick "enough" to go see a physician, or do you just need a day of rest? Your family has a history of cancer. Should you be worried? There is no single answer to these questions. The "right time" to get a flu shot may well depend on when you have a day off. Whether you "need" a flu shot may depend on your occupation. But … if you wear a smartwatch, you're already taking a step toward an AI-assisted healthcare future. That smartwatch already monitors basic health indicators (pulse, respirations, sleep patterns, stress, etc.), but that information isn't being shared. Imagine if your primary care physician were routinely notified of your ongoing health. Now imagine asking the same questions. The "right" time to get your flu shot comes down to a combination of your physician's interpretation of your latest health indicators and the general health of the local population. If the flu is "going around" and your body is "telling" the physician you're not feeling your best, it may be the "right" time to take a day off and rest – or whatever treatment the physician believes necessary. The point is, AI can, in this imaginary future, provide physicians with sufficient information for them to take individualized, personal action.

6.7 CHALLENGES AND LIMITATIONS

6.7.1 What Ethical Concerns Must Be Addressed in AI Healthcare?

Bias in AI Algorithms: In a 2021 paper, authors Fazelpour and Danks discuss the issue of bias with AI algorithms and, importantly for our discussions here, the impact such bias has on "sensitive domains, including healthcare" (Fazelpour & Danks, 2021, Conclusion section). It isn't difficult to see how using an AI model that has a bias toward any specific person or group would negatively impact their health. It's for this reason that any AI model we use in healthcare must be beyond reproach. Those in charge of ensuring the model uses only evidence-based facts must be vigilant. As noted earlier, gaining the trust of people using a new AI tool is only part of the battle in adoption. If the model turns out to push misinformation against any class or population, not only is the model likely to be thrown out, but AI and its use will be impacted, and we'll end up worse off than we are now.

6.7.2 How Can AI Models Be Updated in Low-Resource Settings?

In many nations, the "always on" internet, high-speed fiber or cable connections, reliable electricity, etc., don't exist. Unknown resource availability, if not built into the overall AI plan, will create issues. While some issues can be relatively minor (ex: to get past the issue of a lack of available energy for your smartwatch, we can use solar power), other issues, such as downloading a major software update that is gigabytes in size, require out-of-the-box thinking. Perhaps rural clinics with only an SMS service require someone to physically deliver a thumb drive with the updates. Perhaps upgrades are broken into sufficiently small pieces that even old-school dial-up internet works. The point: issues are solvable.

6.8 FUTURE DIRECTIONS AND RECOMMENDATIONS

AI is just beginning to make its presence known in much of the world. In the developed world, we're seeing a move toward data gathering and manipulation as a marketing tool. In the developing world, AI will play a major role in filling the provider shortage gap. Two different uses of a tool that is just beginning to be understood.

6.8.1 What Role Should Healthcare Leaders Play in AI Adoption?

Patients are human beings undergoing a difficult, if not life-altering, experience. The physician is the "get better or worse" gatekeeper. They are trusted members of our society whose opinions we value over any other. Though current events (particularly in many developed nations) have pushed for a "science or education-free" society, these views are, thankfully, confined to the extremists among us. Unfortunately, this uneducated or divisive rhetoric is putting even greater pressure on healthcare providers to be error-free. Any mistake will certainly be amplified via extremist networks, creating doubt around those very professionals we've asked to provide care. These comments may seem cynical to some, and for a few, they're correct. Not everyone is on the "get rid of science" bandwagon.

Whether or not one agrees with the role or authority given to providers, the unprecedented number of people questioning medical professionals is far too high. This begs the question, "if the doubting patient doesn't trust a provider/physician, who do they trust?" Though it's beyond the scope of this paper to fully address this issue, we must figure it out. For now, we can only ask, "how can we help physicians do their best?" The latest tools in the fanciest of hospitals, surrounded by the world's highest-skilled staff, would be nice, but fanciful. There is a global shortage of providers; those with the greatest monetary resources are pushing for less science, and corporate health systems are pushing profits above all else. If we accept the reality for what it is, we need to think of plan B or C, and we must accept the fact we can't provide the greatest care to everyone. It's brutal. It's unfair. It's cruel. How can so few have so much while the majority have so little? Once again, the authors must take a pass. We can only provide information that, if used correctly, will at least help those in the most need. AI used by urban specialists can help the rural provider and their patients, but it's not a miracle pill.

We've talked about the role of providers, the fairness (or lack thereof) in care access, but not the role of healthcare leaders in AI adoption.

Healthcare leaders are those people with senior levels of experience and/or knowledge in some aspect of healthcare. On the clinical side, we're speaking of MDs, RNs, paramedics, etc. On the non-clinical side, we're speaking of healthcare researchers, hospital executives (CEO, COO, CFO, etc.), ancillary service leaders (e.g., radiology and laboratory directors, etc.), and indirect leaders (e.g., medical suppliers, etc.). It's a broad stroke to be sure. Rather than getting caught up in the full list of "who should be at the decision-making table," a better use of time is to ask, "why do healthcare leaders need to participate in AI adoption?" It may help to understand how AI "learns." In general, AI is provided with information from reputable (hopefully) sources. This information is supplanted by ongoing input by AI prompt engineers (people who pose questions to AI and judge/grade the response). If you're asking AI a question about the best place to eat in Seattle, it's subjective and based on the input of not just the initial information and engineer input, but on widely available information on the web. At worst, you'll have a less-than-wonderful meal in Seattle. At best, the meal is fantastic, you rate your experience on some platform, and the AI incorporates this new information. But what if the question posed to AI was something like, "I'm having chest pains and sweating a lot. What should I do?" Whether you turn to legal or ethical experts, the answer from AI will be "call 911." Within our current environment and the manner in which we use AI tools, this is appropriate. Jump into the future a few years and AI no longer says, "call 911," but provides actual advice? Would you really trust information that has been (at least partially) gathered through Twitter conversations? Or from an engineer with a background in construction? We're not pushing for a fully autonomous AI solution, we're simply pointing out the need for healthcare leaders to be the ones providing the information AI relies upon.

Though accepting a "we must do something" approach to care isn't what most healthcare providers desire, it is a harsh reality.

And so, as a global society, we must have full faith and trust in those appointed to provide us with care.

Healthcare leaders must guide AI adoption to ensure solutions remain ethical and evidence-based. Let's take a step back. AI is, at its heart, information. This information drives AI output, which then explains the options received by, in our situation, the urban-based specialist. If the information within the AI is "bad" or based on half-truths or outright lies, the options passed to the specialist will also be "bad." In healthcare, this is an unacceptable outcome.

6.8.2 Ethical, Infrastructure, and Policy Considerations

AI has the potential to strengthen health systems in resource-poor settings, but adoption requires alignment with governance frameworks and equity principles (Wahl et al., 2018). Even the most advanced AI will fail without three foundational pillars: ethics, infrastructure, and policy. These elements determine whether AI serves as a tool for health equity or reinforces existing gaps. Getting this right is not an abstract or theoretical debate – it's the difference between meaningful adoption and catastrophic missteps or outright failure.

6.8.2.1 Ethical Considerations: More Than Compliance

Trust is not a given; it must be earned. For patients, questions around consent, data privacy, and algorithmic bias are not theoretical; they're personal. A system that predicts medication adherence or triages based on risk scores may sound promising, but what if its recommendations skew against rural patients because the training data was urban-centric?

Ethical safeguards must do more than check a box; they must demonstrate fairness in real-world situations. Transparent, explainable, and accountable frameworks are essential. This means patients should know when AI is involved in their care and how decisions are made. Bias audits, independent oversight, and patient education are critical steps in building confidence that these tools serve all communities equally, not just the most connected or affluent ones. Without such measures, even accurate predictions will face justified pushback.

These ethical considerations must be matched with equally thoughtful infrastructure planning and policy design.

6.8.2.2 Infrastructure Considerations: Potential Barrier to Bold Ideas

AI adoption doesn't fail because models are weak; it fails because of one of the oldest adages in the books: a system is only as strong as its weakest link. In many low-resource settings, bandwidth limitations, on-again/off-again power, and old/outdated hardware are harsh realities. The solution isn't to scale back ambition; it's to design AI systems with modular updates, offline capabilities, and lightweight architecture that doesn't assume a group of top technicians are standing by waiting to fix any issues.

We also need interoperability (yes, the "i" word which far too many companies say exists, but doesn't) standards that allow local health systems to integrate new tools without costly overhauls. Infrastructure is not glamorous, but it's the difference between a promising pilot project and a national rollout. Without robust foundations, even the best AI project or initiative becomes another abandoned experiment and, sadly, yet another reason for some to gloat or complain about technical or medical professional failure.

We envision, expect, and strongly encourage the creation of transparent, patient-centered guidelines that are not only ethically sound but adaptable to local realities.

6.8.2.3 Policy Considerations: Promoter or Roadblock

Regulations can be either a cheerleader or a roadblock. The EU's AI Act (European Commission [EU Commission], 2024), the U.S. AI Bill of Rights (White House Office of Science and Technology Policy [OSTP], 2022), and Africa's Digital Transformation Strategy (African Union [AU], 2020) all signal government involvement and regulation, but the plans are vastly different. In Africa, a well-intentioned policy can stall for years because of funding or political policy changes.

Policy cannot be a "someday" or one-off conversation; it needs to adapt to, and along with, implementation. Incentives for ethical AI use, clear liability frameworks, and region-specific guidelines are not optional; they are non-negotiable for both trust and sustainability. Governments, private innovators, and health institutions must coordinate to ensure regulatory alignment rather than fragmentation.

Delaying action is not an option. AI-enabled bidirectional communication can transform healthcare from a privilege into a guarantee of equity – but only if ethics, infrastructure, and policy move forward in lockstep with political will. The success of an intelligent healthcare system depends on building these three pillars as deliberately as the technology itself.

6.9 CONCLUSION

Recent public discussions in South Africa have raised concerns about the impact of AI and automation on healthcare staff employment. Fears of job loss or displacement, though understandable, must be discussed transparently, in the open, and before any action occurs. AI implementation behind closed doors will only contribute to public mistrust of a system designed to assist healthcare providers, not replace them.

As AI technologies are developed and pushed mainstream, the discussions must be about more than cost savings. We must discuss the improvements and enhancements that will arise from a system designed for efficiency and quality. Thoughtful leadership and strategic integration will allow us to strengthen, not weaken, healthcare throughout the world.

REFERENCES

African Union. (2020). *The digital transformation strategy for Africa: 2020 – 2030.* https://au.int/en/documents/20200518/digital-transformation-strategy-africa-2020-2030

Alshamrani, M. (2022). Iot and artificial intelligence implementations for remote healthcare monitoring systems: A survey. *Journal of King Saud University – Computer and Information Sciences*, *34*(8), 4687–4701. https://doi.org/10.1016/j.jksuci.2021.06.005

Al-Shamsi, M. (2017). Addressing the physicians' shortage in developing countries by accelerating and reforming the medical education: Is it possible? *Journal of Advances in Medical Education & Professionalism*, *5*(4), 210–219. https://pubmed.ncbi.nlm.nih.gov/28979916/

Andigema, A. S., Cyrielle, N., Laetitia, N., & Ekwelle, E. (2024). Transforming healthcare in Africa: The role of artificial intelligence in combatting infectious diseases, neglected tropical diseases, and antimicrobial resistance. *International Journal of Health Policy Planning*, *3*(3), 1–5. Retrieved March 30, 2025, from https://doi.org/10.33140/ijhpp.03.03.01

Bajgain, B., Lorenzetti, D., Lee, J., & Sauro, K. (2023). Determinants of implementing artificial intelligence-based clinical decision support tools in healthcare: A scoping review protocol. *BMJ Open*, *13*(2), e068373. https://doi.org/10.1136/bmjopen-2022-068373

European Commission. (2024). *Regulation (EU) 2024/1689 of the European parliament and of the Council of 13 June 2024* (Document 32024R1689) [Regulation]. https://eur-lex.europa.eu/eli/reg/2024/1689/oj/eng

Fazelpour, S., & Danks, D. (2021). Algorithmic bias: Senses, sources, solutions. *Philosophy Compass*, *16*(8). https://doi.org/10.1111/phc3.12760

Garcia-Vidal, C., Sanjuan, G., Puerta-Alcalde, P., Moreno-García, E., & Soriano, A. (2019). Artificial intelligence to support clinical decision-making processes. *eBioMedicine*, *46*, 27–29. https://doi.org/10.1016/j.ebiom.2019.07.019

Mohammadiaghdam, N., Doshmangir, L., Babaie, J., Khabiri, R., & Ponnet, K. (2020). Determining factors in the retention of physicians in rural and underdeveloped areas: A systematic review. *BMC Family Practice*, *21*(1). https://doi.org/10.1186/s12875-020-01279-7

Piggott, T., Nowak, A., Brignardello-Petersen, R., Cooke, G. S., Huttner, B., Schünemann, H. J., Persaud, N., Magrini, N., & Moja, L. (2022). Global status of essential medicine selection: A systematic comparison of national essential medicine lists with recommendations by who. *BMJ Open*, *12*(2), e053349. https://doi.org/10.1136/bmjopen-2021-053349

Runnels, V., Labonté, R., & Packer, C. (2011). Reflections on the ethics of recruiting foreign-trained human resources for health. *Human Resources for Health*, *9*, 2. Retrieved April 13, 2025, from https://doi.org/10.1186/1478-4491-9-2

Saluja, S., Rudolfson, N., Massenburg, B., Meara, J. G., & Shrime, M. G. (2020). The impact of physician migration on mortality in low and middle-income countries: An economic modelling study. *BMJ Global Health*, *5*(1), e001535. https://doi.org/10.1136/bmjgh-2019-001535

Strehle, E. M., & Shabde, N. (2006). One hundred years of telemedicine: Does this new technology have a place in paediatrics? *Archives of Disease in Childhood*, *91*(12), 956–959. Retrieved April 12, 2025, from https://doi.org/10.1136/adc.2006.099622

Tang, X., Hacker, N., Danish, A., & Chen, S. (2021). Patient-reported outcome+ platform for remote symptom management, featuring automated triage system. *International Journal of Radiation Oncology*Biology*Physics*, *111*(3), e98–e99. https://doi.org/10.1016/j.ijrobp.2021.07.489

Wahl, B., Cossy-Gantner, A., Germann, S., & Schwalbe, N. R. (2018). Artificial intelligence (AI) and global health: How can AI contribute to health in resource-poor settings? *BMJ Global Health*, *3*(4), Article e000798. Retrieved July 21, 2025, from https://doi.org/10.1136/bmjgh-2018-000798

Wang, X., Lin, X., & Shao, B. (2022). How does artificial intelligence create business agility? Evidence from chatbots. *International Journal of Information Management*, *66*, 102535. Retrieved April 27, 2025, from https://doi.org/10.1016/j.ijinfomgt.2022.102535

White House Office of Science and Technology Policy. (2022). *Blueprint for an AI bill of rights: Making automated systems work for the American people* [Policy Framework]. https://bidenwhitehouse.archives.gov/ostp/ai-bill-of-rights/

World Health Organization. (2021). *Ethics and governance of artificial intelligence for health* (9789240029200) [Guidance Document]. WHO.

Part III

AI Applications in Healthcare Practice

7 Integrating Artificial Intelligence in Disease Preparedness

Wasswa Shafik

7.1 INTRODUCTION

Disease epidemics and pandemics represent an all-hazards risk that can occur with little warning, anytime, anywhere. The consequences of an uncontrolled infectious disease outbreak can be economically costly, disrupting trade and economic output, and have long-term economic consequences. As healthcare technology has developed, we have seen a parallel growth in the global prevalence of emerging and re-emerging infectious diseases. In managing such threats, the public and global health community faces a clear challenge despite advances in infectious disease detection, surveillance, and response (Bhaskar, 2023). Outbreaks of infectious diseases have shown common themes, including weaknesses in global and domestic response systems in coping with a multisectoral public health disaster and a lack of robust disease-preparedness plans that might have served to minimize the impact of outbreaks. In an increasingly global, technology-driven world, it is vitally important to ensure that our responses to future global health risks are agile, robust, evidence-based, and fully representative of new technological potentials. Artificial intelligence and machine learning, which hold significant promise for improving predictive analytics and pattern recognition on a scale not possible using normal human analytical abilities, represent one key development in technology that has not hitherto been fully explored in the context of direct application to global public health problem-solving (Jeyakumar et al., 2023). As a whole, we are underprepared for future health risks and lack robust, evidence-based plans designed to allow rapid, efficient, and well-coordinated responses at a national, regional, and global level. This is particularly critical given the potential amplification of such risks that result from ever-increasing international travel, connectivity, and urbanization. There is, therefore, an urgent need for research and development of robust, evidence-based disease-preparedness strategies to enhance public health security (Ienca, 2019).

Disease-preparedness is a field involving long-term public health strategies that aim to prevent the spread of disease, effectively monitor for the occurrence of disease, and respond in an organized and efficient way should a disease be detected in

DOI: 10.1201/9781003624875-10

the community. Being prepared for disease is important because infectious disease threats are increasing, both in frequency and in geographic spread. As we become more globally connected, either through trade or through travel, it becomes quicker and easier for diseases to spread around the world (Shafik, 2024c, 2025b). Diseases that were once unique to very specific corners of the globe now regularly pop up in a growing number of places. This makes the disease a "when" problem, not an "if" problem. Consequently, it makes good public health sense to be ready to deal with cases if or when they arrive. At a very high level, preparedness involves doing a number of specific things related to programmatic functions. These include building surveillance, information systems, community engagement, education, planning, communication, and laboratory and diagnostic capacity (Simsek & Kantarci, 2020). In terms of implementation, work in public health varies from country to country due to the fact that the disease risk, sociopolitical climates, resources, and cultures are different from location to location. It is within these frames and functions that AI technologies will be studied and discussed in further detail throughout the remainder of this thesis. Advance your preparedness planning and work in the public health field, utilizing more sophisticated tools that will not only help identify problems but also aid in the design and implementation of policies and responses (Farooq et al., 2022). AI systems could add a unique and new approach to these issues to help prepare for better future diseases. They could also give the public health field, which is mainly prevention-oriented, the tools needed to justify their efforts. Thus, the impacts of integrating AI tools into public health are potentially as far-reaching as the effects of public health itself. Because public health is fundamentally concerned with prevention, contagion control and health promotion are potentially wide-reaching issues (Tambo et al., 2021).

7.2 UNDERSTANDING ARTIFICIAL INTELLIGENCE FUNDAMENTALS

Artificial intelligence (AI) serves as an umbrella science for a wide range of problem-solving, human-like cognition, and perception tasks and has a broad spectrum from computing systems and robotics to machine learning and computer vision. Machine learning is a subset of AI that allows software applications to become more accurate at predicting outcomes independently through learning from data patterns. Deep learning is an advanced topic within machine learning that uses artificial neural networks to learn from large amounts of data (Shafik, 2023). Deep learning has shown superior performance in drug discovery, robotics, and computer vision, among other tasks, and outperforms humans in several image classification tasks. Machine learning techniques include supervised and unsupervised learning, where the former relies on annotated data to make predictions or decisions, while the latter does not. Semi-supervised learning and reinforcement learning are other techniques that are applied when small or large amounts of annotated data instances are available (Rahman et al., 2022). A major application of deep learning in healthcare is medical imaging, for example, to propose patient diagnoses from medical images and to differentiate diseased cells from healthy ones. Text data that is largely free-text reports constitute unstructured data. Natural Language Processing (NLP) is a subfield of AI focusing on the interaction between computer languages and human languages. It aims to extract meaningful insights from these unstructured reports (Shafik, 2024g). Unlike many other forms of data, the tidying step is highly non-trivial in unstructured text data and requires highly advanced linguistic techniques. Therefore, one major challenge lies in extracting structured information from this unstructured data. It utilizes AI, machine learning, deep learning, and semi-supervised and transfer learning techniques. Despite the rapid progress in the corresponding technologies, its integration into disease-preparedness frameworks has been lagging. AI is an interdisciplinary science with significant contributions from computer science, statistics, and domain expertise (Swayamsiddha et al., 2021).

7.2.1 Machine Learning and Deep Learning Basics

Machine learning and deep learning are two core constituents of artificial intelligence that facilitate computational systems to learn from data and make predictions or decisions. Machine learning is a method of data analysis that automates analytical model building. It is an application of artificial intelligence that provides systems the ability to learn and improve from experience. By applying complex, AI-driven algorithms to vast data troves, we can also accomplish the process of data mining that extracts insights from the processed data (Geanta et al., 2022). One of the specialized domains of machine learning is deep learning. It uses advanced deep learning structures known as neural networks to understand and identify patterns present in data. These two separate strands of artificial intelligence exist side by side, complementing each other in their rights and finding applications in healthcare. This ability to classify and predict makes machine learning and deep learning pivotal in the development of predictive models that predict patient outcomes, such as patient admissions, finance, and claims for targeted interventions. In recent years, machine learning systems, which enable computers to process and analyze large data sets, have made a growing impact in healthcare (Parija & Poddar, 2024). Digital health companies and organizations leverage machine learning algorithms to develop a model that can predict emergency room visits four hours ahead of the onset of symptoms. The model, trained on existing medical records and data, produced patient risk assessments at an 83% accuracy rate. Researchers also use similar machine learning techniques to develop a model to predict patient length of stay in ICU with 85% accuracy. Such systems require large amounts of historical data to learn the difference between a patient who will or will not be admitted to the hospital (Shafik, 2025a; Uohara et al., 2020). Through this, machine learning-based models can provide evidence-based interventions to prevent the inappropriate use of emergency room resources and to address patient admissions.

7.2.2 Natural Language Processing in Healthcare

In the healthcare domain, natural language processing (NLP) and text mining techniques have been widely utilized to automatically analyze biomedical and clinical texts, such as clinical notes, prescription records, registered claims, published research articles, grant-funded projects, and disease outbreak news. Different from structured data processing, which handles data that would normally fit into a database, NLP aims to enable computers to derive valuable insights from human natural language data. Human language is the primary form in which knowledge is expressed and documented (Ambas et al., 2024). Despite making up roughly 80% of the world's total knowledge, most of the valuable information is stored in unstructured or semi-structured data forms, which makes it hard for systematic interpretation. Therefore, a substantial wealth of health and medical knowledge derived from the free text remains untapped. Furthermore, most biomedical NLP research focuses on data-driven hypothesis generation for new facts and relationships; yet another valuable application of NLP tools is to extract the semantic structure of health information for improving clinical decision-making (Shafik, 2024d; Zaidan, 2023). In healthcare settings, if the information related to patients and diseases contained in the unstructured texts can be automatically processed and summarized, it can significantly contribute to enhancing the healthcare system and even ad-hoc public health surveillance. Moreover, the application of NLP emphasizes the adoption of tools for summarizing text-based patient information. The subsequent incentives program motivates the upsurge in the utilization of NLP-based technologies in the form of applications and systems for processing and other clinical-related tasks (Farooq et al., 2022; Shafik, 2024f). Medical research articles are one of the most important resources in the management and control of newly emergent diseases. In disease information management, exploring and collecting scattered information from valuable articles is indispensable when there are sudden outbreaks of diseases that require a rapid response. With the purpose of knowledge discovery and analysis, various integrated, semi-automated, and human-computer-supported methods and tools utilizing NLP and AI have been developed. We demonstrate various NLP-based systems that are developed specifically for timely disease response and supporting a potential strategy for assisted preparedness (Ambas et al., 2024; Shafik, 2024e).

7.3 CURRENT CHALLENGES IN DISEASE PREPAREDNESS

Disease-preparedness is a persistent challenge across the globe. Many health systems rely on data siloed into independent data systems, and governments cannot consistently collect, integrate, and validate accurate disease data. As issues linger in data collection, information systems also require significant investment to ensure fair sharing and access to relevant information. This challenges a coordinated response in outbreak management because of a high degree of variability across agencies, from case identification to case tracking (Shafik, 2024b; Simsek & Kantarci, 2020). Even with serviceability and accessibility to preparedness information, the challenge of acknowledging the unknowns in one's environment and linking environmental data known to action requires significant financial resources. Considerations for peacetime production of agricultural commodities, regular healthcare services, and strategies for night markets are imperative; safe and ethical concerns must also be addressed because viruses with eventual human adaptation concerns are not yet human-transmissible. Resources have not been allocated in sufficient supply for disease-preparedness and readiness (Parija & Poddar, 2024). Funding preparedness for global health security is limited at the governmental level, and a business model for sustainable preparedness does not exist for the wider health market. Any organization, public or private, operating with a limited budget far below its actual preparedness needs can expect to be stressed by emerging threats. Governments are hesitant to provide taxpayer funds for a crisis that is non-existent or not yet identified, thereby shifting resource allocation away from investment in costly breakthrough technology. The staff's practical skill sets, from laboratory investigations through epidemiology, environmental health, infection control, emergency response, and policy-making, also need to be continually honed in concert with public safety preparedness measures (Farooq et al., 2022; Shafik et al., 2024). Pathogenic considerations demonstrate the value of preparedness and global response. Given the interconnected nature of human and animal interactions, understanding the early dynamics of these markets and how risks are changing in the wake of new pathogens and climate shifts should be a critical extension to international preparedness and develop domestic response capability. Globally, efforts are accelerating to do this, but such tasks will also require investment in specialized support for countries to access and use technologies that inform the most effective responses (Ambas et al., 2024; Ganasegeran & Abdulrahman, 2020). With the challenges, it appears that our current approaches to improvement need enhancement.

7.3.1 Data Collection and Integration

Integrating AI for disease-preparedness and response relies on data collection and data integration. The affected countries must gather accurate, timely, and trustworthy data to inform public health responses that terminate and prevent harm. Generally, health sector data are gathered and used by:

a. Government agencies, such as ministries of health, gather clinical data to provide care or model healthcare necessities and pharmaceuticals and to undertake regulatory activities,
b. International organizations that may need to collect data from countries' inputs, as may other bodies and regional governmental organizations; and
c. Private entities, such as businesses, collect and use medical payment and treatment data or mobile location data to model anticipated visits, market goods and services, or manage logistics and customers.

Data then flow throughout the health sector at national and across levels, including to international stakeholders. However, important gaps exist, including in-country situational awareness. There remain problems with data collection activities. Specifically, the collection of clinical trial and post-marketing data remains suboptimal. Preparedness and response efforts appear insufficient to prevent future pandemics. Moreover, disease X could be one of many different diseases. A recent review found that overall, countries often focus on domestic administrative systems (Geanta et al., 2022). Currently, each system within and across countries may use different criteria for data collection and have different priorities in terms of important outputs. These different organizational structures may result in interoperability; systems and facilities might not be connected to give a strong and secure overall policy picture. In fact, the silo effect of standard data collection is clear and does align with the principles. In general, there needs to be a reform of data handling and use within and across most high-income nations if they are to be prepared. AI may present a solution that better integrates and aligns operational data to an organization's smaller, focused outputs through a more comprehensive integrational AI database solution (Simsek & Kantarci, 2020). Consequently, a leap forward in organization-wide disease and response situational awareness is possible.

7.3.2 Resource Allocation and Management

In large-scale infectious disease preparedness frameworks, resource allocation and management present significant challenges. A primary concern is the scarcity of resources—whether they are masks and gloves, healthcare providers, testing capabilities, or funding—which can impede rapid community responses or coordination between neighboring states. The equitable distribution of resources and aid also arises as a significant challenge. Beyond a global pandemic, many regions contend simultaneously with other diseases, public health needs, and natural disasters that may require different or competing resources, yet demand for assistance remaining equitable remains essential (Ambas et al., 2024; Zaidan, 2023). In order to not compromise functionality in other areas of public health, quality and resources allocated to outbreak response must be balanced with the anticipated need. Thus, resource availability must be considered to ensure a proportionate, well-functioning, and timely public health response. Strategic planning must be driven not by the most severe or virulent possible disease threat but rather by the planning scenario that will ensure a well-functioning continuum of public health activities, including response, across a range of disease-severity scenarios and activities (Parija & Poddar, 2024). Hospitals and healthcare providers must also practice clear resource management plans, which may include relocating staff quickly to areas with the greatest need or implementing telemedicine and alternative options for healthcare delivery to limit exposure and use of already short supplies. AI and predictive analytics allow public health and healthcare workers to efficiently manage resource allocation necessary for the immediate and upcoming needs of their constituency, optimizing care and response (Shafik, 2023, 2024a). The value of such tools lies in the ability to immediately apply the model's outcomes and conclusions to intervene in a given situation. The use of AI within predictive analytics modeling is of increasing interest to maximize resource allocation in response to breakout events. By using modeling and prediction, practitioners can anticipate the community's needs in one week, one month, one year, or longer in advance. By forecasting essential human resources, public health officials and their public healthcare system can meet the needs of protecting and saving lives—providing timely intervention and optimum community care—whether the pandemic is large or catastrophic (Bhaskar, 2023).

7.4 APPLICATIONS OF AI IN DISEASE PREPAREDNESS

Artificial intelligence (AI) can be used in various ways to strengthen different aspects of health security and disease preparedness, providing public health decision-makers with more or better information and making many processes cheaper, faster, and easier. A growing body of evidence shows that AI with machine learning algorithms can do a better job than traditional methods when it comes to diagnosing and predicting diseases. Therefore, it would be sensible to look at how AI can be integrated into disease-preparedness strategies in low-resource settings. This section will describe the evidence for the various benefits of AI in disease preparedness, as well as some of the challenges in making use of the new technology (Jeyakumar et al., 2023). It will use case studies from different initiatives to illustrate both a conceptual understanding of the issues and a specific application, particularly in the context of multidisciplinary learning by IT professionals, health informaticians, and public health practitioners. Early detection and diagnosis are crucial in the fight against any epidemic. AI, specifically machine learning, can be useful in identifying patterns in health data more quickly and more exhaustively than humans. Epidemic intelligence uses diverse and often unconventional data sources and data types and machine learning organizations to improve speed and accuracy in the detection of emerging threats (Ienca, 2019). Gathering data from large online or offline populations can give insight into both at-risk populations and prioritized efforts in vaccine and treatment administration and resource deployment to mitigate outbreak impact. Research teams are working with public health officials to create data products and machine learning-driven tools in most of these areas. AI methods are being used to identify strange outbreaks, analyze microbiological potentials of biological agents, forecast the trajectory of an outbreak, support preparation and decision-making, identify communication and health belief needs, and evaluate communication or intervention strategies (Cabatuan & Manguerra, 2020; Gruenwald et al., 2021). Many of these products have been proven to work in the public health research space and are in the process of being adopted into formal public health practice.

7.4.1 Early Detection and Diagnosis

A significant focus of AI for disease surveillance is directed at early detection and diagnosis, utilizing machine learning models that make predictive analytics feasible and, in some cases, real-time. Consequently, the analysis of big data, such as clinical data and reports of mHealth applications, mobilities, or environmental data, is expedited with the transition to data-driven methods, which can capture an earlier signal of a health threat before it escalates. Ample evidence has shown that this real-time or near-real-time approach is critical in improving clinical outcomes for individuals and also in preventing the spread of infectious diseases in the community (Bhakta et al., 2021; Schmid, 2021). Patients who are diagnosed early from an accessible service are more informed and are more likely to comply with treatment provided by a healthcare service director. Tools that complement the work of healthcare providers can improve the likelihood of consistent diagnosis. Early case detection is critically important for simple infectious diseases, such as influenza, that are at their most infectious point immediately after clinical onset (Farooq et al., 2022; Krämer et al., 2023). The early introduction of infection prevention and control measures, increasing the number of hospital and outpatient visits, and restricting hospital admissions during the "lead" and "surge" phases is an effective intervention for managing community-level outbreaks. Additionally, early case detection and patient diagnoses can be more successful when effectively handled by combining AI-capable technology that analyzes data with minimal human oversight to be cost-effective, rapidly scaled, and effective (Chiu et al., 2023; Parija & Poddar, 2024).

7.4.2 Epidemic Forecasting and Monitoring

In emergency preparedness, epidemic forecasting or prediction is becoming increasingly important in order to anticipate the outbreak of epidemics, adapt plans concerning response actions, and prepare the logistics necessary to address the situation. Predictive epidemic modeling is used not so much to forecast a specific final size of the epidemic but rather to anticipate crucial disease trends and derive valuable predictions. At a public health level, predictive modeling is important to implement effective public health interventions (Ganasegeran & Abdulrahman, 2020; Su et al., 2021). Epidemic forecasts are based on predictive models analyzing data. In real-time, different models carry out quantitative and statistical comparisons of the disease data against the prediction distributions or algorithms, and they are able to anticipate potential disease trends and generate early warning signals, which may or may not be validated by the occurrence of cases. Consequently, there are now a growing number of tools using AI that aims to link various streams of data analysis, as well as laboratory results, informal reports, official health reports, news, and other health-related reports, in order to relate trends and patterns exhibited in these data with disease dynamics, using machine learning techniques to refine these indicators and detect changes that may signal the onset of an outbreak (Ambas et al., 2024; Geanta et al., 2022). AI-based systems can provide a monitoring tool at a population level throughout the detection and control of outbreaks. The ability of AI tools to make use of computing capacity to analyze a wide array of data streams in a progressive, sequential manner allows for the determination of trends and patterns that display important statistical changes. AI usually provides a way to link several data streams at the same time. It links them not because they are associated with one particular disease, but rather several situations can be observed, like spikes in absenteeism in a school district indicating a potential problem for outbreaks of influenza or stomach flu, or water quality issues perhaps being related to recreational water use-related infections (Syrowatka et al., 2021; Zaidan, 2023). AI provides a layer of analysis that involves groupings of data associated with symptoms exhibited by several groups.

7.5 ETHICAL AND LEGAL CONSIDERATIONS

Though the existing AI's potential to outpace current capabilities provides an opportunity for innovation in ethics and healthcare procedures, it is pivotal that the risks of disengagement outweigh the need for the creation of a constantly evolving ethical and legal foundation. Research has predicted that inaccuracies produced by the optical coherence tomography guesses could cause a misdiagnosis by healthcare professionals. Not only is it unreasonable to oversee this plethora of cases, but it is also problematic to permit such potentially falsified conclusions. The primary concern of introducing AI for disease-preparedness revolves around the issue of health and privacy (Ismail et al., 2022). An essential connection exists between the state of the ethical and legal framework in disease preparedness and AI characteristics when conducting preventive healthcare procedures. This is particularly important when considering international interests and subsequent confidentiality, secrecy, religion, politics, security, and, of paramount importance, cultural and ethical values. Public health systems are under pressure, which necessitates timely revision in addressing AI health priorities and gathering a pool of public readiness for global, especially unknown, outbreaks of disease (Chen et al., 2021; Simsek & Kantarci, 2020). In light of recent outbreaks, the intersection between disease preparedness and disease diagnosis is most apparent in the diagnosis phase, considering the risk of disease stigma. This is particularly concerning in the current threat landscape, as concerted international interests in ethics have failed to be equitably distributed in the global health paradigm. Suppose AI tools for disease preparedness are to be made. In that case, it is essential that a revised legal framework be organized to address these ethical queries and guarantee transparency and the protection of those prematurely identified (Bartoletti et al., 2024; Nunes et al., 2024). Novel, robust frameworks must be created to address ethical issues in preventive preparedness for healthcare.

Issues involving data security and privacy are paramount to the issue of AI disease preparedness. DNA collection and retention are subject to legislation designed to prevent the abuse and mishandling of data. All stakeholders must respect human rights and the law in their use of AI, having data and other health policies to safeguard health data from any illegal interference and use statistical data. Information should be anonymized to ensure that patient anonymity is retained. Another significant legal aspect of concern is human rights. Beyond the realm of international politics, recent controversies have sparked an ongoing discussion concerning gender and racial bias in data interpretation (Possas et al., 2021; Swayamsiddha et al., 2021). If AI is to improve diagnostic performances, with data entry, are the diagnoses of different patients to be based on the same entry data ultimately unique? Awaiting bias leads to a lack of transparency. These factors demonstrate the necessity for independent and multifaceted regulations that question whether AI-generated inferences are innovative and, on the one hand, are often valuable for equitable performance of healthcare services and treatments, and on the other hand, cross-continent and data-less diagnoses struggle with shortcomings. Systems might be developed to organize feedback conferences, with national working groups engaging with different stakeholders to handle these concerns. In AI, industry regulators and manufacturers ought to engage in these conferences to negotiate a compromise between comprehensive, automated, and involved data quality validation therein. Bipartite recommendations should be approved at national, regional, and international conferences (Malik et al., 2021; Tambo et al., 2021). As an AI system matures, these guidelines should be revisited at least once in its system lifecycle.

7.5.1 Privacy and Data Security

Introducing AI within the healthcare organizational environment means specifically addressing patient privacy issues. AI in healthcare also involves working with different types of patient data, including demographic data, lab data, clinical observations data, insurance data, and free-text data. Free-text data can contain nursing or physician notes, patient history, and other unstructured clinical information. Using AI in healthcare is also a challenge because government agencies regulate this data and require adherence to legal and compliance standards. It pertains to the reliability and trustworthiness of data sources, data storage, data accessibility, and data transmission in clinical practice. It is also important to establish policies on how different key stakeholders and players in the healthcare system share their data (Rahman et al., 2022). In order to be used effectively and safely within the health domain, the system must be able to identify sensitive data and protect against the Piecemeal Disclosure Attack. AI in disease management requires a component, such as a web-based application or a mobile application, which can be used by patients or healthcare staff for effective and efficient service delivery. Applications must be able to recognize their users and create meaningful user experiences. Healthcare stakeholders must also ensure that data is safe and secure from unauthorized access. Adequate cybersecurity measures could save the healthcare domain upfront costs as well as indirect costs of data theft (Bartoletti et al., 2024). Failing to do so, as has been shown in many cases, breaches public trust in hospitals as well as in related AI systems. Consequently, the healthcare domain is also concerned about how hacking affects patient safety when patient data falls into untrusted hands. Encrypting data does not guarantee concealment of the nature of the data being used, so the staff educating and understanding of all the implications also needs to be addressed. Staff should be able to educate the public about AI and scan-based healthcare devices that women encounter and should be able to provide ways to address them. Full managerial commitment is also required in order to ensure health worker awareness (Chiu et al., 2023).

7.5.2 Bias and Fairness in AI Algorithms

AI algorithms that are used in the design of health interventions, as in the event of a disease outbreak, can also be biased. Bias refers to when the model makes systematically different (and often thereby false) predictions or classifications for one subgroup than for others. They can be inaccurate, especially for subpopulations, or can rigidify existing inequalities, further disadvantaging less privileged groups. A central rule of machine learning is that biased data can lead to biased results. Bias can inadvertently be introduced into AI algorithms at various points of design, development, and deployment of the AI system (Ambas et al., 2024). The first occurs during the data wrangling and preprocessing steps, training and updating of algorithms with biased data, or the measures used to evaluate AI. Another area where bias may be introduced is the choice of framing the system. The framing of the task can impact how bias is expressed and the output of the algorithm. In healthcare, AI distortion often relates to inequalities in healthcare access, vulnerabilities in healthcare settings, and coverage of reference values for data informing the algorithm. Skewed input signals are fed to an AI system that further exacerbates the problem. In healthcare, where diverse minorities and patients are involved, much care is needed (Bartoletti et al., 2024). For instance, researchers demonstrated bias and inaccuracy that led to racial discrimination in healthcare software. The use of an AI-driven hiring program was scrapped as it was giving biased feedback and not employing females. More transparent artificial intelligence, enough humans in the loop, and diverse datasets are needed to limit bias. The effective presentation of robots and chatbots and recommendations based on an AI model could be discussed with diverse groups for opinions by the programmers (Possas et al., 2021). Participation of a diverse group of users for regular evaluations would also spot the system's biases and areas of inaccuracy.

7.6 CASE STUDIES AND SUCCESS STORIES: HOW AI ASSISTED IN OUTBREAKS

Artificial intelligence has proven helpful in several outbreaks. For many AI applications, especially those used in the field during an outbreak, evaluations have been applied and adapted to specific situations. At the intersection between public health systems and AI are people on the ground, medical personnel, official agencies, and researchers willing to test safe, efficient, and ethical methods for improving their disease preparedness. However, these practitioners can be skeptical, and not all AI methods work (Tambo et al., 2021). It requires effectively communicated evidence to convince a health system to use an AI-driven solution; stakeholders must see the methods as both effective and able to integrate seamlessly into the existing regional infrastructure. Success stories can demonstrate to these practitioners the value of AI methods in outbreak situations. Two AI solutions have progressed real-world activities in two separate evaluations. These implementations have provided valuable insights into how AI methods can have an impact (Parums, 2023). The first is an AI-driven Rapid Diagnostic presenting an example of computing as:

- The potential to modify the comfortable workflow of healthcare for healthcare practitioners;
- A potential point in the workflow where public health systems are most likely to implement such AI;

- An example of an AI approach that is ready for sustainable implementation.

A more recent example of the potential to use AI in public health systems is the EpiMate project. In the EpiMate project, AI researchers collaborated with disease-modeling epidemiologists who were directly involved on the ground during an outbreak. The AI approaches they developed could aid officials in determining where to cluster vaccinations for people identified to be close to infected individuals. They could also be used for real-time infectious disease risk assessment from disease-specific signals collected during an outbreak (Parija & Poddar, 2024).

7.6.1 AI Applications in Ebola Outbreaks

Although many of the applications have been more observational and useful for early detection and tracking of infected individuals, some have also been very well received. The early Ebola outbreaks saw the development of coordination strategies among healthcare workers, and such exercises have been greatly enhanced by the application of AI technologies. The systems have even won public kudos for the accuracy of pollutant tracking in subsequent releases. Likewise, AI surveillance tools might have been the reason that the next well-published release was named Tndazu (Bhaskar, 2023; Jeyakumar et al., 2023). This AI software was the result of a week-long collaboration between public health and a technology company that had developed real-time predictive integration tools. The biggest takeaway messages in all these examples are the need to develop a rapid data-driven response and the development of AI tools in partnership with public health experts. One popular Measles app has collated data on current returns, mapping and selecting data based on outbreak trends. Further detailed analysis of the data concerning the initial phases of the Ebola outbreak in 2014 has facilitated both the understanding and preparation for the need for resources in the later stages of the epidemic (Cabatuan & Manguerra, 2020; Uohara et al., 2020).

7.6.2 COVID-19 Response and AI Innovations

In response to the COVID-19 pandemic, there have been a number of innovative AI interventions across each phase of response: disease surveillance, case detection, resource allocation, intervention development, and community and individual well-being. To assist in tracking the spread of the disease, monitoring virus mutations, and even predicting future waves of the virus, scientists around the world have built reliable AI models to analyze large collections of data. Using machine learning, deep learning techniques, or natural language processing, scientists are able to decode the genetic sequence of SARS-CoV-2, create large surveillance platforms to scale tracking of cases and preventions, as well as make the pipelines of vaccine and drug development more efficient and cheaper (Farooq et al., 2022). Throughout the pandemic, there has been rapid development in using psychological and behavioral healthcare, whether to personalize coping strategies, identify mental health trends, or track the virus's spread and outbreaks. Mental health AI has shown itself as a new tool at our disposal to limit harm during the pandemic and foster better patient outcomes. Exemplifying numerous innovations, the COVID-19 pandemic also offered numerous examples of the challenges and potential harms of not thoroughly, ethically, and equitably deploying such technologies. There are myriad challenges, including data quality, collection, and use, the role of AI in addressing health equity, and the potential for a changing policy environment that could leave these tools in a precarious position (Chiu et al., 2023; Parija & Poddar, 2024). As the world moves from the acute phase of the COVID-19 pandemic and into shaping long-term strategies to prevent a resurgence of COVID-19 and address unexpected impacts of other health crises, AI-powered tools will be essential. Furthermore, artificial intelligence shows vast potential and benefits while considering the integration of real-time national, regional, and local health data, like electronic health records and pharmacy records, with vaccine distribution status and patient circumstances (Ambas et al., 2024). It can help in the synchronization of the demand for vaccination for those who need it most with the supply of vaccine doses. AI-driven vaccine planning can take into consideration growing age and chronic disease data and complex distribution and storage logistics alongside a fast-changing environment like SARS-CoV-2, anticipating the forthcoming situation on multiple outcomes to make important strategic choices today. By documenting these interventions and ethical considerations, this report aims to robustly demonstrate the invaluable benefits of using AI within a public health context and stresses the need for continued investment in public health preparedness (Parums, 2023; Rahman et al., 2022).

7.7 FUTURE DIRECTIONS AND EMERGING TECHNOLOGIES

Many newer technologies are likely to shape the role of AI in public health preparedness in the coming years. Some of these, although not specific to AI, are likely also to impact the integration of AI into public health preparedness. AI-driven precision medicine has the potential to completely revolutionize the area of healthcare because it aims to provide tailor-made treatment strategies to each individual that will be suitable given their genome and the environmental risks. The concurrent application of pharmacogenomics and epigenomics will further enrich the information provided in the data lakes. A secure and integral data lake is possible with the emergence of blockchain technology (Bhaskar, 2023; Jeyakumar et al., 2023). This technology has found application in healthcare data management. The objective of combining resources is to stimulate and formulate research ideas based on current information as well as future trends in AI. The idea is that such research on future health challenges must be undertaken well before these problems emerge in the public sphere. With health monitoring becoming an increasingly important everyday concern for just about every consumer, the convergence of AI with IoT to develop an innovative and enhanced health monitoring system becomes an obvious choice. Despite being encouraged by the government, industry, and academic details, the role of AI during health monitoring is minimal, especially in the area of disease epidemiology and its preparedness. AI does not appear as an enabling technology for the beleaguered field of public health and preparedness (Chiu et al., 2023). This is likely the result of poor business schemas or lack of a proactive strategy. This is a clear area that requires further intervention from all stakeholders.

7.7.1 AI-Driven Precision Medicine

Precision medicine is forward-looking. Instead of focusing on diagnosing and treating acute disease outcomes, precision medicine orients its technological infrastructure toward preventing disease and disorders before they have had a chance to manifest. A computer system that uses natural language processing and machine learning to reveal insights from large amounts of unstructured data can analyze genetic, substance, and imaging data of individual patients and find specific driver mutations or pathways before computing potential drug combinations using a large evidence-based compendium to predict which treatments would be most effective for the patients (Ganasegeran & Abdulrahman, 2020). Precision medicine combines genetic, environmental, and lifestyle information unique to an individual to provide a tailored medical approach and may increase patient compliance and mitigate side effects associated with unguided interventions that may not work. This avenue of work will, in turn, pave the way for more nuanced, complex, and ultimately effective health-promoting interventions that may work differently from one individual to the next, taking genetics, lifestyles, environment, and mental predispositions into account. Although a good deal of technological development remains ahead, the case studies presented demonstrate considerable potential for AI applications already in early clinical use (Bhaskar, 2023; Jeyakumar et al., 2023). Other existing systems provide support for medical decision-making that may bear upshots for those suffering from chronic or acute disease. There are, of course, several barriers to the clinical integration of data analytics tools broadly, and the predictive output of AI-based models in particular. In particular, technological issues pertain to privacy and security risks, and data sharing and interoperability of healthcare software and digital infrastructure. These technological issues interface with questions of validation and efficacy because before any AI model can be accepted and endorsed into practice through regulatory channels, data systems, data labs, and reports have to be created that can compare and validate data. Most importantly, the intervention must be safe (Syrowatka et al., 2021; Zaidan, 2023). Ethics, or the ethical and societal implications of precision medicine, focus on questions of consent, patient needs, and health equity.

7.7.2 Blockchain in Healthcare Data Management

Blockchains are a type of data structure and serve as a continuously growing list of records (blocks), which are linked and secured using cryptography. Within this framework, blocks are tamper-proof and decentralized. This database can contain a broad range of data and can verify the sources and ensure data integrity so that data cannot be tampered with securely and transparently. In healthcare, develop blockchain-based solutions that improve patient privacy and healthcare data management.

The primary idea is to decentralize and, therefore, break down the data silos that occur when electronic health record providers, clinics, hospitals, labs, insurance companies, and state healthcare systems all run their database products and store patient information in different and non-interoperable ways, reducing the flow of data and preventing collaboration (Chen et al., 2021). Standardized public blockchains can format, store, and give secure access to data, which can be shared as accountable and immutable medical information based on the consensus of a distributed group of stakeholders. This way, multisided networks can work collaboratively without intermediaries to empower interoperability and data integrity, providing unified and reliable views of patient data for various stakeholders and diverse uses. Use cases such as claims management, provider directories, prior authorization, and digital identity are improving services with blockchain in healthcare sectors. The development of this type of infrastructure elucidates that technology offers a greater capacity to build new, innovative, and efficient collaborative health data frameworks (Possas et al., 2021). Future health tech innovation to respond to patient needs should expand this core technological component. The solution is to dash earlier advances and conventional innovations in interoperability and combine the same technologies to secure a seamless blockchain ecosystem. For this reason, it means making an incremental contribution to disease prevention by providing the most interoperable and secure health data registry solution (Bhakta et al., 2021).

7.7.3 Summary of Findings and Recommendations

In this chapter, we have scanned the current landscape of AI applications for disease preparedness and control. The net benefits of AI to health and healthcare are well signaled, allowing for clearer advances in diagnoses, treatment, and institutional efficiency. The area in which we are still sailing uncharted waters is the potential and pitfalls of integrating AI into screenings for emerging pathogens. This special question was thoroughly illuminated in the case of the first phases of pandemic containment. We have also reviewed ongoing debates regarding how "good" AI in healthcare should be developed. A long list of important AI-specific activities and priorities is collected in the conclusion (Syrowatka et al., 2021). Our most remarkable findings and recommendations are these:

- AI is critical to the main prevention and protection mechanisms of public health and must be developed at both macro and micro scales. AI has potential benefits for the strengthening of healthcare systems for responses to high-impact events by predicting trends and redistributing resources.
- There are concerns that it may exacerbate the problems of earlier healthcare systems (access and quality). These will need to be addressed in view of investment and regulation. There are many cross-cutting recommendations across the seven sections that are likely to be valuable for people in a wide range of roles who are looking to link academic research with the development of policy, practice, or product.

- There is much work required to improve the extensive biological surveillance and verify duplicated data as well as integrate data sets from health, agricultural, environmental, social, and veterinary sources. The automation of data mediation and horizontal data collection merits emphasis as well. There remain high degrees of data quality concerns.
- There are trade-offs involved in the dynamic reform of a system to accommodate every incident; potential users and local maps should be engaged to discuss what such a service might look like in practice. Governing structures should be established with a view to ensuring regular explicit monitoring of the fairness of any AI systems. These should involve a multidisciplinary collaboration between scientists, policymakers, healthcare practitioners, and representatives of the wider public.
- Given how much capacity building will be required before AI is of use to assist with the majority of low-prevalence conditions, special priority attention should be given to developing and applying AI-driven interventions for diseases with very high emergence or other direct risks that could become pandemics.
- Testing needs to be taken forward to collect descriptive data for assessments of bias in the output of the models. Socioeconomic diversity in study participants might entail a need for finer-grain stratified representative sampling to get a clearer sense of the applicability.
- AI could also be integrated into broader approaches aimed at economic recovery and social partner investment, reducing the barriers to personal help-seeking from general practitioners, mental health practitioners, or otherwise.
- Ongoing stakeholder consultations and policy labs could suggest other niche applications, but these represent significant returns with relatively low effort and could deliver practical benefits. AI in global health governance is firmly linked to the recognition of the global pandemic/health risk. National and international agencies can actively use AI to inform how to invest in capacity building to achieve global health security on a mucosal basis.

7.8 CONCLUSION

The transformative potential of AI in early detection, instant diagnosis, improved treatment, and testing, along with the amplification of the predictive and forecasting capabilities for infectious diseases, are possible contributions that AI and digital platforms can offer to disease preparedness. Through AI, forms of pandemic readiness, disease prevention, and other aspects of pandemic endeavor have been ameliorated. As AI and AI-related technologies evolve, surveillance system requirements, ethical principles, and legal elements for AI deployment in general and, in particular, for healthcare and pandemic readiness can be compiled. Every technological change and innovation assembly presents an array of ethical, legal, and assurance considerations. Legal changes will likely be a major confront for nations looking to leverage AI and Big Data in healthcare. Critical questions remaining include what the future of AI-driven digital health will be and how digital health practitioners can securely authenticate and endorse the output of an AI device. Finally, the significance of system preparedness and resilience should be highlighted. The endorsement of AI-driven technology will require integration to be inclusive of not only some investors but all stakeholders in technological progress, so that the entire population can be protected from future healthcare threats. Promoting innovation in the digital side of health is essential to climate endurance and integrated systems of health. Mutual efforts could surge the capabilities of AI applications across the primary healthcare system, ensuring that vulnerable people and populations do not miss out. To this end, discussions at a premium exploring what is possible with AI and Big Data for pandemic preparedness should be coupled with an examination of norms and values that promote sharing these and other such technologies to support the much-needed efforts toward resilient health systems.

REFERENCE

Ambas, J., Pakpahan, S., Prisusanti, R. D., Pangandaheng, T., & Sukmawaty, M. N. (2024). Innovations in global health: Leveraging technology for disease surveillance and pandemic preparedness. *Global International Journal of Innovative Research, 1*(3). https://doi.org/10.59613/global.v1i3.41

Bartoletti, M., Bussini, L., Bavaro, D. F., & Cento, V. (2024). What do clinicians mean by epidemics' preparedness. *Clinical Microbiology and Infection, 30*(5). https://doi.org/10.1016/j.cmi.2023.05.030

Bhakta, S., Paul, J., Bhattacharya, A., & Choudhury, S. (2021). Vaccine development through reverse vaccinology using artificial intelligence and machine learning approach. In S. Chatterjee (Ed.), *COVID-19: Tackling Global Pandemics through Scientific and Social Tools* (pp. 33–49). Springer. https://doi.org/10.1016/B978-0-323-85844-1.00006-4

Bhaskar, P. (2023). Antibiotic resistance and a dire need for novel and innovative therapies: The impending crisis. *Syncytia, 1*(2). https://doi.org/10.52679/syncytia.2023.0w8yx9

Cabatuan, M., & Manguerra, M. (2020). Machine learning for disease surveillance or outbreak monitoring: A review. *2020 IEEE 12th International Conference on Humanoid, Nanotechnology, Information Technology, Communication and Control, Environment, and Management, HNICEM 2020.* https://doi.org/10.1109/HNICEM51456.2020.9400088

Chen, J., Lim, C. P., Tan, K. H., Govindan, K., & Kumar, A. (2021). Artificial intelligence-based human-centric decision support framework: An application to predictive maintenance in asset management under pandemic environments. *Annals of Operations Research, 350.* https://doi.org/10.1007/s10479-021-04373-w

Chiu, K. H. Y., Sridhar, S., & Yuen, K. Y. (2023). Preparation for the next pandemic: Challenges in strengthening surveillance. *Emerging Microbes and Infections, 12*(2). https://doi.org/10.1080/22221751.2023.2240441

Farooq, Z., Rocklöv, J., Wallin, J., Abiri, N., Sewe, M. O., Sjödin, H., & Semenza, J. C. (2022). Artificial intelligence to predict West Nile virus outbreaks with eco-climatic drivers. *The Lancet Regional Health – Europe, 17.* https://doi.org/10.1016/j.lanepe.2022.100370

Ganasegeran, K., & Abdulrahman, S. A. (2020). Artificial intelligence applications in tracking health behaviors during disease epidemics. *Behaviour Analysis Using Intelligent Systems* 6, 141–155. https://doi.org/10.1007/978-3-030-35139-7_7

Geanta, M., Tanwar, A. S., Lehrach, H., Satyamoorthy, K., & Brand, A. (2022). Horizon scanning: Rise of planetary health genomics and digital twins for pandemic preparedness. *OMICS A Journal of Integrative Biology*, *26*(2). https://doi.org/10.1089/omi.2021.0062

Gruenwald, L., Jain, S., & Groppe, S. (2021). Leveraging artificial intelligence in global epidemics. In *Leveraging Artificial Intelligence in Global Epidemics*. Elsevier. https://doi.org/10.1016/B978-0-323-89777-8.00015-4

Ienca, M. (2019). Brain-machine interfacing: Reflections on neurotechnology and neurorights. *Notizie Di Politeia*, *35*(133), 52–62.

Ismail, L., Materwala, H., Al Hammadi, Y., Firouzi, F., Khan, G., & Azzuhri, S. R. Bin. (2022). Automated artificial intelligence-enabled proactive preparedness real-time system for accurate prediction of COVID-19 infections — Performance evaluation. *Frontiers in Medicine*, *9*. https://doi.org/10.3389/fmed.2022.871885

Jeyakumar, V., Sundaram, P., & Ramapathiran, N. (2023). Artificial intelligence-based predictive tools for life-threatening diseases. In G. R. Kanagachidambaresan, D. Bhatia, D. Kumar, & A. Mishra (Eds.) *System Design for Epidemics Using Machine Learning and Deep Learning* (Signals and Communication Technology). Springer. https://doi.org/10.1007/978-3-031-19752-9_8

Krämer, M., Ingwersen, M., Teichgräber, U., & Güttler, F. (2023). Added value of chest CT in a machine learning-based prediction model to rule out COVID-19 before inpatient admission: A retrospective university network study. *European Journal of Radiology*, *163*. https://doi.org/10.1016/j.ejrad.2023.110827

Malik, Y. S., Sircar, S., Bhat, S., Ansari, M. I., Pande, T., Kumar, P., Mathapati, B., Balasubramanian, G., Kaushik, R., Natesan, S., Ezzikouri, S., El Zowalaty, M. E., & Dhama, K. (2021). How artificial intelligence may help the Covid-19 pandemic: Pitfalls and lessons for the future. *Reviews in Medical Virology*, *31*(5). https://doi.org/10.1002/rmv.2205

Nunes, M. C., Thommes, E., Fröhlich, H., Flahault, A., Arino, J., Baguelin, M., Biggerstaff, M., Bizel-Bizellot, G., Borchering, R., Cacciapaglia, G., Cauchemez, S., Barbier-Chebbah, A., Claussen, C., Choirat, C., Cojocaru, M., Commaille-Chapus, C., Hon, C., Kong, J., Lambert, N., … Coudeville, L. (2024). Redefining pandemic preparedness: Multidisciplinary insights from the CERP modelling workshop in infectious diseases, workshop report. *Infectious Disease Modelling*, *9*(2). https://doi.org/10.1016/j.idm.2024.02.008

Parija, S. C., & Poddar, A. (2024). Artificial intelligence in parasitic disease control: A paradigm shift in health care. *Tropical Parasitology*, *14*(1). https://doi.org/10.4103/tp.tp_66_23

Parums, D. V. (2023). Editorial: Infectious disease surveillance using artificial intelligence (AI) and its role in epidemic and pandemic preparedness. *Medical Science Monitor*, *29*. https://doi.org/10.12659/MSM.941209

Possas, C., Marques, E. T. A., Risi, J. B., & Homma, A. (2021). COVID-19 and future disease X in circular economy transition: Redesigning pandemic preparedness to prevent a global disaster. *Circular Economy and Sustainability*, *1*(4). https://doi.org/10.1007/s43615-021-00060-x

Rahman, M. S., Safa, N. T., Sultana, S., Salam, S., Karamehic-Muratovic, A., & Overgaard, H. J. (2022). Role of artificial intelligence-internet of things (AI-IoT) based emerging technologies in the public health response to infectious diseases in Bangladesh. *Parasite Epidemiology and Control*, *18*. https://doi.org/10.1016/j.parepi.2022.e00266

Schmid, A. (2021). Preventing pandemics and containing disease: A proposed symptoms-based syndromic surveillance system. *HPHR Journal*, *31*. https://doi.org/10.54111/0001/ee21

Shafik, W. (2023). Wearable medical electronics in artifcial intelligence of medical things. In *Handbook of Security and Privacy of AI-Enabled Healthcare Systems and Internet of Medical Things*. CRC Press. https://doi.org/10.1201/9781003370321-2

Shafik, W. (2024a). Artificial Intelligence-Enabled Internet of Medical Things (AIoMT) in modern healthcare practices. In *Clinical Practice and Unmet Challenges in AI-Enhanced Healthcare Systems* (pp. 42–69). IGI Global. https://doi.org/10.4018/979-8-3693-2703-6.ch003

Shafik, W. (2024b). Artificial Intelligence-Enabled Internet of Medical Things for enhanced healthcare systems. In *Smart Healthcare Systems* (pp. 119–134). CRC Press. https://doi.org/10.1201/9781032698519-9

Shafik, W. (2024c). Connected healthcare—the impact of Internet of Things on medical services. In *Artificial Intelligence and Internet of Things based Augmented Trends for Data Driven Systems* (pp. 181–217). CRC Press. https://doi.org/10.1201/9781003497318-10

Shafik, W. (2024d). Digital healthcare systems in a federated learning perspective. In *Federated Learning for Digital Healthcare Systems* (pp. 1–35). Elsevier. https://doi.org/10.1016/B978-0-443-13897-3.00001-1

Shafik, W. (2024e). IoT-enabled secure and intelligent smart healthcare. In *Secure and Intelligent IoT-Enabled Smart Cities* (pp. 308–333). IGI Global. https://doi.org/10.4018/979-8-3693-2373-1.ch015

Shafik, W. (2024f). Smart health revolution: Exploring artificial intelligence of Internet of Medical things. In *Healthcare Industry Assessment: Analyzing Risks, Security, and Reliability* (pp. 201–229). Springer. https://doi.org/10.1007/978-3-031-65434-3_9

Shafik, W. (2024g). The future of healthcare: AIoMT—Redefining healthcare with advanced artificial intelligence and machine learning techniques. In *Artificial Intelligence and Machine Learning in Drug Design and Development* (pp. 605–634). Wiley. https://doi.org/10.1002/9781394234196.ch19

Shafik, W. (2025a). Revolutionizing skin cancer diagnosis with artificial intelligence: Insights into machine learning techniques. In *Impact of Digital Solutions for Improved Healthcare Delivery* (pp. 167–194). IGI Global.

Shafik, W. (2025b). Smart biomedical devices for smart healthcare. In *Machine Learning Models and Architectures for Biomedical Signal Processing* (pp. 421–448). Elsevier. https://www.sciencedirect.com/science/chapter/edited-volume/abs/pii/B978044322158300017X?via%3Dihub

Shafik, W., Tufail, A., Liyanage, C. D. S., & Apong, R. A. A. H. M. (2024). Medical robotics and AI-assisted diagnostics challenges for smart sustainable healthcare. In *AI-Driven Innovations in Digital Healthcare: Emerging Trends, Challenges, and Applications* (pp. 304–323). IGI Global. https://doi.org/10.4018/979-8-3693-3218-4.ch016

Simsek, M., & Kantarci, B. (2020). Artificial intelligence-empowered mobilization of assessments in COVID-19-like pandemics: A case study for early flattening of the curve. *International Journal of Environmental Research and Public Health, 17*(10). https://doi.org/10.3390/ijerph17103437

Su, Z., McDonnell, D., Bentley, B. L., He, J., Shi, F., Cheshmehzangi, A., Ahmad, J., & Jia, P. (2021). Addressing biodisaster x threats with artificial intelligence and 6G technologies: Literature review and critical insights. *Journal of Medical Internet Research, 23*(5). https://doi.org/10.2196/26109

Swayamsiddha, S., Prashant, K., Shaw, D., & Mohanty, C. (2021). The prospective of Artificial Intelligence in COVID-19 Pandemic. *Health and Technology, 11*(6). https://doi.org/10.1007/s12553-021-00601-2

Syrowatka, A., Kuznetsova, M., Alsubai, A., Beckman, A. L., Bain, P. A., Craig, K. J. T., Hu, J., Jackson, G. P., Rhee, K., & Bates, D. W. (2021). Leveraging artificial intelligence for pandemic preparedness and response: A scoping review to identify key use cases. *NPJ Digital Medicine*, *4*(1). https://doi.org/10.1038/s41746-021-00459-8

Tambo, E., Djuikoue, I. C., Tazemda, G. K., Fotsing, M. F., & Zhou, X. N. (2021). Early stage risk communication and community engagement (RCCE) strategies and measures against the coronavirus disease 2019 (COVID-19) pandemic crisis. *Global Health Journal*, *5*(1). https://doi.org/10.1016/j.glohj.2021.02.009

Uohara, M. Y., Weinstein, J. N., & Rhew, D. C. (2020). The essential role of technology in the public health battle against COVID-19. *Population Health Management*, *23*(5). https://doi.org/10.1089/pop.2020.0187

Zaidan, A. M. (2023). The leading global health challenges in the artificial intelligence era. *Frontiers in Public Health*, *11*. https://doi.org/10.3389/fpubh.2023.1328918

8 Personalization in Healthcare Using AI

Ekta Bhaggi, Lalit Banger, and Simran Kaur Sandal

8.1 INTRODUCTION

AI has truly come of age and is now controlling every domain. AI uses techniques that utilize the ability of machines and systems to perform tasks that classically require human aptitude, such as learning, problem-solving, decision-making, and communication. The progress of AI is driven by improvements in computing power, big data analytics, and machine learning algorithms. AI is already widely being used in the business world to improve customer service and drive innovation. AI can figuratively free up human employees through the automation of routine tasks and decision-making processes; it can also free up human staff to focus on higher-level tasks that require creativity and critical thinking [1]. Additionally, AI can scrutinize the vast amount of data to identify patterns and trends, which would be difficult for humans to distinguish, resulting in better decision-making and business outcomes.

8.2 AI IN HEALTHCARE

In the arena of healthcare, as the amount of health data exponentially grows, AI will become a crucial tool for healthcare workers, helping them deliver better care to patients. AI has been used to develop new treatments, improve patients' outcomes, and reduce costs. AI can assist doctors by looking at medical records of patients to make more precise detections and can develop personalized treatment plans [2]. With technological advancements daily, AI is also rapidly changing and becoming more innovative [3]. Three main principles for the successful adoption of AI in healthcare include data and security, analytics and insights, and shared expertise. An individual's health is heavily influenced by lifestyle, nutrition, environment, and access to care. These behavioral and social determinants can be tracked and measured by wearables and a range of medical devices, which account for 60% of health outcomes of a person, whereas 30% is based on genes and the rest 10% accounts for medical history.

For about 300 million books of personal and health-related data would generate in our lifetime, which in conclusion would lead to a longer and healthier life [4]. Furthermore, AI boosts clinical decision-making, detects adverse events, and predicts patients' readmissions using electronic health record (EHR). Healthcare

DOI: 10.1201/9781003624875-11

TABLE 8.1
Contributors to Health Outcomes and Their Estimated Influence

Contributor	Percentage
Lifestyle, nutrition, etc.	60%
Genetic (genes)	30%
Medical history	10%

policymakers and government use AI-based tools to control and predict infections and outbreaks. One such actual application is FINDER, a machine-learning model that is practiced for the real-time detection of foodborne illness using anonymous and collected web search as well as location data [5]. Yet another application is the combined data hub and care-management solution using IBM Connect360 and IBM Watson Care Manager that Sonoma County, California government agencies used to renovate health and healthcare for socially disadvantaged groups and other displaced individuals during a time of community-wide crisis [6]. This solution aided the integration of isolated data and services into a unified citizen status view, credentials of clinical and social determinants of health from structured and unstructured sources, construction of algorithms to match clients with services, and restructuring of care coordination during the 2017 and 2019 Sonoma County wildfires. Such models can be used in the global pandemic coronavirus disease 2019 to predict at-risk populations in such a way AI has played a big role in helping to manage public health and respond to the crisis excellently [7].

8.3 PRECISION MEDICINE

AI technologies in medicine can take many forms ranging from virtual systems (e.g., deep-learning-based decision-support) to cyber-physical systems such as robotic surgical assistance [8]. AI has the capability to perceive complex patterns and veiled structures by enabling many image-based detection and diagnostic systems in healthcare that are better than clinicians in some cases effectively [9]. A subject of precision medicine is providing a new advancement in the field of AI in healthcare; it aims to personalize care for every person by providing treatments to each individual based on their unique genetic makeup, lifestyle, and environmental factors. Integration of AI in this is to completely transform healthcare, making it more effective. Well, it is possible that the most suitable effect of precision medicine in health industry today is genotype-guided treatment; as a result, a correct dose of warfarin can be easily determined by this kind of information [10].

AI plays a vital role in the precision medicine field by analyzing massive datasets from large-scale data repositories such as UK Biobank, Biobank Japan, and the Australian Genomics Health Alliances. Through machine learning algorithms, AI

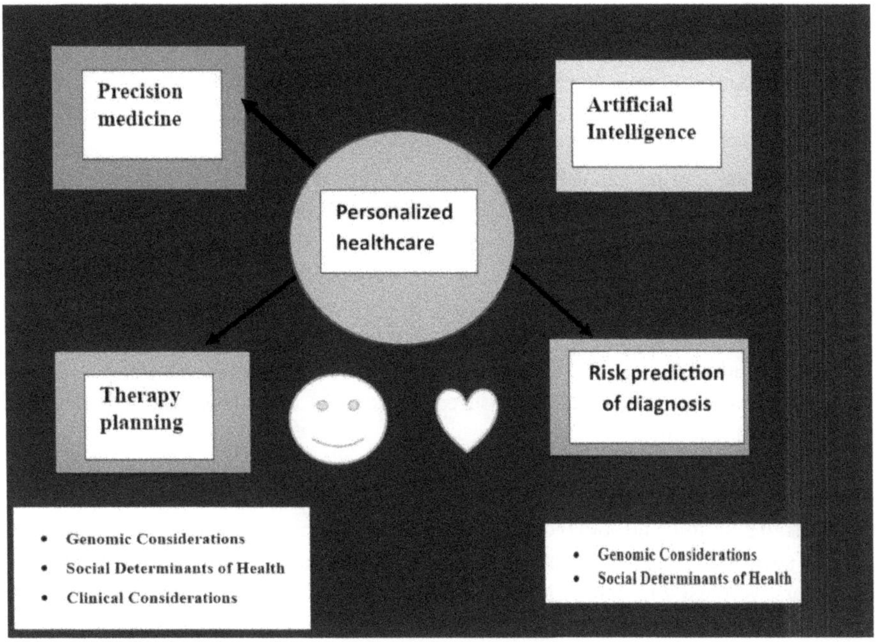

FIGURE 8.1 Applications of AI in healthcare for decision-making, outbreak detection, and population risk prediction.

can not only estimate diseases but also assist in detecting diseases with precise accuracy and can optimize treatment plans to maximize safety and reliability.

8.3.1 AI and Precision Medicine

AI and precision medicine are collaborating to assist in solving the most intricate difficulties in personalized care. Figure 8.1 illustrates the four aspects of personalized healthcare that are particularly amenable to advancement through AI [11–13].

8.3.1.1 Genomic Considerations

In therapy planning, genome-informed advising is one of the foremost areas to demonstrate the influence of precision medicine at measure [14]. Nevertheless, its accomplishment depends upon the machine-learning algorithms that will predict which patient is in need of medications related to the genomic data, as such practices personalizing medicine and related dosages require the advanced knowledge to genotype the patients [15].

Furthermore, AI has shown remarkable potential in the field of radiogenomics, which combines cancer imaging with gene expression data to predict the outcomes of radiotherapy, for instance, genetic mutation in glioma and its relevance in breast, liver, and colorectal cancers [16–19]. Using gene expression data, AI models such as support vector machines can predict patients' responses to chemotherapy. It is also necessary to note that more studies and robust data are required to improve AI-driven results. Beyond genomic considerations, social and environmental factors also significantly influence personalized healthcare outcomes.

8.3.1.2 Social Considerations

Environmental and personal factors are important to consider for patients' wellbeing. The major troublesome issue includes addressing homelessness, which demands frequent updates in demographic data for the issues of transportation, medications that require refrigeration, and tools that require electricity. In resource-limited settings, AI has become an operative enabler that not only enhances treatment but also tailors the possibilities of therapy [20–22]. Up until now, deep learning models have successfully identified malaria, cervical cancer, predicted infectious outbreaks, and estimated environmental toxin exposures. Hence, AI can bridge the gap between expertise and resources.

8.3.1.3 Clinical Considerations

Aside from genomic and social determinants of health, clinical factors are also important for successful therapy planning. In one study, it was found that machine learning classifiers were used to detect 30 comorbidities to identify critically ill patients who require prolonged ventilation and tracheostomy placement [23]. Another algorithm has been used to monitor the adverse events at bedside to predict organ dysfunction or failure [24, 25].

8.3.1.4 Genomic Considerations in Risk Prediction or Diagnosis

Taking genomics factors into account, they are vital in risk and disease prediction as well as for diagnoses. Genome-validated risks stimulate personalized preventive care strategies. Predictive modeling in fields such as cardiovascular medicine has been used for decades and proven beneficial to assess patient risk, and recent developments allow for the prediction of heart failure and other cardiac events even in symptomless individuals [26]. These models, incorporated with personalized prevention strategies, perhaps can eventually reduce disease occurrence and improve outcomes. Composite diseases like cardiovascular disease have a mix of genetic, environmental, and lifestyle factors; thus, AI has proven effective in the recognition of the complex relationships between these variables [27, 28]. The incorporation of multiple data types, including EHR and genetic information, improves predictive accuracy, as in the case of studies conducted at Vanderbilt [29]. A rapid whole-genome sequencing and NLP-enabled automated phenotyping can accurately and rapidly diagnose the suspected genetic disease in infants (seriously ill) [30].

8.3.1.5 Nongenomic Considerations in Risk Prediction or Diagnosis

Practically, the detection of early dementia, cognitive impairment, and Parkinson's disease can be done with the help of natural language processing, which is continuously driving advancements in automated speech analytics [31–34]. Researchers are also working on trailing the mental health changes using smartphone sensors [35]. Additionally, AI is also making a substantial contribution in guiding the decisions between cesarean sections and vaginal deliveries, aiming to reduce the complications of stillbirths [35]. Further advancements in disease prediction and diagnosis with wearable and home monitoring can greatly help in tracking chronic diseases, facilitate decentralized clinical trials, and can be helpful in detecting residual disease [36].

8.4 LIMITATIONS OF AI IN PERSONALIZED HEALTHCARE

8.4.1 Data Quality

It is one of the most important factors that will make personalized health care effective. The accuracy and dependability are highly dependent on the quality of the data just because AI models are used to identify the patterns in the data and make predictions. If the data on which the AI model is trained is incomplete, then the performance of the model will degrade [37–39]. For example, an AI model may not perform well for other groups if it is trained on data that is mainly composed of a specific racial or socioeconomic group. This could lead to disparities in healthcare outcomes. Similarly, incomplete data can also compromise the performance of the model [37]. For instance, if an AI system is intended to forecast the probability of a patient acquiring a specific illness, but crucial information like family health background is absent, the predictions made by the AI system might be unreliable.

8.4.2 Privacy Concerns

Similar to any technology that utilizes personal information, the application of AI in healthcare brings forth crucial privacy issues. Patients rightfully worry about how their personal health data is collected, stored, and utilized. The possible dangers of data breaches, data misuse, or unauthorized access are considerable and can have serious repercussions for patients. The privacy concerns associated with the use of AI in healthcare make it probable for patient data to be used without their knowledge or consent. Patients will be hesitant about the security of their data.

Healthcare providers need to guarantee the secure and ethical management of patient information by adopting strategies such as encryption, access restrictions, and data oversight to avert abuse. Being transparent and obtaining patient consent is crucial when utilizing personal data. Moreover, AI technology in healthcare encounters privacy issues tied to bias, which may stem from unbalanced training data or flawed algorithm development, possibly leading to unequal healthcare outcomes [40, 41].

8.4.3 Lack of Human Interactions

We know that AI offers so many benefits in healthcare, but concerns exist about compact collaboration. Individuals appreciate the compassion and tailored care that only healthcare professionals can provide, particularly for emotional assistance during critical health issues. The understanding of communication distinctions like facial expressions and body language is something that only human caregivers are good at in comparison to AI models and mother mechanic robots. The unique assistance is also something that only humans can provide. The human connection, value insights, and personalization are something that AI systems cannot provide. AI systems that provide healthcare must ensure the integration of human-centered care and the comfort of the patient. The only way to provide the best care is by balancing the use of technology and healthcare.

8.4.4 Ethical Consideration

As AI becomes more prevalent in healthcare, so does the concerns around the ethical considerations associated with its use. Artificial intelligence models can raise ethical issues, particularly concerning discrimination, when they are trained on biased datasets. These biases may lead to inequalities in healthcare, especially affecting underserved communities. It is essential to guarantee that the training data is varied, inclusive, and reflects the patient population to address these concerns.

The deployment of AI in the healthcare sector brings forth issues regarding the responsibility and accountability of both medical professionals and AI creators. Healthcare providers are obligated to ensure that the use of AI adheres to ethical principles, safeguarding patient data in a secure and impartial manner, and developing algorithms that represent the diversity of the population. AI developers are tasked with building systems that are transparent, comprehensible, and capable of being audited, which facilitates an understanding of their operations and recommendations, while also allowing for the detection of biases or inaccuracies.

The application of AI in healthcare brings forward significant ethical issues, such as the possibility of bias, the need for accountability among healthcare providers and AI developers, and the danger of making choices that may not prioritize patients' well-being. Healthcare institutions must guarantee that AI systems are implemented in accordance with ethical guidelines and optimal practices, involving patients in the design and execution of AI technologies. By tackling these ethical challenges, healthcare institutions can ensure that AI's role in healthcare is both efficient and morally sound.

8.4.5 Cost and Accessibility

The use of AI systems in healthcare can be costly, which can be a barrier to adoption for smaller healthcare providers. The cost of implementing AI includes obtaining and maintaining the most important hardware and software, as well as cost of employing personnel to develop the AI systems. Additionally, the problem of not accessing the technology by every person is also a big issue, as patients in rural or low-income areas may not be able to use the internet or basic devices to access the AI systems. This could result in unequal access to healthcare resources.

Healthcare professionals need to tackle the financial implications and accessibility of AI technologies by associating to distribute costs or collaborating with providers to develop cost-effective options. It is essential for policies to guarantee that the deployment of AI does not exacerbate health inequalities, focusing on fair access to care for every patient.

The expense and availability of AI systems can be important barriers to adopting healthcare providers. Also, it could be true that not every person has the technology that is required to use AI systems, which could exacerbate health disparities. The healthcare providers must take care of the cost and accessibility and work to ensure that these systems do not exacerbate existing health disparities. Cloud-based solutions may provide cost-effective solutions and accessible options for healthcare implementing AI systems.

8.5 CONCLUSION

By accurate and precise diagnosis, individualized treatment plans, and artistic answers to challenging medical obstacles, the integration of AI into personalized healthcare has revolutionary prospects for enhancing health outcomes. AI has shown promise in disease prediction, treatment plan optimization, and the analysis of large datasets. Data quality, privacy difficulties, limited human connection, ethical dilemmas, and cost accessibility are some of the most important problems to its widespread use in healthcare. Proper mitigation of these gaps is, however, essential in totally harnessing AI for healthcare—that is in terms of a diversity of the data used and with strong guarantees for privacy to prevent exploitation in such systems that also ensure adequate balance between people-centered care, ethics, costs, and fairness. Addressing these gaps thus may ensure that healthcare delivery could be equitable, effective, and available to many through personalized interventions.

REFERENCES

1. Y. Juhn and H. Liu, "Artificial intelligence approaches using natural language processing to advance EHR based clinical research," *J. Allergy Clin. Immunol.*, vol. 145, no. 2, pp. 463–469, Feb. 2020.
2. C. Friedman, "Discovering novel adverse drug events using natural language processing and mining of the electronic health record," Artificial Intelligence in Medicine: 12th Conference on 2009.
3. R. Lulubelle, "Exploratory study of artificial intelligence in healthcare," *Int. J. Innov. Res. Technol.*, vol. 3, no. 1, pp. 1–10, 2016.
4. IBM and partners to transform personal health with watson and open cloud. 2015. https://www.prnewswire.com/news-releases/ibm-and-partners-to-transform-personal-health-with-watson-and-open-cloud-300065025.html
5. A. Sadilek et al., "Machine-learned epidemiology: Real-time detection of foodborne illness at scale," *NPJ Digit. Med.,* vol. 1, p. 36, 2018.
6. J. L. Snowdon, et al., "Empowering caseworkers to better serve the most vulnerable with a cloud-based care management solution," *Appl. Clin. Inform.*, vol. 11, pp. 617–621, 2020.
7. R. Vaishya, et al., "Artificial intelligence (AI) applications for COVID-19 pandemic," *Diabetes Meta. Syndr.,* vol. 14, pp. 337–339, 2020.

8. P. Hamet and J. Tremblay, "Artificial intelligence in medicine," *Metabolism,* vol. 69S, pp. S36–S40, 2017.
9. E. J. Topol, *Deep Medicine: How Artificial Intelligence Can Make Healthcare Human Again,* Basic Books, New York, NY, 2019.
10. A. L. Jorgensen, et al., "Implementation of genotype-guided dosing of warfarin with point-of-care genetic testing in three UK clinics: A matched cohort study," *BMC Med.*, vol. 17, p. 76, 2019.
11. D. O. Arnar and R. Palsson, "Precision medicine and advancing clinical care: Insights from Iceland," *JAMA Intern. Med.,* vol. 179, pp. 139–140, 2019.
12. J. M. Pulley, et al., "Accelerating precision drug development and drug repurposing by leveraging human genetics," *Assay Drug Dev. Technol.,* vol. 15, pp. 113–119, 2017.
13. O. Gottesman, et al., "The Electronic Medical Records and Genomics (emerge) Network: Past, present, and future," *Genet. Med.,* vol. 15, pp. 761–771, 2013.
14. J. M. Pulley, et al., "Operational implementation of prospective genotyping for per signalized medicine: The design of the Vanderbilt PREDICT project," *Clin. Pharmacal. Ther.,* vol. 92, pp. 87–95, 2012.
15. J. S. Schildkraut, et al., "A prognostic model based on readily available clinical data enriched a pre-emptive pharmacogenetic testing program," *J. Clin. Epidemiology.,* vol. 72, pp. 107–115, 2016.
16. E. Trivialise, et al., "Artificial intelligence Radiogenomics for advancing precision and effectiveness in oncologic care (Review)," *Int. J. Oncol.,* vol. 57, pp. 43–53, 2020.
17. Z. Zhu, et al., "Deep learning for identifying Radiogenomics associations in breast can car," *Compute. Biol. Med.,* vol. 109, pp. 85–90, 2019.
18. J. E. Gibault, et al., "Deep learning and Radiomics predict complete response after neo-adjuvant chemoradiation for locally advanced rectal cancer," *Sci. Rep.,* vol. 8, pp. 12611, 2018.
19. E. Trivialise, et al., "Extending 2-D convolutional neural networks to 3-D for advance Ing deep learning cancer classification with application to MRI liver tumour different tuition," *IEEE J. Biomed. Health Inform.,* vol. 23, pp. 923–930, 2019.
20. D. J. Biederman, et al., "Identifying patients experiencing homelessness in an Elec tonic health record and assessing qualification for medical respite: A five-year retrospective review," *J. Health Care Poor Underserved,* vol. 30, pp. 297–309, 2019.
21. M. Brown, et al., "Applying a time-patterned typology of homelessness among Indi visuals with mental illness," *Am. J. Community Psychol.,* vol. 59, pp. 306–315, 2017.
22. L. Roy, et al., "Occupation-based practices and homelessness: A scoping review," *Can. J. Occupy. Ther.,* vol. 84, pp. 98–110, 2017.
23. J. Parece, et al., "Using artificial intelligence to predict prolonged mechanical Venti lotion and tracheostomy placement," *J. Surg. Res.,* vol. 228, pp. 179–187, 2018.
24. Q. Qiu, et al., "Development and validation of three machine-learning models for pre ducting multiple organ failure in moderately severe and severe acute pancreatitis," *BMC Gastroenterol.,* vol. 19, pp. 118, 2019.
25. A. Silva, et al., "Rating organ failure via adverse events using data mining in the intensive care unit," *Arif. Intel. Med.,* vol. 43, pp. 179–193, 2008.
26. S. K. Low, et al., "Breast cancer: The translation of big genomic data to cancer precis Sion medicine," *Cancer Sci.,* vol. 109, pp. 497–506, 2018.
27. J. D. Schwalm, et al., "Resource effective strategies to prevent and treat Cardiovasc collar disease," *Circulation,* vol. 133, pp. 742–755, 2016.
28. G. J. August and A. Gewirtz, "Moving toward a precision-based, personalized frame work for prevention science: Introduction to the special issue," *Prev. Sci.,* vol. 20, pp. 1–9, 2019.

29. J. Zhao, et al., "Learning from longitudinal data in electronic health record and eg nitic data to improve cardiovascular event prediction," *Sci. Rep.*, vol. 9, pp. 717, 2019.
30. M. M. Clark, et al., "Diagnosis of genetic diseases in seriously ill children by rapid whole-genome sequencing and automated phenotyping and interpretation," *Sci. Transl. Med.*, vol. 11, pp. eaat6177, 2019.
31. A. Konig, et al., "Automatic speech analysis for the assessment of patients with pre dementia and Alzheimer's disease," *Alzheimer's Dement. (Mast.).*, vol. 1, pp. 112–124, 2015.
32. A. M. Garcia, et al., "How language flows when movements don't: An automated anal lysis of spontaneous discourse in Parkinson's disease," *Brain Lang.*, vol. 162, pp. 19–28, 2016.
33. A. Konig, et al., "Use of speech analyses within a mobile application for the assess mint of cognitive impairment in elderly people," *Curr. Alzheimer Res.*, vol. 15, pp. 120–129, 2018.
34. C. M. Corcoran, et al., "Prediction of psychosis across protocols and risk cohorts using automated language analysis," *World Psychiatry,* vol. 17, pp. 67–75, 2018.
35. P. Fergus, et al., "Classification of caesarean section and normal vaginal deliveries using foetal heart rate signals and advanced machine learning algorithms," *Biomed. Eng. Online,* vol. 16, pp. 89, 2017.
36. M. Gold, et al., "Digital technologies as biomarkers, clinical outcomes assessment, and recruitment tools in Alzheimer's disease clinical trials," *Alzheimer's Dement. (NY),* vol. 4, pp. 234–242, 2018.
37. M. A. Veronin, R. P. Schumaker, R. R. Dixit, P. Dhake, and M. Ogwo, "A systematic approach to 'cleaning' of drug name records data in the FAERS database: A case report," *Int. J. Big Data Manage.*, vol. 1, no. 2, p. 105, 2020.
38. R. Dixit, M. Ogwo, and R. P. Schumaker, "Irony of the FAERS database: An analysis of data input errors and potential consequences," IIMA/ICITED Joint, 2018.
39. M. A. Veronin, R. P. Schumaker, and R. Dixit, "The irony of MedWatch and the FAERS database: An assessment of data input errors and potential consequences," *J. Pharm. Technol.*, vol. 36, no. 4, pp. 164–167, Aug. 2020.
40. J. Shaw, F. Rudzicz, T. Jamieson, and A. Goldfarb, "Artificial intelligence and the implementation challenge," *J. Med. Internet Res.*, vol. 21, no. 7, p. e13659, Jul. 2019.
41. T. Davenport and R. Kalakota, "The potential for artificial intelligence in healthcare," *Future Healthc. J.*, vol. 6, no. 2, pp. 94–98, Jun. 2019.

Part IV

Advanced AI Technologies and Clinical Applications

9 Harnessing Deep Learning for Swift Abdominal Trauma Diagnosis, Injury Assessment, and Streamlined Patient Care

Rajendra Hegadi, Sudeepto Chatterjee, Prathamesh P. Pai, Prakash Agarwal, and Ashis J. Kalathil

9.1 INTRODUCTION

Traumatic injuries represent a significant global public health concern, being the primary cause of mortality in individuals within the first four decades of life (Gad et al., 2012).

Among these injuries, blunt force trauma, notably from motor vehicle accidents, frequently leads to abdominal trauma, causing internal damage and bleeding in critical organs like the liver, spleen, kidneys, and bowel (Simon et al., 2023;Clancy et al., 2001). Swift and precise diagnosis of these injuries is vital for effective treatment, with a considerable number of patients requiring urgent surgery. Computed tomography (CT) has emerged as an invaluable tool for evaluating suspected abdominal injuries due to its ability to generate detailed cross-sectional images (Hassan & Abd Aziz, 2010). However, interpreting these CT scans for abdominal trauma presents complexities, especially in identifying multiple injuries or subtle bleeding sites (Gong et al., 2017; Yun et al., 2017; Bruno et al., 2015; Ersoydan et al., 2023; Ruikar et al., 2019a). To address this diagnostic challenge, this research explores the potential of Artificial Intelligence (AI), Machine Learning (ML), and Deep Learning (DL) to assist medical professionals in swiftly and accurately detecting these injuries and determining their severity. This study underscores the significance of DL models in expediting the diagnosis of abdominal trauma, seeking to significantly enhance patient care and health outcomes in emergency settings.

DOI: 10.1201/9781003624875-13

9.2 LITERATURE REVIEW

Willmann et al. (2002) studied the role of multidetector CT in identifying active hemorrhage post-blunt abdominal trauma. They evaluate its effectiveness in diagnosing bleeding in patients with abdominal injuries, emphasizing timely detection, crucial in incidents like motor vehicle accidents. The research examines CT's capability to pinpoint ongoing hemorrhage within the abdomen, providing detailed cross-sectional images. The authors discuss advantages, such as revealing potential bleeding sources and assessing the severity of injuries to organs like the liver, spleen, kidneys, and bowel.

Lynch et al. (2018) and Ruikar et al. (2023) reviewed the distinctive features, challenges, and considerations of pediatric abdominal trauma. They examined its causes, mechanisms, and common sources, highlighting differences from adult cases. The spectrum of injuries covers various accidents like falls, bicycle mishaps, sports injuries, and abuse. Additionally, they discussed specific diagnostic and management considerations for pediatric abdominal trauma.

Jansen et al. (2008) examines diagnostic strategies for blunt abdominal trauma, discussing evaluation techniques and clinical signs. It covers trauma causes like accidents or assaults, potential injuries to organs, and challenges in diagnosis due to symptom variability. Diagnostic modalities such as imaging and laboratory tests are explored for their strengths and limitations in various clinical contexts.

Ersoydan et al. (2023) investigated the temporal changes in clinical reasoning quality of abdominal CT scans over a period of 15 years from 2005 to 2019. They observed that during this period, the number of abdominal CT scans significantly increased, while the quality of clinical reasoning significantly decreased.

Bruls and Kwee (2020) in their research on workload for radiologists during 2006 to 2020 have shown that CT studies increased by more than 500% in large general hospitals in Western Europe. Hence there is a need for advanced technologies like AI to provide tools to radiologists to match this ongoing increasing trend to avoid potential burnout and to maintain quality and safety of radiological care.

Ghaffar Nia et al. (2023) have discussed recent advancements in AI techniques for diagnosing and predicting various diseases. This research suggests these AI techniques seek to enhance higher precision compared to human specialists, with minimal human error.

Meena et al. (2023) proposed advanced deep learning methods for identifying diseases from CT lung scans. This study has demonstrated quick pneumonia screening and the identification of high-risk patients through the analysis of pneumonia-related CT images.

9.3 OBJECTIVES

The literature survey indicates there is a need for AI, ML, and DL tools and techniques to assist radiologists in precisely evaluating abdominal CT scans. These tools and techniques can enhance diagnostic accuracy, streamline workflow, and improve patient outcomes by providing additional support to healthcare professionals in interpreting medical imaging data.

The primary objective of this research is to create sophisticated DL models specialized in detecting and classifying severe injuries and areas of active internal bleeding within abdominal CT scans. These models should be adaptive, efficient, and accurate in their analysis. The intent is to expedite the diagnosis process, which typically involves meticulous visual interpretation by healthcare professionals. Proposed models should significantly reduce the time required for the identification and classification of injuries, enabling swift and precise diagnoses.

9.3.1 Reducing Diagnostic Errors and Improving Diagnostic Accuracy

Improving diagnostic accuracy in the context of diagnosing abdominal trauma using AI models is fundamental for precise and reliable identification of injuries within the abdomen. Traditional diagnostic processes heavily rely on visual interpretation by healthcare professionals, which can be subject to human error and potential variations in interpretation. Therefore, the integration of AI models with diagnosis seeks to enhance accuracy by mitigating these potential errors (Ghaffar et al., 2023; Al-Antari, 2023; Richens et al., 2020; Aggarwal et al., 2021; Kulkarni & Singh, 2023).

AI models are trained using extensive datasets of abdominal CT scans showcasing a diverse range of injury types and severities. These models employ sophisticated AI algorithms to recognize distinctive patterns, anomalies, and specific features associated with various injuries. The objective of this research is to accurately identify and categorize injuries within the abdominal organs, encompassing fractures, contusions, lacerations, hematomas, and areas of internal bleeding.

The proposed DL models are trained not only to identify injuries but also to differentiate their severity. Distinguishing between minor and severe injuries is critical in determining the urgency and type of intervention required. Thus, these models are trained to assign severity levels to the identified injuries, aiding healthcare professionals in prioritizing patient care and intervention strategies. By achieving a high level of diagnostic accuracy, DL models reduce the variability and subjectivity often inherent in human interpretation, leading to more consistent and dependable diagnoses. This improvement in accuracy and reliability has a direct impact on patient care. Accurate identification and classification of injuries facilitate faster and more informed treatment decisions, potentially reducing delays in interventions and thereby contributing to improved patient outcomes, particularly in emergency scenarios involving abdominal trauma.

9.3.2 Enhancing Emergency Care

Enhancing emergency care through the implementation of AI in diagnosing abdominal trauma is pivotal for expediting the diagnostic process and improving patient outcomes in critical situations (Emami & Javanmardi, 2023; Piliuk & Tomforde, 2023). In emergency scenarios, swift and accurate diagnosis plays a crucial role in determining timely and appropriate interventions (Vearrier et al., 2022). The integration of AI strives to significantly reduce the time taken for the diagnosis of abdominal trauma, a process that traditionally relies on visual interpretation by healthcare professionals. AI models trained on diverse CT scans can swiftly detect injuries and bleeding in key abdominal organs.

The primary goal of this research is to reduce delays between diagnosis and intervention, which can be lifesaving in emergency situations. Through DL-assisted interpretations, the identification and severity grading of injuries can be swiftly achieved, enabling healthcare professionals to make more informed and timely decisions regarding patient care and treatment strategies. The expedited diagnostic process, enabled by DL, has the potential to significantly impact patient survival rates in emergency settings. By providing quick and accurate insights, the DL approach minimizes the time required for decision-making, allowing for quicker initiation of appropriate treatments, ultimately leading to improved patient outcomes and potentially reducing mortality rates associated with abdominal trauma in critical care situations. This advancement in emergency care can be transformative, particularly in scenarios where time is a critical factor in determining patient survival and recovery.

9.4 MOTIVATION

The motivation for undertaking this research stems from the critical need to address traumatic injuries, particularly abdominal trauma, which stands as a significant global public health concern, being a leading cause of mortality, particularly among individuals in the first four decades of life. The timely and accurate diagnosis of these injuries plays a pivotal role in determining appropriate interventions, profoundly influencing patient outcomes and survival rates.

Computed tomography (CT) has emerged as an invaluable tool in evaluating suspected abdominal injuries, providing detailed cross-sectional images crucial for diagnosis. However, the interpretation of CT scans for abdominal trauma presents substantial challenges, especially in cases involving multiple injuries or subtle areas of internal bleeding. Harnessing the capabilities of AI, ML, and DL in this context offers a promising avenue for revolutionizing trauma care.

This research is driven by the need for timely and accurate identification of internal injuries in abdominal trauma. By leveraging DL, the goal is to streamline the diagnostic process, reducing delays in identifying severe injuries in critical abdominal organs like the liver, spleen, kidneys, and bowel.

Our motivation lies in equipping healthcare professionals with advanced DL models capable of swiftly and accurately identifying injuries and grading their severity within CT scans. This research is centered on significantly impacting patient care and health outcomes in emergency settings by expediting the identification of traumatic injuries, ensuring timely and appropriate interventions. The potential of AI to enhance diagnostic accuracy, minimize errors, and expedite decision-making in emergency scenarios is the driving force behind this research endeavor. The primary motivation is to improve survival rates, decrease treatment delays, and ultimately contribute to advancing global public health by integrating DL driven diagnostic tools into the realm of abdominal trauma care. Through this pursuit, we intend to catalyze a paradigm shift in trauma care, potentially saving lives and enhancing patient outcomes on a global scale.

9.5 EXPERIMENTAL DESIGN

We used Kaggle's RSNA 2023 Abdominal Trauma Detection data set (Colak et al., 2023), hosted by Kaggle for the RSNA 2023 Abdominal Trauma Detection competition; it is a resource for research in advanced medical imaging technology for the diagnosis of abdominal trauma. Comprising a diverse collection of anonymized medical images, this dataset offers a glimpse into the complexities of abdominal injuries, providing researchers and practitioners with invaluable insights for improving diagnostic accuracy and patient outcomes.

Deep Learning models are employed in the following five steps as shown in Figure 9.1.

a) Data Preparation
b) Data Augmentation
c) Model Architecture
d) Training and Evaluation
e) Model saving and best epoch metric

The following sections describe the steps involved in the implementation of DL models.

9.5.1 Data Preparation

The data preparation phase is a meticulous process, crucial for organizing and structuring the dataset to facilitate effective model training and evaluation. To streamline this process, a vector is utilized to store image addresses that link to the dataset as shown in Figure 9.2.

In the medical domain, *patientID* and *scan IDs* play a pivotal role in distinguishing and accessing specific images related to individual patients and their various scans (Ruikar et al., 2021). This dataset organization method follows a hierarchical structure, with *patientIDs* serving as the primary identifier, followed by corresponding *scan IDs*, and multiple instances associated with each scan, representing different images or slices obtained from the imaging technology. The vector efficiently manages these hierarchies by storing the addresses or paths to the images, providing

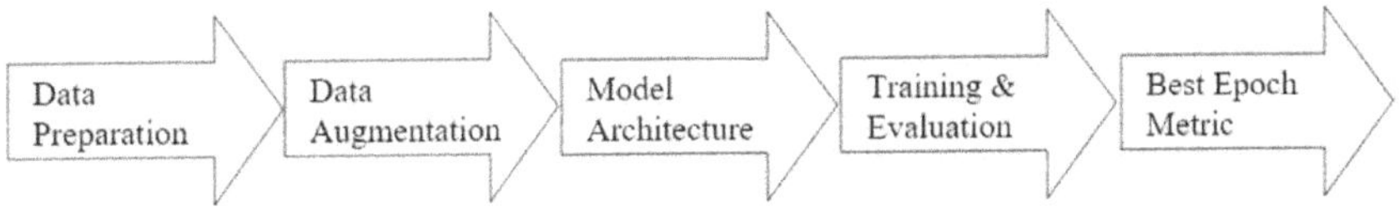

FIGURE 9.1 Procedures for implementing Deep Learning techniques on the dataset.

Patient ID (*Primary Identifier*)	Scan IDs	Image Address

FIGURE 9.2 The dataset vectors.

a structured and easily accessible linkage to the dataset. Each address in the vector corresponds to a specific image and is constructed based on the *patientIDs* and *scan IDs*. This arrangement allows for swift and accurate retrieval of images associated with particular patients and their respective scans during model training and validation.

This vector-based approach ensures the dataset is systematically organized, facilitating streamlined access to specific image instances within the dataset. It allows for the retrieval and utilization of relevant images during the modeling process, essential for training neural networks. It also enables the avoidance of redundancies and inconsistencies in data representation, ensuring data integrity and uniform access to images from various scans related to distinct patients. In essence, by employing a vector to store image addresses based on patient and *scan IDs*, the data preparation phase optimizes the dataset's organizational structure, allowing for efficient access, retrieval, and utilization of pertinent images crucial for the development and evaluation of models for abdominal trauma detection.

9.5.2 Data Augmentation

Dataset augmentation in the context of abdominal trauma detection involves a critical process to enhance the dataset's diversity and robustness by artificially creating variations or scenarios that might be encountered in real-world situations (Ruikar et al., 2019b). In this particular augmentation process, a technique is employed to simulate a synthetic or "fake" injury within the images. Each image instance is augmented by incorporating a simulated injury represented by a black pixel.

While the use of black pixels to simulate synthetic injuries presents a straightforward and computationally inexpensive method for augmenting the dataset, we acknowledge its limited clinical realism. In real-world scenarios, abdominal injuries manifest in various forms—such as contrast extravasation, tissue lacerations, and organ swelling—which are visually and structurally more complex than single-pixel anomalies. The simplistic nature of black pixel augmentation may not accurately reflect the diversity of actual trauma patterns, potentially biasing the model to focus on artifacts rather than meaningful clinical features. Therefore, although this technique helped increase data variability and provided an initial direction for injury localization, future studies should adopt more anatomically and radiologically accurate augmentation strategies. These could include using generative models or simulation-based perturbations informed by radiologist feedback to better replicate the nuanced appearance of abdominal trauma on CT scans.

The purpose behind this augmentation method is to provide the Deep Learning model with a diverse range of examples that mimic injury scenarios within the

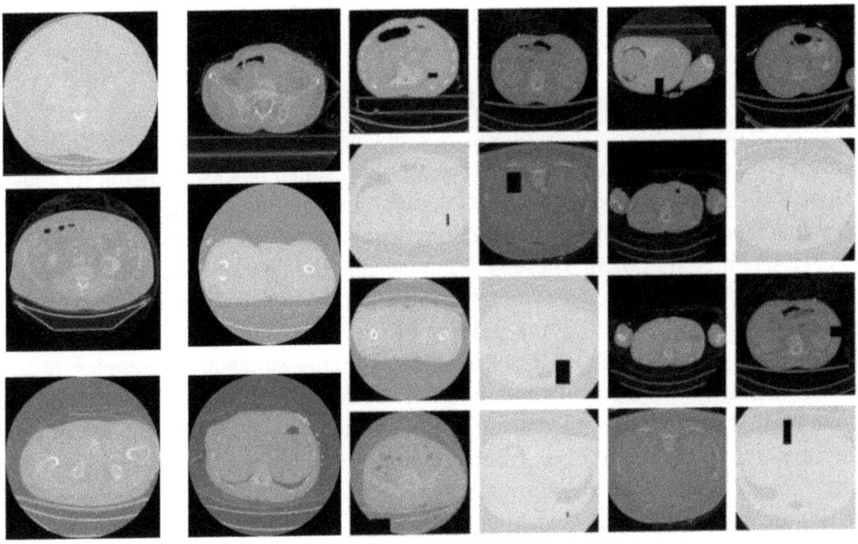

FIGURE 9.3 CT scan images of various organs from dataset (a) Original images; (b) Augmented images.

abdominal images. By artificially introducing a black pixel to denote a simulated injury in each image, the model is trained to recognize this visual cue as an abnormality or traumatic lesion. This augmentation technique strives to enrich the dataset with variations representing different injury instances that might occur in clinical settings, ultimately improving the model's ability to accurately detect and classify trauma-related abnormalities during training.

Through this process, the Deep Learning model is exposed to a broader spectrum of instances that mimic potential injuries, allowing it to learn to differentiate between normal and abnormal patterns within the images. While the 'fake' injuries are simulated using black pixels, they serve as representative features mimicking potential traumatic abnormalities, aiding the model in recognizing and classifying similar abnormalities during its training phase as shown in Figure 9.3a and 9.3b. This form of dataset augmentation is essential in training the model to accurately identify and classify trauma-related lesions or abnormalities, providing a more diverse set of scenarios for the model to learn from. It contributes to the model's ability to generalize and make informed predictions when presented with real-world instances of abdominal trauma in medical images.

9.5.3 Model Architecture

The selection of different pre-existing neural network architectures, such as ResNet, EfficientNet, and VGG-16, is a crucial component in the development of Deep Learning models for abdominal trauma detection. Each architecture brings distinct advantages and features, contributing to the overall robustness and effectiveness of the model.

9.5.3.1 ResNet (Residual Network) Model

ResNet, short for Residual Network, is renowned for its revolutionary "residual learning" approach. It introduced the concept of residual blocks, allowing for much deeper neural network models without encountering the vanishing gradient problem. Residual blocks consist of skip connections or shortcuts that bypass one or more layers (Hasanah et al., 2023). These shortcuts enable the flow of information directly from the initial layers to deeper layers, facilitating the maintenance and propagation of information, thus enabling the training of very deep networks with hundreds of layers. This characteristic of ResNet makes it highly suitable for complex image recognition tasks, where depth and accuracy are crucial (Shafiq & Gu, 2022). In the context of abdominal trauma detection, ResNet aids in capturing intricate patterns and features in medical images, allowing for more accurate identification and classification of trauma-related abnormalities.

Figure 9.4 is the ResNet model that we generated on the data set with the specified input parameters. In the top layer input (64, 512, 512, 3) the first parameter (64) is the batch size i.e. number of the images; the second, third, and fourth parameters refer to the size of each image which in this case is 512*512*3.

9.5.3.2 EfficientNet Model

EfficientNet represents a family of neural network architectures developed to optimize both accuracy and efficiency. It uses a compound scaling method that uniformly scales different dimensions (depth, width, and resolution) to build highly efficient yet accurate models. This approach helps in achieving state-of-the-art performance using significantly fewer parameters, enabling faster training and inference. The EfficientNet architecture is well suited for tasks in computer vision and medical imaging due to its ability to balance model complexity and performance, making it a compelling choice for abdominal trauma detection (Yue et al., 2023). It provides a trade-off between accuracy and computational efficiency, offering the potential for streamlined model deployment and real-time analysis, essential in medical settings.

Figure 9.5 shows the EfficientNet model that we generated on the data set with the specified input parameters.

9.5.3.3 VGG-16 (Visual Geometry Group) Model

VGG-16 is a classic deep convolutional neural network known for its simplicity and effectiveness. It consists of 16 layers, including 13 convolutional layers and three fully connected layers, using small (3x3) convolutional filters throughout the network. VGG-16 excels in learning and extracting intricate features from images. Its straightforward architecture makes it easy to understand and implement, which can be beneficial for training models in medical imaging tasks (Kode & Barkana, 2023). While it might not be as computationally efficient as some newer architectures, VGG-16's ability to capture diverse image features makes it a valuable choice

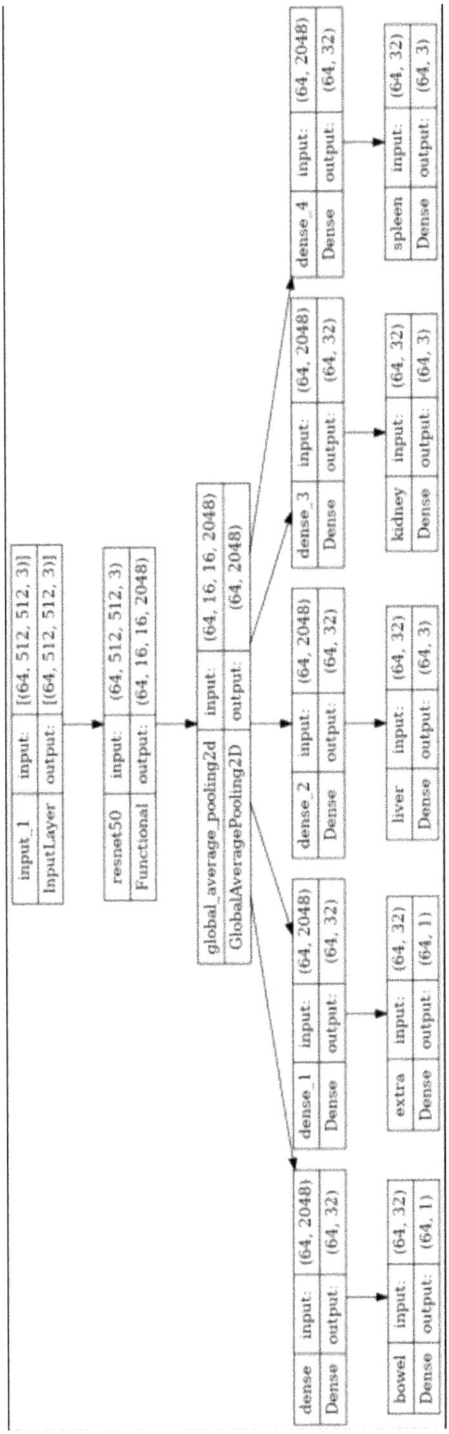

FIGURE 9.4 ResNet Architecture for RSNA 2023 dataset.

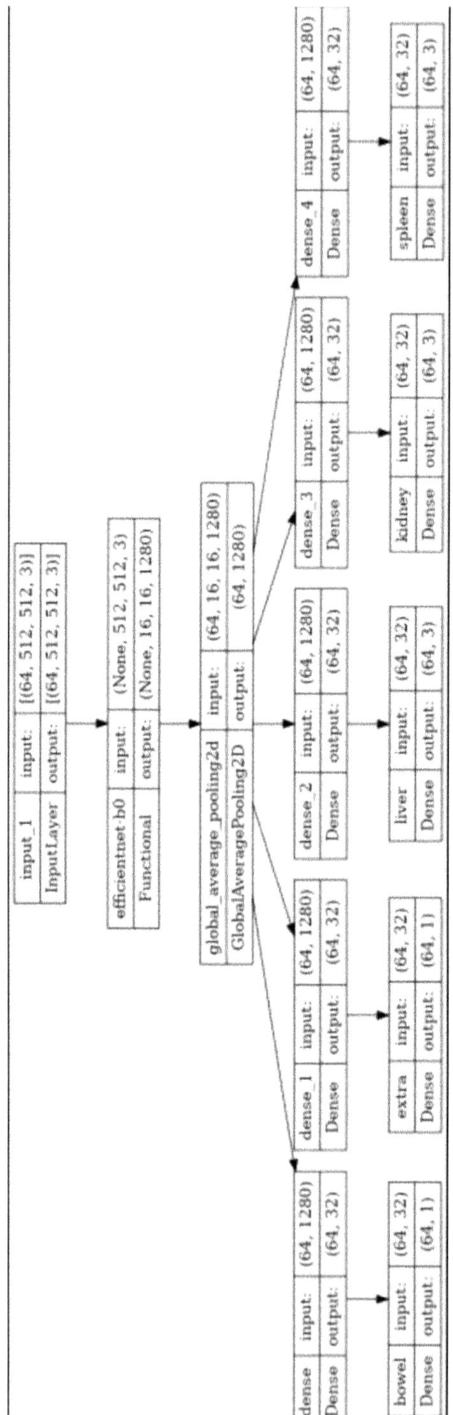

FIGURE 9.5 EfficientNet Architecture for RSNA 2023 dataset.

in recognizing and classifying complex patterns and abnormalities in abdominal trauma images Figure 9.6.

9.5.4 Training and Evaluation

The training and evaluation phase of the abdominal trauma detection models involving VGG-16, EfficientNet, and ResNet employs a method known as the Cosine Decay learning rate schedule. This schedule regulates the learning rate during training, optimizing the model's ability to converge and fine-tune its parameters effectively. In the training phase, the models start off by initializing with pretrained weights obtained from their corresponding architectures. The Cosine Decay learning rate schedule is implemented, adjusting the learning rate over epochs in a cosine manner. The learning rate gradually decreases, following a cosine curve, seeking to facilitate smoother optimization and model convergence. This method allows the models to slowly adapt and refine their parameters without making abrupt changes, ultimately aiding in achieving more accurate and stable results. Simultaneously, the models are trained on the augmented dataset that incorporates the simulated injuries, providing a diverse range of examples to learn from.

Training involves feeding the dataset into the models and iteratively updating the model's weights based on the information provided by the images and their associated injuries. Throughout the training process, various metrics such as accuracy and loss are computed on both the training and validation sets. These metrics measure the model's performance and its ability to correctly predict and classify trauma-related abnormalities. Accuracy represents the model's overall correctness in its predictions, while loss quantifies the difference between predicted and actual values. The evaluation phase involves assessing how well the trained models generalize to unseen data. The validation set, which the model has not seen during training, is employed to measure the model's performance. This is crucial for ensuring that the models have not simply memorized the training data but have truly learned to recognize and classify trauma-related injuries.

9.5.5 Model Saving and Best Epoch Metric

Once the training process is completed, the trained models, having learned from the dataset and adjusted their parameters, are saved for future use or deployment. This ensures that the models, with their learned patterns and optimized parameters, can be easily reloaded and utilized without needing to retrain from scratch. Saving the models in this way allows for their preservation, sharing, or further analysis without the need to redo the extensive training process.

During the training phase, the models' performance metrics are typically recorded and monitored over multiple iterations or epochs. The best epoch represents the point at which the model achieved its peak performance on the validation set, showcasing the most optimal trade-off between accuracy and generalization to unseen data. The epoch with the lowest loss or the highest accuracy on the validation set is often

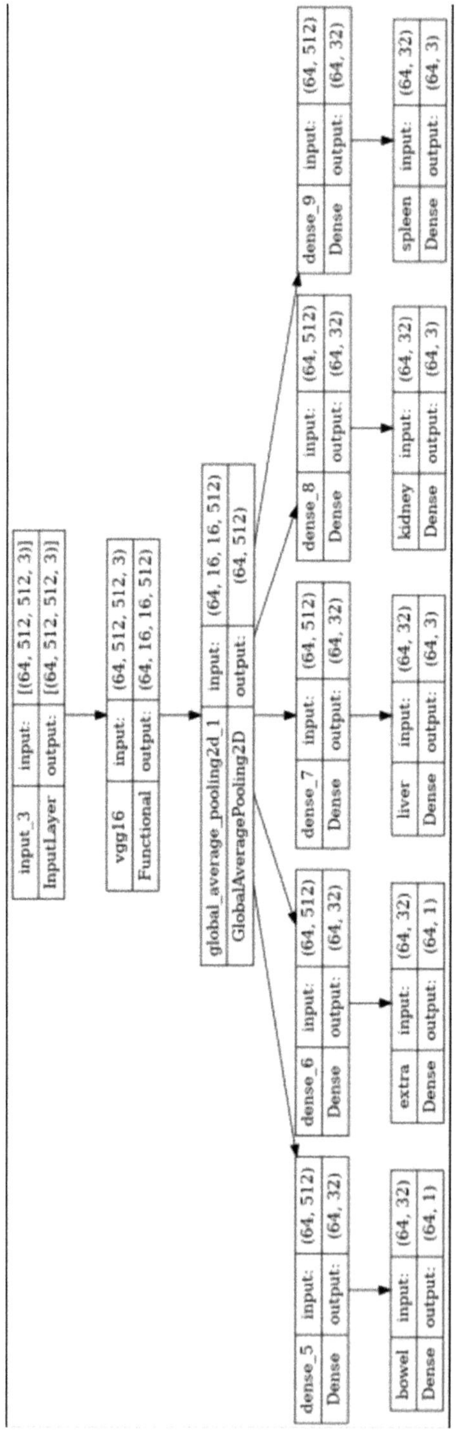

FIGURE 9.6 VGG-16 Architecture for the RSNA 2023 dataset.

considered the best epoch. This metric serves as an indicator of the model's ability to generalize and make accurate predictions on new, unseen data.

Additionally, organ-specific accuracies are determined and reported. These accuracies represent the model's performance in specifically identifying and classifying trauma-related abnormalities in various abdominal organs, such as the liver, spleen, kidneys, and bowel. Recording these organ-specific accuracies is essential as it provides insights into the model's proficiency in accurately detecting specific abnormalities within different regions of the abdomen. By tracking the best epoch metrics and organ-specific accuracies, developers and researchers gain a comprehensive understanding of the model's performance at different stages of training. It aids in selecting the most optimal model state, ensuring its readiness for deployment while offering insights into its performance in distinguishing specific traumatic lesions in different abdominal organs. The saved models, along with these key metrics, form a valuable asset for further analysis, comparison, and potential deployment in clinical or research settings.

9.6 RESULTS AND DISCUSSION

In the culmination of our research endeavors focusing on abdominal trauma detection, the performance metrics of the developed models, namely EfficientNet, ResNet, and VGG-16, were diligently assessed. The obtained results shed light on the models' accuracies and the respective epochs at which the peak accuracies were achieved.

The experimental results are tabulated in Table 9.1 and Table 9.2. The EfficientNet, a model renowned for its balance between efficiency and accuracy, exhibited a notable best accuracy of 73%. This peak accuracy was attained during the 8th training epoch. Simultaneously, the ResNet model demonstrated commendable performance, securing a best accuracy of 71.5%, also realized at the 8th epoch. On the other hand, VGG-16, a classic architecture known for its depth and ability to recognize diverse image features, achieved a similar best accuracy of 71.5%. Notably, VGG-16 reached its pinnacle performance at the 2nd training epoch.

The observed variations in performance and epochs at which the best accuracies were obtained among the models offer valuable insights. EfficientNet exhibited the highest accuracy, signifying its capability to effectively discern trauma-related abnormalities within abdominal images. ResNet closely followed, demonstrating strong accuracy at a similar epoch, showcasing its competency in recognizing

TABLE 9.1
Results of Efficiency, Accuracy and Epoch from the Deep Learning Models

	ResNet	EfficientNet	VGG-16
Best Loss	4.911	3.816	3.711
Best Accuracy	0.715	0.730	0.715
Best Epoch	7	7	1

TABLE 9.2
Accuracy Results for the Organs Obtained from the Deep Learning Models

	ResNet	EfficientNet	VGG-16
Bowel	0.520	0.520	0.520
Extravasation	0.697	0.696	0.697
Liver	0.870	0.870	0.870
Kidney	0.811	0.835	0.811
Spleen	0.677	0.729	0.677

intricate patterns within the dataset. Conversely, VGG-16, while achieving a comparable accuracy, reached its peak performance notably earlier, highlighting its quick learning or sensitivity to the dataset's characteristics in the initial epochs.

These results indicate the diverse capacities and learning behaviors of the distinct architectures in identifying trauma-related anomalies. EfficientNet's higher accuracy emphasizes its suitability for this task, while the differences in the epoch at which the peak accuracies were achieved provide useful insights into the learning efficiency and timely adaptation of the models to the given dataset. These findings are instrumental in understanding the relative strengths of these models and inform decisions regarding model selection for accurate abdominal trauma detection in medical imaging.

9.7 CONCLUSION

In conclusion, our research endeavors in abdominal trauma detection using Deep Learning models, namely EfficientNet, ResNet, and VGG-16, have unveiled valuable insights and implications. The primary focus was to harness neural network models to accurately identify and classify trauma-related abnormalities within abdominal images, intended to strengthen medical diagnostics and patient care.

The utilization of diverse architectures demonstrated varying degrees of success. EfficientNet emerged as the most proficient model, achieving the highest accuracy of 73%, showcasing its robust ability to discern traumatic lesions. This architecture's balance between efficiency and accuracy positions it as a promising candidate for accurate detection and classification of abdominal trauma, potentially enhancing clinical decision-making and patient outcomes. ResNet and VGG-16, while achieving slightly lower but comparable accuracies of 71.5%, also exhibited commendable performance. ResNet's notable performance at the 8th epoch emphasizes its capacity to recognize intricate patterns within the dataset. VGG-16, although reaching a similar accuracy, displayed its quick learning capability by achieving its peak accuracy as early as the 2nd epoch. The differences in accuracy and epochs at which the best accuracies were achieved highlight the diverse learning behaviors and efficiencies of these models. EfficientNet's superior accuracy, ResNet's deep learning capabilities, and VGG-16's sensitivity in the early epochs provide nuanced perspectives on their performance and learning adaptability.

These findings emphasize the potential of Deep Learning in medical imaging, particularly in abdominal trauma detection, where accurate and prompt diagnosis is critical for initiating timely interventions. The high accuracy levels attained by these models signify their potential to aid healthcare professionals in efficiently identifying traumatic injuries, guiding appropriate interventions, and potentially reducing diagnostic errors. While our study showcases promising results, further investigations could explore ensemble methods or fine-tuning techniques to enhance the models' performance. This research contributes to the growing field of medical imaging and serves as a foundation for developing robust models capable of precise and efficient abdominal trauma detection, ultimately contributing to improved patient care and diagnostic accuracy.

9.8 DEPLOYMENT AND INTEGRATION IN CLINICAL SETTINGS

For any AI-based diagnostic system to be impactful, seamless integration into hospital systems is critical. The models developed in this study are designed with scalability in mind, and their computational efficiency (particularly EfficientNet) makes them suitable for real-time inference in clinical environments. Deployment into hospital PACS (Picture Archiving and Communication System) and integration with existing DICOM workflows are key next steps.

Additionally, real-world validation is essential. Our current work has been validated on a public dataset, but prospective clinical validation involving radiologist feedback and retrospective cohort studies across multiple institutions will be crucial to assess generalizability. Such validation would also allow model performance to be benchmarked against clinical gold standards. Further collaboration with radiology departments is planned to assess usability, interpretability, and trustworthiness, addressing key adoption barriers such as explainability, medico-legal accountability, and integration with emergency triage systems.

Moreover, the implementation of user-friendly front-end systems that provide real-time decision-support to radiologists (e.g., highlighting suspected injury regions or severity scores) will be vital for clinical uptake. These steps form the backbone of translating this research into a tangible, deployable AI tool for abdominal trauma diagnosis.

9.9 CHALLENGES AND FUTURE SCOPE

An imbalanced distribution of injuries within the dataset complicated the learning process. Certain injury types were overrepresented while others were underrepresented, potentially biasing the model's learning toward more frequent injuries and impacting its ability to accurately identify rarer traumatic lesions. However, these challenges have opened avenues for future advancements in our research. One potential future scope involves training models from scratch rather than relying solely on transfer learning models. This approach may offer a more tailored learning experience, potentially improving the models' ability to detect subtle or less common trauma-related anomalies.

Leveraging the entire dataset for training from scratch could yield more comprehensive insights into the dataset, potentially enabling the models to adapt better to its diversity. Moreover, utilizing ensemble learning techniques stands as a promising future direction. Ensemble learning involves combining predictions from multiple models, potentially leading to more accurate and robust results. Implementing ensemble methods could enhance the models' ability to generalize and accurately classify a broader spectrum of traumatic injuries. These future scopes hold the potential to address the challenges we encountered and propel our research to more effective and comprehensive solutions for abdominal trauma detection.

Data Availability Statement: For our research we built DL models using Kaggle's RSNA 2023 Abdominal Trauma Detection dataset, available at: https://kaggle.com/competitions/rsna-2023-abdominal-trauma-detection.

Experimental code, results are available in GitHub repository at: https://github.com/prakash02dec/Abdominal-Trauma-Detection

REFERENCES

Aggarwal, R., Sounderajah, V., Martin, G., et al. (2021). Diagnostic accuracy of deep learning in medical imaging: A systematic review and meta-analysis. *npj Digital Medicine*, 4, 65. https://doi.org/10.1038/s41746-021-00438-z

Al-Antari, M. A. (2023). Artificial intelligence for medical diagnostics-existing and future AI technology! *Diagnostics (Basel)*, 13(4), 688. https://doi.org/10.3390/diagnostics13040688

Bruls, R. J. M., & Kwee, R. M. (2020). Workload for radiologists during on-call hours: Dramatic increase in the past 15 years. *Insights Imaging*, 11, 121. https://doi.org/10.1186/s13244-020-00925-z

Bruno, M. A., Walker, E. A., & Abujudeh, H. H. (2015). Understanding and confronting our mistakes: The epidemiology of error in radiology and strategies for error reduction. *Radiographics,* 35, 1668–1676. https://doi.org/10.1148/rg.2015150023

Clancy, T. V., Gary Maxwell, J., Covington, D. L., Brinker, C. C., & Blackman, D. (2001). A statewide analysis of level I and II trauma centers for patients with major injuries. *Journal of Trauma*, 51(2), 346–351. https://doi.org/10.1097/00005373-200108000-00021

Colak, E., Lin, H.-M., Ball, R., Davis, M., Flanders, A., Jalal, S., Magudia, K., Marinelli, B., Nicolaou, S., Prevedello, L., Rudie, J., Shih, G., Vazirabad, M., & Mongan, J. (2023). *RSNA 2023 Abdominal Trauma Detection*. Kaggle. https://doi.org/10.1148/ryai.240334

Emami, P., & Javanmardi, K. (2023). Enhancing emergency response through artificial intelligence in emergency medical services dispatching; a letter to editor. *Archives of Academic Emergency Medicine*, 11(1), e60. https://kaggle.com/competitions/rsna-2023-abdominal-trauma-detection

Ersoydan, S., Yakar, D., Kasalak, Ö., et al. (2023). Did medical doctors who order abdominal CT scans during on-call hours truly become worse at clinical reasoning? Yes, they did. *European Radiology,* 33, 1015–1021. https://doi.org/10.1007/s00330-022-09121-7

Gad, M. A., Saber, A., Farrag, S., Shams, M. E., & Ellabban, G. M. (2012). Incidence, patterns, and factors predicting mortality of abdominal injuries in trauma patients. *North American Journal of Medicine and Science*, 4(3), 129–134. https://doi.org/10.4103/1947-2714.93889

Ghaffar Nia, N., Kaplanoglu, E., & Nasab, A. (2023). Evaluation of artificial intelligence techniques in disease diagnosis and prediction. *Discover Artificial Intelligence*, 3, 5. https://doi.org/10.1007/s44163-023-00049-5

Gong, J., Mei, D., Yang, M., Xu, J., & Zhou, Y. (2017). Emergency CT of blunt abdominal trauma: Experience from a large urban hospital in Southern China. *Quantitative Imaging in Medicine and Surgery*, 7(4), 461–468. https://doi.org/10.21037/qims.2017.08.03

Hasanah, S. A., Pravitasari, A. A., Abdullah, A. S., Yulita, I. N., & Asnawi, M. H. (2023). A deep learning review of ResNet architecture for lung disease identification in CXR image. *Applied Sciences*, 13, 13111. https://doi.org/10.3390/app132413111

Hassan, R., & Abd Aziz, A. (2010). Computed Tomography (CT) imaging of injuries from blunt abdominal trauma: A pictorial essay. *Malaysian Journal of Medical Sciences*, 17(2), 29–39. PMID: 22135535; PMCID: PMC3216157.

Jansen, J. O., Yule, S. R., & Loudon, M. A. (2008). Investigation of blunt abdominal trauma. *BMJ*, 336(7650), 938–942. https://doi.org/10.1136/bmj.39534.686192.80

Kode, H., & Barkana, B. D. (2023). Deep learning- and expert knowledge-based feature extraction and performance evaluation in breast histopathology images. *Cancers (Basel)*, 15(12), 3075. https://doi.org/10.3390/cancers15123075

Kulkarni, P. A., & Singh, H. (2023). Artificial intelligence in clinical diagnosis: Opportunities, challenges, and hype. *JAMA*, 330(4), 317–318. https://doi.org/10.1001/jama.2023.11440

Lynch, T., Kilgar, J., & Al Shibli, A. (2018). Pediatric abdominal trauma. *Current Pediatric Reviews*, 14(1), 59–63. https://doi.org/10.2174/1573396313666170815100547

Meena, K., Veeramakali, T., Singh, N. H., et al. (2023). Deep learning techniques for prediction of pneumonia from lung CT images. *Soft Computing*, 27, 8481–8491. https://doi.org/10.1007/s00500-023-08280-z

Piliuk, K., & Tomforde, S. (2023). Artificial intelligence in emergency medicine. A systematic literature review. *International Journal of Medical Informatics*, 180, 105274. https://doi.org/10.1016/j.ijmedinf.2023.105274

Richens, J. G., Lee, C. M., & Johri, S. (2020). Improving the accuracy of medical diagnosis with causal machine learning. *Nature Communications*, 11, 3923. https://doi.org/10.1038/s41467-020-17419-7

Ruikar, D., Kamble, P., Ruikar, A., et al. (2023). DNN-Based knee OA severity prediction system: Pathologically robust feature engineering approach. *SN Computer Science*, 4, 58. https://doi.org/10.1007/s42979-022-01476-4

Ruikar, D. D., Santosh, K. C., & Hegadi, R. S. (2019a). Automated fractured bone segmentation and labeling from CT images. *Journal of Medical Systems*, 43, 60. https://doi.org/10.1007/s10916-019-1176-x

Ruikar, D. D., Santosh, K. C., & Hegadi, R. S. (2019b). Contrast stretching-based unwanted artifacts removal from CT images. In K. Santosh & R. Hegadi (eds.), *Recent Trends in Image Processing and Pattern Recognition*. RTIP2R 2018. Communications in Computer and Information Science, vol 1036. Springer, Singapore. https://doi.org/10.1007/978-981-13-9184-2_1

Shafiq, M., & Gu, Z. (2022). Deep residual learning for image recognition: A survey. *Applied Sciences*, 12, 8972. https://doi.org/10.3390/app12188972

Simon, L. V., Lopez, R. A., & King, K. C. (2023). *Blunt Force Trauma*. https://www.ncbi.nlm.nih.gov/books/NBK470338/

Vearrier, L., Derse, A. R., Basford, J. B., Larkin, G. L., & Moskop, J. C. (2022). Artificial intelligence in emergency medicine: Benefits, risks, and recommendations. *The Journal of Emergency Medicine*, 62(4), 492–499. https://doi.org/10.1016/j.jemermed.2022.01.001

Willmann, J. K., Roos, J. E., Platz, A., Pfammatter, T., Hilfiker, P. R., & Marincek, B. (2002). Weishaupt D. Multidetector CT: Detection of active hemorrhage in patients with blunt abdominal trauma. *American Journal of Roentgenology*, 179(2), 437–444. https://doi.org/10.2214/ajr.179.2.1790437

Yue, W., Liu, S., & Li, Y. (2023). Eff-PCNet: An efficient pure CNN network for medical image classification. *Applied Sciences*, 13, 9226. https://doi.org/10.3390/app13169226

Yun, S. J., Kim, H. C., Yang, D. M., Kim, S. W., Rhee, S. J., & Ahn, S. E. (2017). Diagnostic errors when interpreting abdominopelvic computed tomography: A pictorial review. *British Journal of Radiology*, 90(1073), 20160928. https://doi.org/10.1259/bjr.20160928

10 Transparent-ATC-DNN

Deep Neural Networks–Based ATC Drug Class Prediction Using 17 Molecular Properties and Transparency Analysis

Anushka Chaurasia, Deepak Kumar, and Yogita

10.1 INTRODUCTION

The Anatomical Therapeutic Chemical (ATC) system, developed by the World Health Organization (WHO 2003), is internationally used to monitor medication usage across different populations and time frames (Chen et al. 2012; Cheng et al. 2017) It classifies active pharmaceutical substances into distinct groups based on their specific target organ or system of action and their chemical, pharmacological, and therapeutic properties. Predicting ATC drug classes is vital for multiple reasons, as it accelerates drug development and repurposing, enabling faster identification of therapeutic uses based on molecular properties (Lublóy 2014). Further, it enhances drug safety by anticipating potential interactions or side effects, increasing patient safety. In the realm of personalized medicine, ATC class prediction helps tailor drug therapies to individuals, improving therapeutic results. Additionally, it aids regulatory agencies in monitoring and managing drug utilization.

The prediction of ATC drug classes is of significant importance. Various properties of drugs exert distinct effects on pharmacological and pharmacokinetic (D'Souza et al. 2023) processes. Consequently, different chemical properties, such as fingerprints (Gallo et al. 2022), chemical-chemical interactions (Liu et al. 2015), 17 molecular properties (Das and Hussain Mazumder 2021) and SMILES structures, respectively, are employed for this purpose. Although the molecular properties of drugs provide significant insights into a drug's potential mechanism of action, pharmacokinetics, and pharmacodynamics (Longuespée et al. 2021), these properties have not been thoroughly analyzed for this purpose. Most of the existing works related to ATC drug class prediction have focused on different ML techniques. While these methods demonstrate remarkable accuracy and low loss values, they suffer from a lack of precision due

DOI: 10.1201/9781003624875-14

to a high false positive rate. ATC drug class is a multi-label classification problem that involves multiple therapeutic effects and targets different body systems simultaneously. For instance, acetylsalicylic acid, known as aspirin (used in pain reduction and blood-thinning, which can reduce the ability of platelets to stick together and form clots while affecting multiple physiological areas), exemplifies this multi-label scenario as it is classified into C (cardiovascular system), B (blood and blood-forming organs), N (nervous system), and M (musculoskeletal system) at the same time (Wishart et al. 2018). Furthermore, it contends with the issue of class imbalance, where drug instances across different labels are distorted. Additionally, the absence of transparency analysis makes it challenging to discern which properties contribute to the observed performance metrics.

The objectives of the present work are mentioned below:

1. To reduce the false positive rate in the prediction of ATC drug class prediction using 17 molecular properties.
2. To analyze the contribution of different molecular properties by transparency analysis and to categorize them into different baskets depending on their relevance in their drug class prediction.

To achieve these stated objectives, a multi-label deep neural network-based framework (Transparent-ATC-DNN) has been proposed, which deploys MLSMOTE for addressing the issue of class imbalance and performs transparency analysis by employing the SHAP method. Further, the molecular properties were categorized into different baskets and ranked from high to low depending on the relevance of the molecular properties. The proposed framework has been applied to 17 molecular properties extracted from the PubChem database and ATC data obtained from the SIDER database. It has been compared with four state-of-the-art methods in terms of hamming loss, recall, ROC-AUC, accuracy, f1-score, and precision.

The structure of the subsequent sections of the paper is as follows: Section 10.2 provides an overview of the existing literature in the field. The proposed framework is presented in Section 10.3, encompassing four components, namely Data Acquisition and Preprocessing, Handling Class Imbalance, Multi-Label Deep Neural Network Architecture, and Transparency Analysis. Section 10.4 of the paper outlines the experimental setup and subsequent analysis of the results. A discussion of the performance measures follows this. Finally, in Section 10.5, the paper concludes with a summary of the findings.

10.2 RELATED WORK

There have been disparate attempts toward ATC drug class prediction in the literature, considering different drug properties and diverse Machine Learning (ML) and Deep Learning (DL) techniques (Das and Hussain Mazumder 2024). Logistic regression has been employed by authors (Liu et al. 2015) to predict ATC classes using a similarity-based method that considers numerous drug properties, including chemical-chemical interactions, chemical structures, side effects, gene expressions, and drug target proteins. Additionally, drug molecular targets and ATC classes have been predicted by examining 3D similarity, fragment occurrence, physicochemical properties, and molecular fingerprints, specifically FP24, MDL (166), and ECFP4, by authors (Gallo et al. 2022; Guo et al. 2023) using logistic regression, support vector machine (SVM), k-nearest neighbors (KNN), decision tree (DT), Gaussian naive Bayes, and random forest (RF). Vaidya et al. (2018) have used LibSVM based on over 1700 drug-like properties for ATC class prediction. Das and Hussain Mazumder (2021) uses 17 molecular properties for predicting the ATC drug classes using four machine learning classifiers, namely ETC, KNN, DT, and RF. An information extraction (IE) and machine learning (ML) based framework was introduced by Gurulingappa et al. (2009) to categorize drugs into ATC classes based on text data encompassing pharmacological, systemic, therapeutic, and chemical details. A data-driven network-based label space partition (NLSP) approach is used by Wang et al. (2019) for multi-label prediction of ATC. It utilizes structural and fingerprint similarities and chemical-chemical interactions with other compounds from diverse ATC categories. Community detection algorithms enhance the model's performance by identifying label clusters. The jackknife method is employed for model validation in the multi-label learning framework. While Peng et al. (2021) proposed a network-based approach by using seven types of fingerprints and protein targets interaction network to predict ATC codes for drugs, validated the models, and applied them to predict potential activities on heart failure, which were further verified through in vitro experiments. While Chen et al. (2018), inferring presented a network-based method that combined the shortest path and random walk with restart approaches to forecast ATC classes of pharmaceuticals using chemical-chemical relationships. Olson and Singh (2017) used tiered learning, an architecture of machine learning to predict ATC classes from chemical structure, chemical-chemical association, and chemical target association.

In the realm of deep learning, various innovative approaches have been developed. Zhao et al. (2020) proposed a deep residual network that utilizes structural similarity to predict ATC drug classes, highlighting the integration of advanced neural architectures for specific classification tasks. Additionally, an ensemble-based method involving a convolutional neural network (CNN) and long short-term memory (LSTM) models was introduced by Nanni et al. (2020) for ATC class classification, utilizing chemical structure, fingerprints, and chemical-chemical interactions. Furthermore, Lumini and Nanni (2018) developed a CNN-based multi-label classifier system, which has demonstrated superior prediction quality across five metrics—aiming, coverage, accuracy, absolute true rates, and absolute false rates—signaling a promising advancement in addressing ATC classification challenges.

The necessity of transparency analysis in deep learning models for a better understanding of the trained model with respect to data has been considered in different applications, namely adverse drug reactions, disease-gene (Madeddu et al. 2020), polypharmacy (Rajakumar et al. 2021), drug treatment, drug repurposing (Fang et al. 2018), etc. An ensemble SVM method for predicting adverse drug reactions, incorporating SHAP for interpreting the model's logic, was implemented by Joshi et al. (2021). Furthermore, the XGBoost algorithm was applied by Petsis et al. (2022) to forecast the number of emergency department (ED) visits at the University Hospital of Ioannina, Greece, considering factors such as historical data, temporal patterns, holidays, and weather conditions. In these instances, the SHAP framework has been instrumental in enhancing the understanding of the decision-making processes within the models. A methodology employing an RNN with an attention mechanism to provide interpretable explanations in the medical context of adverse drug event predictions and to compare its results with those obtained using SHAP was proposed by Rebane et al. (2021). Across these studies, the SHAP framework has significantly contributed to an enhanced understanding of the decision-making processes of the models.

Overall, based on the literature survey, it can be stated that ATC drug class prediction using ML and DL techniques is an important task for which different types of drug properties, namely drug-likeness properties, 17 molecular properties, chemical interaction, chemical structure, gene expression, drug target proteins, and fingerprints have been considered in a number of works, but the 17 molecular properties for drugs are still underexplored. However, the 17 molecular properties need to be further investigated, as these properties are capable of reflecting the drug-likeness and pharmacological properties of a compound, which relate to its therapeutic and chemical classification. While ML techniques are improving in performance, they require handcrafted properties that necessitate domain expertise. In contrast, DL techniques do not require handcrafted properties but have an opaque nature that necessitates the transparency analysis of DL models considering the 17 molecular properties of drugs for ATC drug class prediction. This observation frames the motivation for the present work.

10.3 METHODOLOGY

The proposed Transparent-ATC-DNN framework, illustrated in Figure 10.1, has been divided into four modules: Data Acquisition and Preprocessing, Handling Class Imbalance, Multilabel Deep Neural Network Architecture, and Transparency Analysis. Each module has been described in detail in the following sections.

10.3.1 Datasets Acquisition and Preprocessing

The dataset acquisition and preprocessing module has comprised two steps: data acquisition and data preprocessing. In the data acquisition step, data related to ATC drug classes and molecular drug properties have been initially extracted from SIDER (Kuhn et al. 2016) and PubChem (Kim et al. 2016), respectively. This database includes PubChem IDs and categorizes drugs into 14 distinct anatomical classes, including Antiparasitic products (P), Antineoplastic, Immunomodulating agents (L), as shown in Figure 10.2. The 17-MD (Molecular Descriptors/properties) have been extracted from PubChem IDs. This extraction, conducted using the Python package PubChemPy, includes molecular weight, XLogP, and other descriptors as detailed in Figure 10.2, with data sourced from PubChem (Kim et al. 2016). Subsequently, a comprehensive dataset has been compiled by mapping these molecular properties

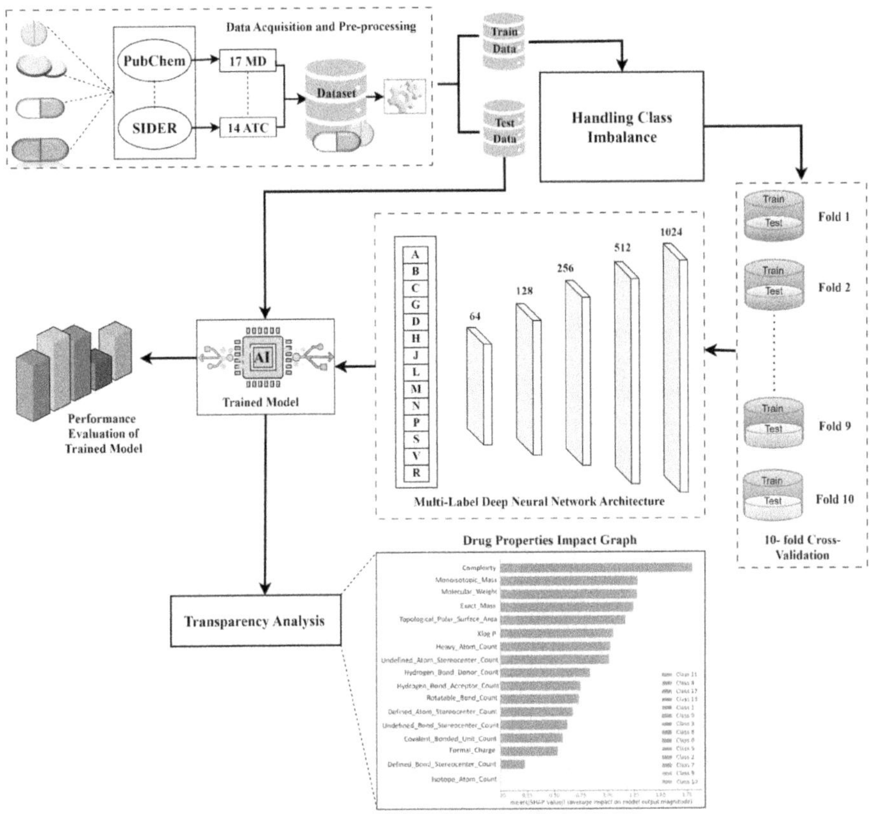

FIGURE 10.1 Architecture of the Proposed Transparent-ATC-DNN Framework.[1]

with ATC drug classes using drug_id. This dataset encompasses 1118 distinct medications and includes 17 computed physical and chemical properties of the drugs, alongside their corresponding 14 ATC class labels (Das et al. 2022). In the preprocessing steps, it has been observed that the XLogP column contained missing values. To address this, the mean value of the XLogP column has been calculated and used to fill in these missing entries. This approach ensures consistency in the dataset, allowing for more accurate analysis and interpretation of the drug properties in relation to their ATC classifications.

10.3.2 Handling Class Imbalance

The dataset exhibits class imbalance as a result of the uneven distribution of data samples among different labels. Class P has precisely 25 samples, Class N has precisely 250 samples, and Class D has precisely 50 samples as seen in Figure 10.3. This problem often leads to subpar predictive performance that requires resolution.

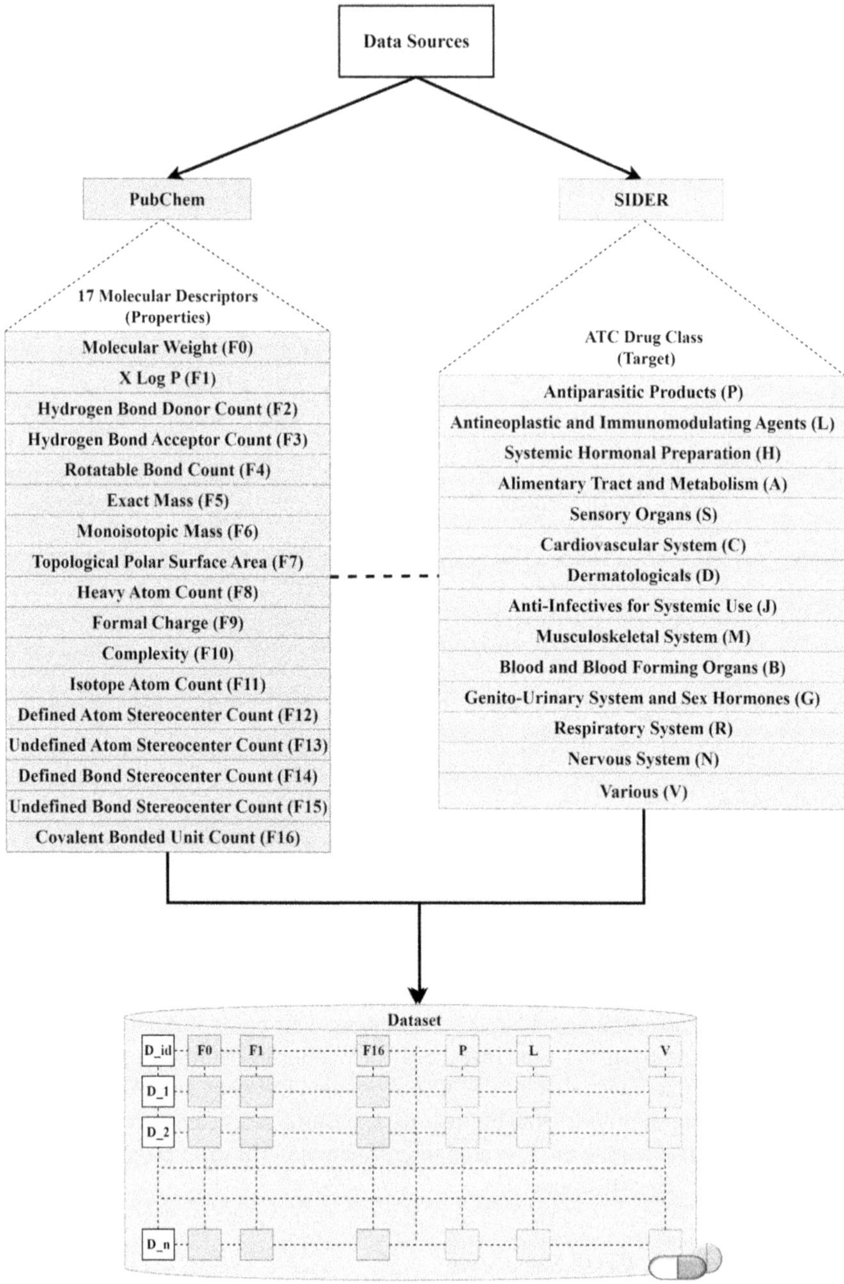

FIGURE 10.2 Data Acquisition Process.

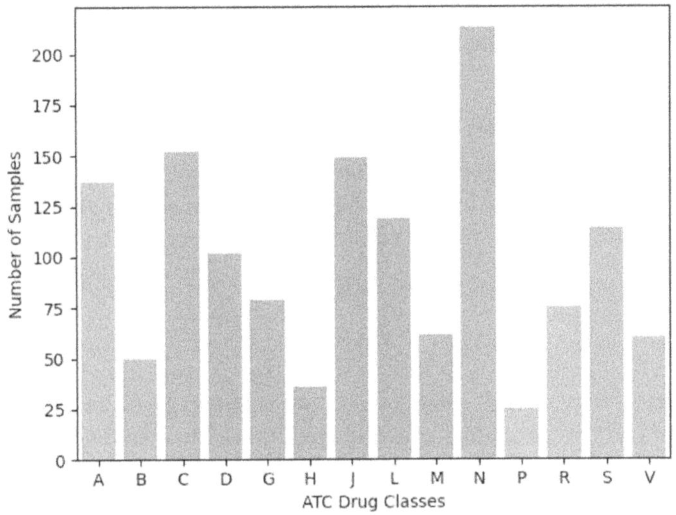

FIGURE 10.3 Total Number of Samples in Each Class.

Multilabel Synthetic Minority Over Sampling Technique (MLSMOTE) is applied to tackle the mentioned challenge (Charte et al. 2015). It focuses on augmenting data for underrepresented classes, balancing their distribution, and consequently improving the effectiveness of the classifier algorithm.

The technique involves selecting a minority class instance randomly, nearest neighbor search, and synthetic dataset generation. In minority class instance selection, the mean imbalance ratio and IRLbl (imbalance ratio per label) of each label are calculated using Equations 10.1 and 10.2, where X′ is the dataset that contains properties and labels, T is the set of labels, T_t is the last label in the set, and Y_j is the label sets associated with the jth instance in X′.

$$IRLbl(t) = \frac{argmax_{t`=T_1}^{T_{|T|}} \left(\sum_{j=1}^{|X'|} f(t`, Y_j)\right)}{\sum_{j=1}^{|X'|} f(t, Y_j)}, h(t, Y_j) = \begin{cases} 1\, for\, t \in Y_j \\ 0\, otherwise \end{cases} \tag{10.1}$$

$$Mean\ Imbalance\ Ratio = \frac{1}{|T|} \sum_{t=T_1}^{T_{|T|}} \left(IRLbl(t)\right) \tag{10.2}$$

If the IRLbL value exceeds the mean imbalance ratio, the label is identified as a minority label. This identification continues until all minority labels are isolated and saved in 'labelsets.' For each sample within the minority label, the Euclidean distance is computed with neighbors. From these neighbors, 'n' instances are chosen, and synthetic samples are generated, preserving their original property dimensions.

These newly created samples receive labels through a majority voting method and are smoothly merged into the primary dataset.

10.3.3 Multi-Label Deep Neural Networks Architecture

This section presents the proposed architecture that employs deep neural networks to predict ATC drug classes based on 17-MD properties, as depicted in Figure 10.4. Given X is the input matrix, where each row represents one of the 17-MD properties, i.e.,

$$X \in \mathbb{R}^{n\times17} \tag{10.3}$$

In this context, n is defined as the number of instances. These properties are used as the input layer of the architecture and are followed by five hidden layers whose node sizes are 1024, 512, 256, 128, and 64, respectively. For each hidden layer ℓ, the output H_ℓ is represented in Equation 10.4.

$$\mathrm{H}_\ell = \mathrm{ReLU}\left(W_\ell \cdot H_{\ell-1} + b_\ell\right) \tag{10.4}$$

Where W_ℓ is the weight matrix, b_ℓ is known as the bias vector for the layer ℓ, and H_ℓ is the input X. The activation function rectified linear unit (ReLU) (Agarap 2018), is utilized by these layers, allowing nonlinearity to be handled effectively by the model. Following the hidden layers, a dense output layer containing 14 neurons is introduced, corresponding to the total number of classes in the dataset, as shown in Equation 10.5.

$$\mathrm{H}_\ell = \sigma\left(W_\mathrm{o} \cdot H_{\ell\mathrm{ast}} + b_\mathrm{o}\right) \tag{10.5}$$

Where W_o is the weight matrix, b_o is the bias vector for the output layer, and σ is the sigmoid function. A sigmoid activation function (Maxwell et al., 2017) is well suited to multilabel classification because it outputs independent probabilities for each label and pairs seamlessly with the common architectures and loss functions used in these tasks. L2 regularization with weight decay (0.0001) is applied to each hidden layer, as described in Equation 10.6. By adding a penalty term to the loss function proportional to the weights' square, the regularization method prevents the model from overfitting the data. It also aids in making the model more generalized.

$$L2_{penalty} = \lambda \sum_{i,j} \left(w_{\ell\mathrm{ij}}\right)^2 \tag{10.6}$$

The model comprises a total of 716,622 trainable parameters. These parameters are optimized using the Adam optimizer with a learning rate of 0.001, coupled with a binary cross-entropy loss function.

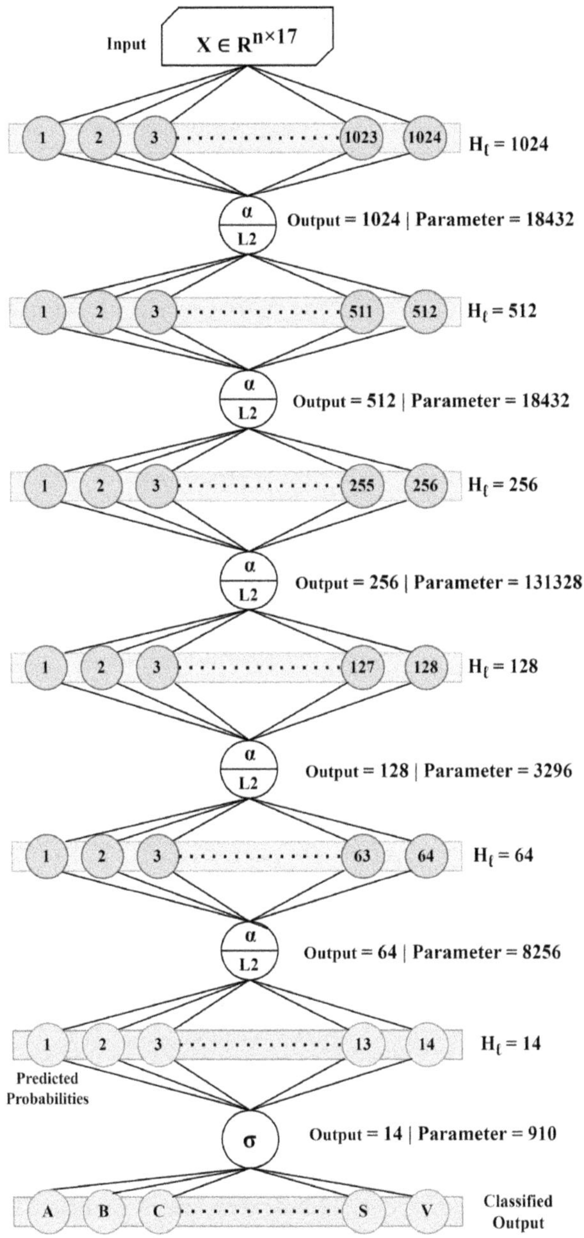

FIGURE 10.4 Multi-Label Deep Neural Networks Architecture.

10.3.4 Transparency Analysis

Deep learning models often lack transparency, so it is crucial to analyze how the proposed multi-label deep neural network architecture makes decisions based on its input variables (Agarwal and Das, 2020). The suggested framework employs SHAP, based on the optimum shapley values derived from game theory (Lundberg and Lee 2017). The outcomes of this approach illustrate the impact of each characteristic on the anticipated output. According to Chen (2021), SHAP sees the Shapley value as a mechanism for attributing properties to a model. It considers the model's predictive value to be the sum of the attribute values of each input property:

$$M(f`) = \varnothing_0 + \sum_{i=1}^{X`} \varnothing_i f`_i \tag{10.7}$$

In this context, M signifies the proposed multi-label DNN model, while $f' \in 0,1^M$ symbolizes the observability of each specific property (1 for observable, 0 for non-observable). X′ represents the total quantity of inputs, and each property's attribution value or SHapley value is denoted as $\phi_i \in R$. The constant of the proposed model, represented by ϕ_0, is calculated as the predicted mean of all training samples. When discussing global interpretability, the aggregated SHAP values illustrate the extent to which each predictor impacts the outcome variable. The significance of property j, specifically, is determined as follows:

$$\varnothing_j \equiv \frac{1}{|D|!} \sum_{F \subseteq X \setminus \{j\}} |F|!(|D| - |f| - 1)!A \tag{10.8}$$

$$A = \left[O(F \cup \{j\}) - O(F)\right] \tag{10.9}$$

In this context, O (F) denotes the interpretation of a proposed model's output utilizing a property set F, while D stands for the exhaustive list of all properties. The influence of a particular property, denoted as j (ϕ_j), is calculated by averaging its impact across all potential permutations of a property set.

10.4 EXPERIMENTAL SETUP AND RESULT ANALYSIS

10.4.1 Experimental Setup

The proposed Transparent-ATC-DNN framework, which predicts ATC drug classes using 17 molecular properties, has been implemented in scikit-learn and evaluated on Windows 10 (64-bit) with an Intel i7-5300U CPU, 64 GB RAM, and an NVIDIA Quadro P600 GPU (64 GB). Visualization and transparency analyses have been conducted using matplotlib, seaborn, and the SHAP library. The hyperparameters of ML models have been exhibited in Table 10.1 where the SVM model has utilized a radial basis function (rbf) kernel for its computational operations. Concurrently, the

TABLE 10.1
Hyperparameter of XGBoost and SVM on 17 Molecular Properties Dataset

Models	Hyperparameter
XGBoost	estimator: 50, learning rate: 0.001
SVM	C: 100.0, kernel: 'rbf', gamma: 5.86416154e-08, probability: True

TABLE 10.2
Hyperparameter of Deep Learning Models on 17 Molecular Properties Dataset

Models	Epochs	Hidden Layers	AF	Optimizer	Learning Rate
1D-CNN	150	Conv (32,64) MaxPool (2,2) Kernel size (3,3)	ReLU	Adam	0.001
LSTM	150	LSTM (75,50,50)	ReLU	Adam	0.001

XGBoost algorithm has been trained with a learning rate of 0.001 and 50 estimators to enhance prediction accuracy.

Table 10.2 illustrates the hyperparameters of the deep learning architectures evaluated in this study. Both the 1D convolutional neural network (1D-CNN) and the long short-term memory (LSTM) model are trained for 150 epochs and employ the Adam optimizer with a learning rate of 0.001 and Rectified Linear Unit (ReLU) activations in their hidden layers. The 1D-CNN comprises two convolutional layers with 32 and 64 filters, respectively, each using a 3×3 kernel, followed by a 2×2 max-pooling layer to downsample feature maps. In contrast, the LSTM architecture consists of three stacked recurrent layers with 75, 50, and 50 units; the second layer is configured to return full sequences, while the third outputs only its final state. By holding the optimizer, learning rate, and activation function constant, this configuration isolates the impact of convolutional versus recurrent architectures on multilabel classification performance.

10.4.2 Performance Metrics

The predictive capabilities of the proposed Transparent-ATC-DNN framework, compared to ML, ensemble, and DL models, are analyzed using five key performance measures: accuracy, precision, recall, F1 score, ROC-AUC, and hamming loss. Precision has been defined as the ratio of correctly predicted positive labels to the total number of labels predicted as positive across all labels in the dataset. Recall has been calculated for each data sample as the ratio of correctly predicted labels to the actual number of labels, reflecting the ability of the model to identify all relevant instances. The harmonic mean of precision and recall, known as the F1 score, has been used as a comprehensive measure of model performance. Accuracy, or the exact match ratio, has been represented as the fraction of samples for which every label has been correctly predicted, indicating the overall effectiveness of the model. Hamming loss has been described as the average rate at which the model misclassifies labels. The corresponding equations are presented below.

$$Accuracy = \frac{1}{N.K}\sum_{m=1}^{N}\sum_{t=1}^{K} x(a_{m,t} = b_{m,t}) \tag{10.11}$$

$$Hamming\ Loss(H - L) = \frac{1}{N}\sum_{m=1}^{N}\left(\frac{1}{K}\sum_{t=1}^{K} x(a_{m,t} = b_{m,t})\right) \tag{10.12}$$

$$Precision = \frac{1}{N}\sum_{m=1}^{N}\frac{|a_{m,t} \cap b_{m,t}|}{|b_{m,t}|} \tag{10.13}$$

$$Recall = \frac{1}{N}\sum_{m=1}^{N}\frac{|a_{m,t} \cap b_{m,t}|}{|a_{m,t}|} \tag{10.14}$$

$$F1 - Score = \frac{1}{N}\sum_{m=1}^{N}\frac{2|a_{m,t} \cap b_{m,t}|}{|a_{m,t}| + |b_{m,t}|} \tag{10.15}$$

Where N is the count of data samples, K is the count of labels, $a_{m,t}$ is the true label for the tth label of the mth sample, $b_{m,t}$ is the predicted label for the tth label of the mth sample, and x(.) is the indicator function, equating to 1 if $a_{m,t} = b_{m,t}$ and 0 otherwise.

10.4.3 Result Analysis and Discussion

In this section, the performance of the proposed Transparent-ATC-DNN framework is discussed. Additionally, the contributions of the 17 molecular properties to ATC drug class prediction are analyzed and classified as either low or high contributing properties.

10.4.3.1 Performance Analysis of Transparent-ATC-DNN

The performance of the Transparent-ATC-DNN framework has been exhibited in Table 10.3, using 10 distinct experimental folds, with four critical evaluation metrics employed: precision, recall, F1 score, and ROC-AUC. Each metric has provided insights into various aspects of the model's predictive accuracy and reliability in ATC drug class prediction. Notably, in fold 5, all metrics have performed well, with a precision of 96.06%, a TPR of 97.07%, and a F1 score of 96.94%, indicating the model's effective positive prediction capability under the specific dataset conditions. The

TABLE 10.3
Performance Metrics of the Transparent-ATC-DNN Framework Across 10 Folds

Folds	Accuracy	Precision	Recall	F1-Score	ROC-AUC	Hamming Loss
1	0.9814	0.9567	0.9641	0.9603	0.9755	0.01599
2	0.9817	0.9593	0.9738	0.9665	0.9809	0.01472
3	0.9849	0.9605	0.9744	0.9674	0.9813	0.01629
4	0.9851	0.9510	0.9770	0.9639	0.9812	0.01804
5	0.9834	0.9639	0.9724	0.9681	0.9809	0.01453
6	0.9857	0.9542	0.9642	0.9591	0.9755	0.01453
7	0.9817	0.9532	0.9703	0.9616	0.9782	0.01815
8	0.9825	0.9501	0.9708	0.9603	0.9779	0.01653
9	0.9818	0.9515	0.9712	0.9612	0.9783	0.01406
10	0.9822	0.9477	0.9713	0.9594	0.9778	0.01608
Training Time					15.02 sec per fold	

ROC-AUC metric has consistently possessed high discriminative power, peaking notably at 98.12% in fold 5, underscoring the model's robustness in differentiating between classes across a 0.5 threshold. This consistency across various folds suggests that the model is reliable and performs well on different data subsets. The high values in the fifth fold suggest that the model has generalized well in this instance. However, it also highlights the importance of meticulous model tuning to secure consistent predictive accuracy.

Table 10.4 and Figure 10.5 contain the results of the proposed architecture for each 14 ATC classes in the fifth fold. The model has demonstrated strong performance across all single-label subtasks of ATC prediction, achieving a precision, recall, and F1-score of 1.00, particularly for the label of Systemic Hormonal Preparation. Additionally, the ROC-AUC curve shows the balance between the true positive rate (recall or sensitivity) and the false positive rate, with the overall classifier's performance evaluated using the AUC. Class H (Systemic Hormonal Preparation) has attained a ROC-AUC of 1.00, while the remaining nine ATC classes have obtained a ROC-AUC of 0.99, except for classes L (Antineoplastic and Immunomodulating Agents), N (Nervous System), P (Antiparasitic Products), and R (Respiratory System), which have acquired ROC-AUC scores of 0.97, 0.95, 0.96, and 0.98, respectively. This analysis highlights the effectiveness of the proposed methodology in predicting multiple classes of the multi-label ATC prediction problem in a balanced and efficient manner.

Table 10.5 presents the ablation study of the Transparent-ATC-DNN models. The proposed model achieves a high F1-score of 98.47±.003, indicating a well-balanced performance between precision and recall. Regarding hamming loss, the

TABLE 10.4
Evaluation of Single Label Performance for Transparent-ATC-DNN Framework

Classes	Precision	Recall	F1-Score
Alimentary Tract and Metabolism	0.93	0.96	0.94
Blood and Blood-Forming Organs	0.97	0.99	0.98
Cardiovascular System	0.86	0.93	0.9
Dermatologicals	0.96	0.99	0.97
Genitourinary System and Sex Hormones	0.95	0.99	0.97
Systemic Hormonal Preparations, Excluding Sex Hormones and Insulins	1.00	1.00	1.00
Antineoplastic and Immunomodulating Agents	0.96	0.88	0.91
Musculoskeletal System	0.86	0.94	0.95
Anti-Infective for Systemic Use	0.95	0.99	0.97
Nervous System	0.96	0.92	0.94
Antiparasitic Products, Insecticides and Repellents	0.97	1.00	0.98
Respiratory System	0.96	0.98	0.97
Sensory Organs	0.96	0.98	0.97
Various	0.97	1.00	0.98

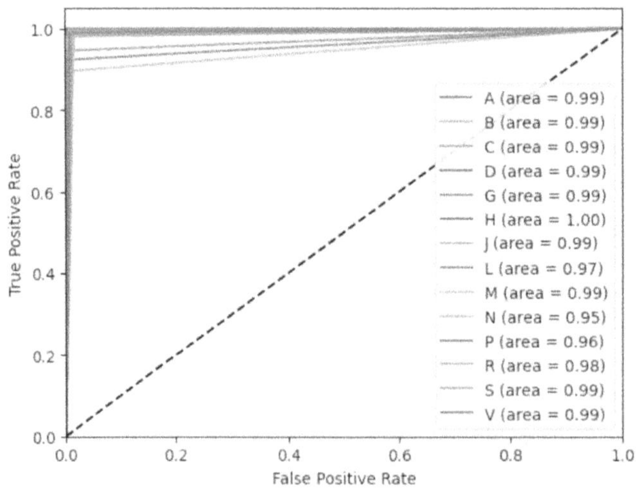

FIGURE 10.5 ROC-AUC of Transparent-ATC-DNN on 17-MD Dataset.[2]

TABLE 10.5
Ablation Study Results for Transparent-ATC-DNN Architecture

Models	Accuracy	Hamming Loss	ROC-AUC	F1-Score
DNN (1024)	91.82±.005	8.17±.005	87.33±.013	81.66±.015
DNN (1024,512)	97.67±.011	2.32±.011	96.76±.022	94.84±.028
DNN (1024,512,256)	98.30±.001	1.69±.001	98.01±.002	96.29±.003
DNN (1024,512,256,128)	98.61±.003	1.60±.003	98.25±.002	97.14±.005
Transparent-ATC-DNN	98.89±.002	1.50±.002	98.47±.003	97.58±.005

Transparent-ATC-DNN model demonstrates excellent performance with a score of 1.05±.002, slightly outperforming the DNN (1024, 5128), which scores 1.60±.002. An examination of accuracy reveals that the DNN (1024) has a lower score of 91.28 compared to the other models, while the proposed Transparent-ATC-DNN model excels with a score of 98.89. The ROC-AUC scores for all the proposed models range from 81% to 96.29%, with the Transparent-ATC-DNN model achieving the highest score of 97.85%. Overall, the proposed Transparent-ATC-DNN model exhibits the most robust performance across multiple metrics, indicating its superiority in accurately predicting ATC drug classes compared to other models.

Table 10.6 has outlined a comparative evaluation showcasing the efficacy of the proposed Transparent-ATC-DNN framework relative to existing state-of-the-art models on a 17-molecular properties dataset and models used in the literature for ATC drug class prediction. Das and Hussain Mazumder (2021) have utilized ML models using 17-MD properties datasets, where the KNN model has reached a maximal accuracy of 98.60±.010, an F1 score of 96.12±.022, an H-L of 1.99±0.010, a ROC-AUC of 97.88±.011, with an execution time of 197.58 seconds. Additionally, among the other state-of-the-art models, SVM has performed the least with the highest hamming loss of 19.25±.003, while 1D CNN, LSTM, and XGBoost have shown comparable performance. Despite good scores in all metrics, the execution times of 1D CNN and LSTM have been high, with 525.21 and 3785.65 seconds, respectively. The proposed Transparent-ATC-DNN framework has outperformed the previously state-of-the-art methods (Das and Hussain Mazumder 2021), exhibiting a higher precision of 97.47±.004, a minimum hamming loss of 1.50±.002, and superior F1 score of 97.58±.005, ROC-AUC of 98.47±.003, and an execution time of 152.12 seconds. From this observation, it can be stated that the precision score has been increased by 3.5%, while the other metrics, namely accuracy, recall, F1 score, and ROC-AUC, have been increased by 0.19 to 3%, and hamming loss has decreased by 0.3%. This outcome has highlighted the significant potential of the deep learning model in ATC drug class prediction.

TABLE 10.6
Comparison of Proposed Transparent-ATC-DNN Framework with Different ML and DL Models

Execution Time	245.56 Secs	189.65 Secs	197.58 Secs	168.78 Secs	567.14 Secs	321.58 Secs	3785.65 Secs	5295.21 Secs	152.12 Secs
ROC-AUC	97.88±.011	97.11±.012	96.91±.013	96.79±.016	62.99±.003	96.07±.002	96.57±.004	96.17±.006	98.47±.003
F1-Score	96.12±.022	95.92±.017	95.69±.018	93.72±.027	41.82±.007	94.27±.002	94.56±.005	93.88±.009	97.58±.005
Recall	97.15±.014	95.39±.021	95.02±.023	93.61±.026	30.45±.006	93.61±.004	94.83±.008	94.29±.011	97.69±.007
Precision	94.87±.031	96.47±.013	96.38±.012	93.84±.029	66.78±.009	94.95±.003	94.28±.007	93.48±.011	97.47±.004
Hamming Loss	1.99±.010	2.13±.007	2.17±.007	3.19±.011	19.25±.003	2.57±.001	2.47±.002	2.80±.004	1.50±.002
Accuracy	98.60±.010	96.89±.007	96.68±.007	95.09±.011	80.74±.003	97.42±.001	97.52±.002	97.19±.004	98.89±.002
Models	KNN (Das and Hussain Mazumder 2021)	ETC (Das and Hussain Mazumder 2021)	RF (Das and Hussain Mazumder 2021)	DT (Das and Hussain Mazumder 2021)	SVM (6)	XGBoost	1D-CNN	LSTM	Transparent-ATC-DNN

10.4.3.2 Analysis and Ranking of 17 Molecular Properties Toward the ATC Drug Class Prediction

The SHAP approach has been utilized to assess the importance and impact of each of the 17 molecular properties in predicting ATC drug classes. This analysis was conducted on four models: XGBoost, 1D-CNN, LSTM, and Transparent-ATC-DNN, as these are the top-performing models in this proposed framework regarding all performance metrics.

Figure 10.6 illustrates the importance of each of the 17 molecular properties in predicting 14 ATC drug classes. In this graph, the x-axis represents the average SHAP values, which indicate the average impact of the models on the output magnitude. These values are calculated by taking the SHAP values for each property across all data points in the dataset and calculating the average. The y-axis represents the 17 molecular properties. The color code defines the total of 14 ATC drug classes, and the color bar denotes the contribution of each property in predicting particular drug classes. The analysis reveals that complexity is the top contributing property in all four models, responsible for predicting 14 drug classes in each model. Specifically, complexity has a high impact on classes 5 and 11 in the XGBoost model, classes 11 and 4 in the LSTM model, classes 1 and 11 in the 1D-CNN model, and classes 4 and 8 in the Transparent-ATC-DNN, respectively. Monoisotopic mass is the second-most contributing property in the LSTM, Transparent-ATC-DNN, and 1D-CNN models.

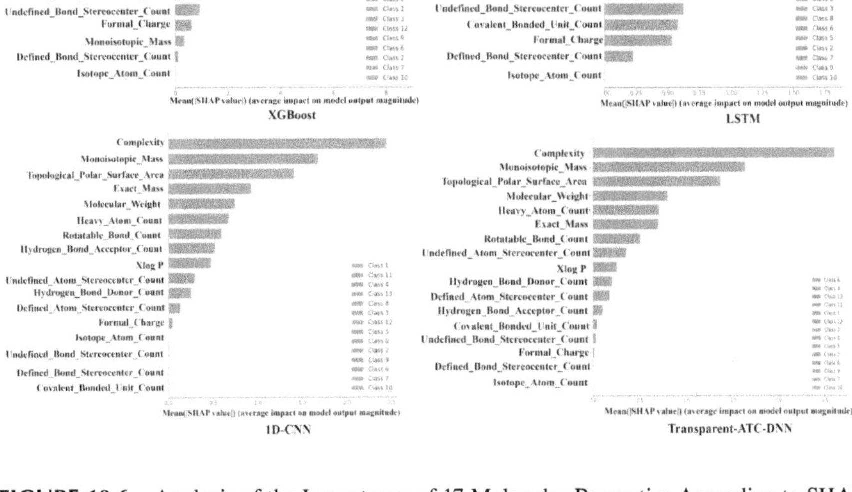

FIGURE 10.6 Analysis of the Importance of 17 Molecular Properties According to SHAP for Models XGBoost, 1D-CNN, LSTM, and Transparent-ATC-DNN.[3]

TPSA and molecular weight are also significant, ranking within the top three and four contributing properties, respectively, in the Transparent-ATC-DNN model. Across XGBoost and Transparent-ATC-DNN, heavy atom count consistently ranks within the top five, while it ranks seventh and sixth in LSTM and 1D-CNN, respectively. The analysis highlights the varying influence of these properties across different classes and models. The least important properties are the isotope atom count in XGBoost, Transparent-ATC-DNN, and LSTM, and the second least important property across all four models is the defined bond stereocenter count. Therefore, it can be stated that the top five contributing properties in the proposed Transparent-ATC-DNN framework are complexity, monoisotopic mass, topological polar surface area, molecular weight, and heavy atom count, as these properties highly contribute to the ATC drug class prediction.

Figure 10.7 has illustrated how properties ranked from the top five through all seventeen (subgroups T5–T17) have influenced performance on the four best models

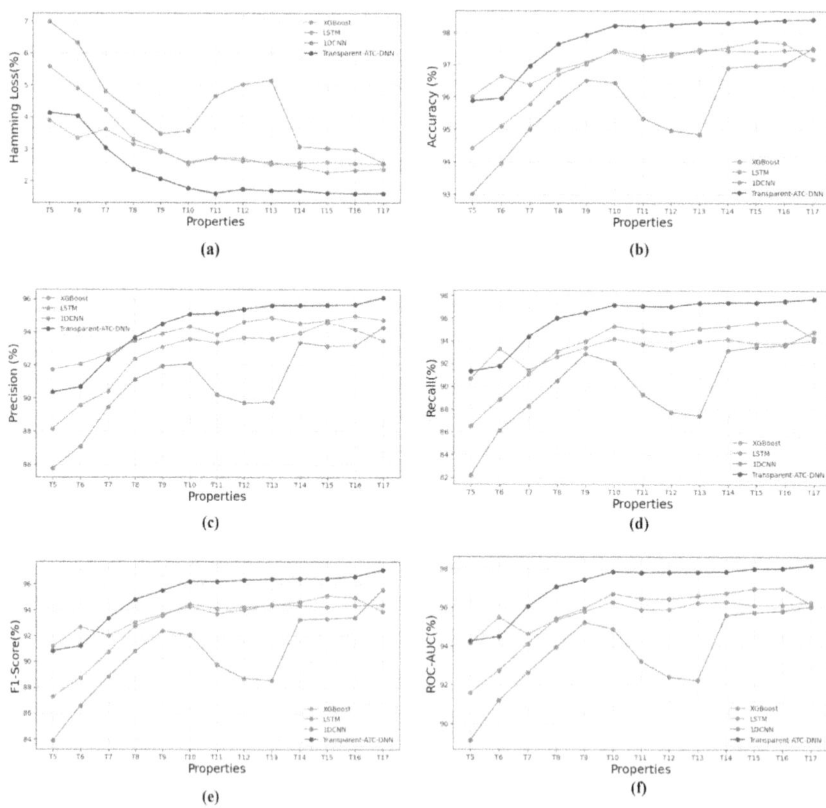

FIGURE 10.7 Analyzing the Impact of Different Features on the Performance of the Proposed Transparent-ATC-DNN Framework Regarding Hamming Loss, Precision, Recall, F1 Score, and ROC-AUC.[4]

(XGBoost, LSTM, 1D-CNN, and Transparent-ATC-DNN). Each subgroup has been used to train these models, and their precision, recall, hamming loss, ROC-AUC, and accuracy have been evaluated. Figure 10.7(a) displays the graph of hamming loss for four models in various subgroups. It reveals that the loss for all four models falls within the range of 4% to 7% at T5, decreases until T10, and then remains stable until T17. In contrast, in the case of 1D-CNN, the loss increases after T10, undergoes a rapid decrease after T13, and then remains relatively stable until T17. This variation is due to the disparities in properties, as the subgroups have been divided based on the properties' contribution in the proposed Transparent-ATC-DNN.

Figures 10.7 (b), (c), (d), (e), and (f) show the graphs of accuracy, precision, recall, F1-score, and ROC-AUC score, respectively, for the four models in various subgroups. At T5, the values of all performance metrics for the three models have ranged from 82% to 96%. As the number of features has increased, the values have risen until T10, reaching between 92% to 98%. After that, the values remained approximately the same until T17, except for 1D-CNN, where the values deviated from T10 and suddenly increased at T14. This is due to the ordering of the properties, as these properties have been divided based on the proposed Transparent-ATC-DNN SHAP graph. It can be concluded from this graph that after T10, there has been no significant change in performance. Additionally, it can also be analyzed that the proposed Transparent-ATC-DNN has shown superior performance in each subgroup compared to the other three models in terms of all performance metrics. Specifically, hamming loss has decreased by 0.12% to 2.48%, while accuracy has improved by 1.08% to 3.27%, precision by 1.48% to 5.05%, recall by 2.55% to 5.89%, F1-score by 2.55% to 6.05%, and ROC-AUC by 2.02% to 5.98%.

Figure 10.8 provides a detailed comparison of T5, T10, and T17 across all five performance metrics for the four leading models. For hamming loss (Figure 10.8 a), T5 has consistently yielded the highest hamming loss, while T10 has achieved a 1–4% reduction for each model; T17 then closely matches T10 for XGBoost, LSTM, and Transparent-ATC-DNN, with only a 1% further drop in the case of the 1D-CNN. In terms of accuracy (Figure 10.8 b), all models attain their lowest scores on T5, improve by 4–5% on T10, and show virtually identical performance on T17 again excepting a modest +1% gain for 1D-CNN. The average precision, recall, and F1 metrics (Figure 10.8 c–e) follow the same trend: T5 delivers the poorest results; T10 produces substantial gains (precision +3–6%, recall +4–10%, F1 +1–8%); and T17 offers only marginal additional benefits (typically +0.3–4%, most pronounced in the LSTM and CNN architectures). Finally, ROC-AUC (Figure 10.8 f) rises by 2–5% from T5 to T10 and remains effectively unchanged for T17, apart from a 1% uptick for 1D-CNN. Collectively, these results indicate that the majority of performance improvements occur when expanding from the top five to the top ten properties, and that using all seventeen adds negligible further value.

Table 10.7 illustrates how ranking molecular properties into high- and low-impact baskets based on their mean SHAP values has elucidated the decision-making processes of our top deep-learning models. By segregating properties into baskets of high and low based on their contributions to ATC drug class prediction, this ranking system serves as a pivotal tool in demystifying the 'black box' nature of these

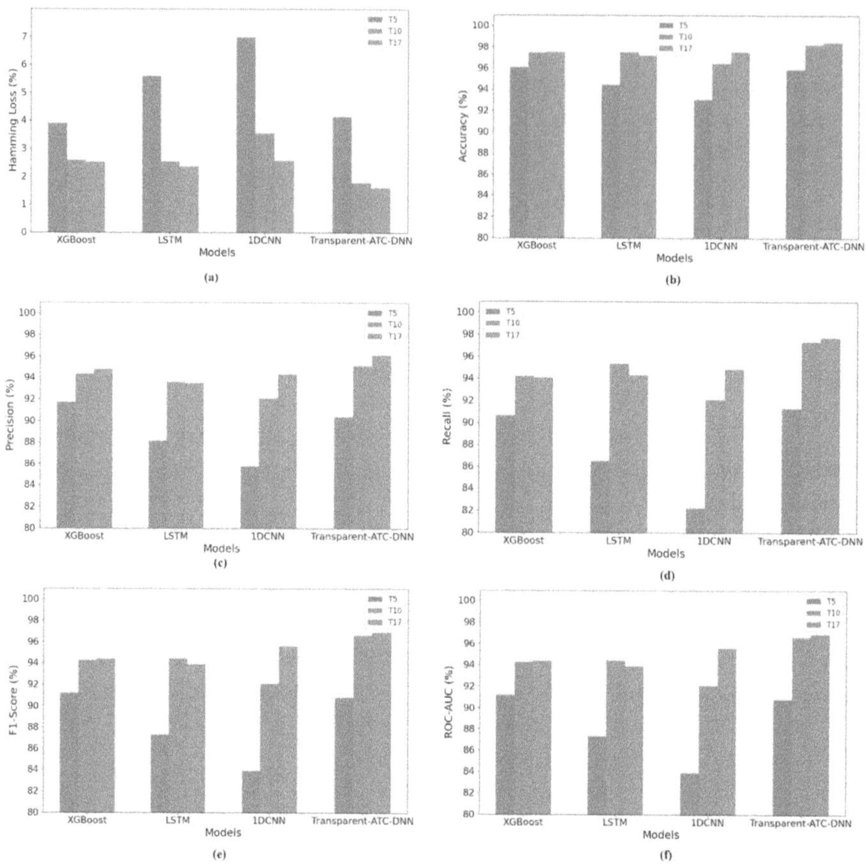

FIGURE 10.8 Comparison of XGBoost, LSTM, 1D-CNN, and Transparent-ATC-DNN Using Top 5, 10, and 17 Properties Using Metrics Hamming Loss, Accuracy, Precision, Recall, F1-Score, and ROC-AUC.[5]

models. The contrast between properties, as shown by their mean SHAP values, gives information on the underlying decision-making processes. Specifically, the identification of 'Complexity' as the property with the highest mean SHAP value of 2.5 highlights its critical role, offering insights into its substantial impact on model predictions. Similarly, the subsequent ranking of properties such as 'Monoisotopic Mass' and 'TPSA', with their respective contributions, provides a nuanced understanding of their relative importance and influence. The inclusion of properties like 'Molecular Weight' and 'Heavy Atom Count' further in the ranking demonstrates a tiered understanding of property influence, ranging from moderate to minimal contributions. Importantly, the delineation of properties with decreasing mean SHAP values beyond the top ranks reveals the diminishing impact on prediction accuracy, thus contributing to a comprehensive understanding of property relevance. The classification of properties like 'Defined Atom Stereocenter Count' and 'Isotope Atom

TABLE 10.7
Property Ranking and Mean SHAP Values (MSV)

Rank	Property Name	Contribution Level	MSV
1	Complexity	High	2.5
2	Monoisotopic mass	High	1.7
3	TPSA	High	1.4
4	Molecular weight	High	0.8
5	Heavy atom count	High	0.8
6	Exact mass	High	0.7
7	Rotatable bond count	High	0.55
8	Undefined atom stereocenter count	High	0.5
9	XlogP	High	0.4
10	Hydrogen bond donor count	High	0.4
11	Defined atom stereocenter count	Low	0.35
12	Hydrogen bond acceptor count	Low	0.3
13	Covalent bonded unit count	Low	0.25
14	Undefined bond stereocenter count	Low	0.15
15	Formal Charge	Low	0.1
16	Defined bond stereocenter count	Low	0.05
17	Isotope atom count	Low	0

Count' into lower tiers of contribution underscores the granularity of this analysis, offering a detailed perspective on the differential impact of various properties. This methodical ranking and categorization not only illuminate the operational intricacies of high-performing deep learning models but also enhance the interpretability of these complex systems, thereby bridging the gap between advanced computational techniques and their practical application in drug class prediction.

10.5 LIMITATIONS AND FUTURE WORK

Although the Transparent-ATC-DNN framework has demonstrated strong predictive performance and interpretability on our curated dataset, its generalizability across structurally diverse or noisy external collections has not yet been assessed, limiting its applicability to novel drug classes and real-world screening scenarios. Furthermore, the multi-layer deep architecture and SHAP-based interpretability have incurred non-trivial inference and explanation times, averaging 152.12 s per fold, posing challenges for high throughput and resource-constrained deployment. In addition, the exclusive reliance on seventeen molecular descriptors has not incorporated potentially informative features such as three-dimensional conformer dynamics or protein–ligand interaction signatures. To address these constraints, the following avenues can be proposed: external validation on publicly available repositories (e.g., ChEMBL, DrugBank) to assess robustness across a broader chemical space; integration of supplementary modalities (such as Protein Sequence and gene-expression profiles) to enrich feature representation; and employment of automated hyperparameter-tuning strategies to optimize network configurations for novel datasets.

10.6 CONCLUSION

A novel framework called Transparent-ATC-DNN, which incorporates a deep neural network and SHAP-based methodology, has been introduced to predict the drug class in ATC. This framework also assesses the importance and impact of 17 properties on the prediction. The Transparent-ATC-DNN framework was compared to state-of-the-art methods using six performance metrics. The results showed a high accuracy of 98.89±0.002, recall of 97.69±.007, precision of 97.47±.004, f1-score of 97.58±.005, ROC-AUC of 98.47±.003, and a low hamming loss of 1.50±0.002. The proposed framework uses the SHAP approach on high-performing models, XGBoost, LSTM, 1D-CNN, and Transparent-ATC-DNN to identify critical attributes that have a major influence on prediction results in order to improve transparency in pharmaceutical analytics. Through analysis of different subsets, ranging from the T5 to the T17, it was found that leveraging the T10 attributes yields similar results to T17. This underscores the crucial significance of these T10 properties in the prediction process. These essential properties were subsequently categorized into high and low contribution buckets. This methodology demonstrates the efficacy of the Transparent-ATC-DNN framework in multi-label classification tasks for drug prediction, providing pharmaceutical companies with a reliable tool to optimize drug research and development procedures. Through focused analysis and property selection, this framework aids in optimizing predictive accuracy and efficiency, thereby accelerating the path to market for new drugs while ensuring a deeper understanding of model decisions in the complex landscape of pharmaceutical research.

NOTES

1. For the color version of Figure 10.1, please see the Support Material page: http://www.routledge.com/9781041036876
2. For the color version of Figure 10.5, please see the Support Material page: http://www.routledge.com/9781041036876
3. For the color version of Figure 10.6, please see the Support Material page: http://www.routledge.com/9781041036876
4. For the color version of Figure 10.7, please see the Support Material page: http://www.routledge.com/9781041036876
5. For the color version of Figure 10.8, please see the Support Material page: http://www.routledge.com/9781041036876

REFERENCES

Abien Fred Agarap. Deep learning using rectified linear units (relu). arXiv preprint arXiv:1803.08375, 2018. **doi:** https://doi.org/10.48550/arXiv.1803.08375.

Namita Agarwal and Saikat Das. Interpretable machine learning tools: A survey. In *2020 IEEE Symposium Series on Computational Intelligence (SSCI)*, pages 1528–1534. IEEE, 2020. **doi:** 10.1109/SSCI47803.2020.9308260.

ATC classification. https://www.who.int/tools/atc-ddd-toolkit/atc-classification, 2003.

Francisco Charte, Antonio J Rivera, María J del Jesus, and Francisco Herrera. Mlsmote: Approaching imbalanced multilabel learning through synthetic instance generation. *Knowledge-Based Systems*, 89:385–397, 2015. **doi:** 10.1016/j.knosys.2015.07.019.

Shikun Chen. Interpretation of multi-label classification models using shapley values. arXiv preprint arXiv:2104.10505, 2021. **doi:** https://doi.org/10.48550/arXiv.2104.10505.

Lei Chen, Tao Liu, and Xian Zhao. Inferring anatomical therapeutic chemical (atc) class of drugs using shortest path and random walk with restart algorithms. *Biochimica et Biophysica Acta (BBA)-Molecular Basis of Disease*, 1864(6):2228–2240, 2018. **doi:** 10.1016/j.bbadis. 2017.12.019.

Lei Chen, Wei-Ming Zeng, Yu-Dong Cai, Kai-Yan Feng, and Kuo-Chen Chou. Predicting anatomical therapeutic chemical(atc) classification of drugs by integrating chemical-chemical interactions and similarities. *PloS One*, 7(4):e35254, 2012. **doi:** 10.1371/journal.pone.0035254.

Xiang Cheng, Shu-Guang Zhao, Xuan Xiao, and Kuo-Chen Chou. iatc-misf: A multi-label classifier for predicting the classes of anatomical therapeutic chemicals. *Bioinformatics*, 33(3):341–346, 2017. **doi:** 10.1093/bioinformatics/btw644.

P. Das and D. H. Mazumder. A comprehensive survey of studies on predicting anatomical therapeutic chemical classes of drugs. *ACM Computing Surveys*, 57(3):1–31, 2024.

Pranab Das and Dilwar Hussain Mazumder. Predicting anatomical therapeutic chemical drug classes from 17 molecules' properties of drugs by multi-label binary relevance approach with mlsmote. In 2021 5th *International Conference on Computational Biology and Bioinformatics*, pages 1–7, 2021. **doi:** 10.1145/3512452.3512453.

Pranab Das, Jerry W Sangma, and Vipin Pal. Predicting adverse drug reactions from drug functions by binary relevance multi-label classification and mlsmote. In *Practical Applications of Computational Biology & Bioinformatics, 15th International Conference (PACBB 2021)*, pages 165–173. Springer, 2022. **doi:** 10.1007/978-3-030-86258-917.

Sofia D'Souza, KV Prema, S Balaji, and Ronak Shah. Deep learning-based modelling of drug-target interaction prediction incorporating binding site information of proteins. *Interdisciplinary Sciences: Computational Life Sciences*, 15(2):306–315, 2023. **doi:** https://doi.org/10.1007/s12539-023-00557-z.

Alex Chengyu Fang, Yemao Liu, Yaping Lu, Jing Cao, and Jingbo Xia. A corpus-oriented perspective on terminologies of side effect and adverse reaction in support of text retrieval for drug repurposing. *International Journal of Data Mining and Bioinformatics*, 21(3):269–286, 2018.

Kathleen Gallo, Andrean Goede, Robert Preissner, and Bjoern-Oliver Gohlke. Superpred3.0: Drug classification and target prediction—a machine learning approach. *Nucleic Acids Research*, 50(W1): W726–W731, 2022. **doi:** https://doi.org/10.1093/nar/gkac297.

Lin Guo, Xiujuan Lei, Ming Chen, and Yi Pan. Msresg: Using gae and residual gcn to predict drug–drug interactions based on multi-source drug features. *Interdisciplinary Sciences: Computational Life Sciences*, 1–18, 2023. **doi:** https://doi.org/10.1007/s12539-023-00550-6.

Harsha Gurulingappa, Corinna Kolárik, Martin Hofmann-Apitius, and Juliane Fluck. Concept-based semi-automatic classification of drugs. *Journal of Chemical Information and Modeling*, 49(8):1986–1992, 2009. **doi:** 10.1021/ci9000844.

Pratik Joshi, Masilamani Vedhanayagam, and Raj Ramesh. An ensembled svm based approach for predicting adverse drug reactions. *Current Bioinformatics*, 16(3):422–432, 2021. **doi:** 10.2174/1574893615999200707141420.

Sunghwan Kim, Paul A Thiessen, Evan E Bolton, Jie Chen, Gang Fu, Asta Gindulyte, Lianyi Han, Jane He, Siqian He, Benjamin A Shoemaker, et al. Pubchem substance and compound databases. *Nucleic Acids Research*, 44(D1):D1202–D1213, 2016. **doi:** 10.1093/nar/gkv951.

Michael Kuhn, Ivica Letunic, Lars Juhl Jensen, and Peer Bork. The sider database of drugs and side effects. *Nucleic Acids Research*, 44(D1):D1075–D1079, 2016. **doi:** 10.1093/nar/gkv1075.

Zhongyang Liu, Feifei Guo, Jiangyong Gu, Yong Wang, Yang Li, Dan Wang, Liang Lu, Dong Li, and Fuchu He. Similarity-based prediction for anatomical therapeutic chemical classification of drugs by integrating multiple data sources. *Bioinformatics*, 31(11):1788–1795, 2015. **doi:** 10.1093/bioinformatics/btv055.

Rémi Longuespée, Dirk Theile, Margaux Fresnais, Jürgen Burhenne, Johanna Weiss, and Walter E Haefeli. Approaching sites of action of drugs in clinical pharmacology: New analytical options and their challenges. *British Journal of Clinical Pharmacology*, 87(3):858–874, 2021. **doi:** https://doi.org/10.1111/bcp.14543.

Ágnes Lublóy. Factors affecting the uptake of new medicines: A systematic literature review. *BMC Health Services Research*, 14(1):1–25, 2014. doi: https://doi.org/10.1186/1472-6963-14-469.

Alessandra Lumini and Loris Nanni. Convolutional neural networks for atc classification. *Current Pharmaceutical Design*, 24(34):4007–4012, 2018. **doi:** 10.2174/13816128246661112113438.

Scott M Lundberg and Su-In Lee. A unified approach to interpreting model predictions. *Advances in Neural Information Processing Systems*, 30, 2017. **doi:** https://doi.org/10.48550/arXiv.1705.07874.

Lorenzo Madeddu, Giovanni Stilo, and Paola Velardi. A feature-learning-based method for the disease-gene prediction problem. *International Journal of Data Mining and Bioinformatics*, 24(1):16–37, 2020.

Andrew Maxwell, Runzhi Li, Bei Yang, Heng Weng, Aihua Ou, Huixiao Hong, Zhaoxian Zhou, Ping Gong, and Chaoyang Zhang. Deep learning architectures for multi-label classification of intelligent health risk prediction. *BMC Bioinformatics*, 18:121–131, 2017. doi: 10.1186/s12859-017-1898-z.

Loris Nanni, Sheryl Brahnam, and Alessandra Lumini. Ensemble of deep learning approaches for atc classification. In *Smart Intelligent Computing and Applications: Proceedings of the Third International Conference on Smart Computing and Informatics*, Volume 1, pages 117–125. Springer, 2020. **doi:** 10.1007/978-981-13-9282-512.

Thomas Olson and Rahul Singh. Predicting anatomic therapeutic chemical classification codes using tiered learning. *BMC Bioinformatics*, 18(8):1–13, 2017. doi: https://doi.org/10.1186/s12859-017-1660-6.

Yayuan Peng, Manjiong Wang, Yixiang Xu, Zengrui Wu, Jiye Wang, Chao Zhang, Guixia Liu, Weihua Li, Jian Li, and Yun Tang. Drug repositioning by prediction of drug's anatomical therapeutic chemical code via network-based inference approaches. *Briefings in Bioinformatics*, 22(2):2058–2072, 2021. **doi:** 10.1093/bib/bbaa027.

Evangelos Kalampokis Spyridon Petsis, Areti Karamanou, and Konstantinos Tarabanis. Forecasting and explaining emergency department visits in a public hospital. *Journal of Intelligent Information Systems*, 59(2):479–500, 2022. **doi:** https://doi.org/10.1007/s1084402 2-00716-6.

Serena Rajakumar, G Kavitha, and I Sathik Ali. Extraction of drug-drug interaction information using a deep neural network. *International Journal of Data Mining and Bioinformatics*, 25(3–4):181–200, 2021.

Jonathan Rebane, Isak Samsten, Panteleimon Pantelidis, and Panagiotis Papapetrou. Assessing the clinical validity of attention-based and shap temporal explanations for adverse drug event predictions. In *2021 IEEE 34th International Symposium on Computer-Based Medical Systems (CBMS)*, pages 235–240. IEEE, 2021. **doi:** 10.1109/CBMS52027.2021.00025.

Pankaj Vaidya, Ankit Gupta, and Varun Jaiswal. Machine learning based prediction of anatomical therapeutic chemical (atc) class of drug like molecule. In *2018 International Conference on Recent Innovations in Electrical, Electronics & Communication Engineering (ICRIEECE)*, pages 1045–1048. IEEE, 2018. **doi:** 10.1109/ICRIEECE44171.2018.9009216.

Xiangeng Wang, Yanjing Wang, Zhenyu Xu, Yi Xiong, and Dong-Qing Wei. Atc-nlsp: Prediction of the classes of anatomical therapeutic chemicals using a network-based label space partition method. *Frontiers in Pharmacology*, 10:971, 2019. **doi:** https://doi.org/10.3389/fphar.2019.00971.

David S Wishart, Yannick D Feunang, An C Guo, Elvis J Lo, Ana Marcu, Jason R Grant, Tanvir Sajed, Daniel Johnson, Carin Li, Zinat Sayeeda, et al. Drugbank 5.0: A major update to the drugbank database for 2018. *Nucleic Acids Research*, 46(D1): D1074–D1082, 2018. doi: 10.1093/nar/gkx1037.

Haochen Zhao, Peng Ni, Cheng Yan, Yaohang Li, and Jianxin Wang. A novel approach based on deep residual learning to predict drug's anatomical therapeutic chemical code. In *2020 IEEE International Conference on Bioinformatics and Biomedicine (BIBM)*, pages 921–926. IEEE, 2020. **doi:** 10.1109/BIBM49941.2020.9313327.

11 Wearable IoT in Healthcare

Transforming Patient Monitoring, Chronic Care, and Independent Living

Krishnendhu Manoharan, Aswathi Bindhu Jawahar, and Philip Eappen

11.1 INTRODUCTION

Wearable technology in healthcare refers to devices that patients attach to their bodies to collect health and fitness data, which they may provide to doctors, health providers, and other providers (1). The smart wearable health devices market was valued at $13.8 billion in 2020 and is expected to balloon to $37.4 billion by 2028 (1). The wearable Internet of Things (WIoT) has the potential to become a vital part of the healthcare system. These devices offer diverse approaches to addressing a range of social and medical issues. They have the potential to reduce healthcare expenses while also improving the delivery of care and quality of life for individuals with disabilities or chronic illnesses. Wearable technology can lower hospitalization rates by promoting independent living or preventing illnesses, which can result in significant savings in healthcare services. Thus, WIoT technology presents substantial financial advantages in the healthcare industry.

Wearable devices are gaining attention due to their significant impact on healthcare practices and their ability to reduce human intervention. These devices can be broadly classified into two categories: medical-grade devices, which must be approved by the US Food and Drug Administration and are used for data collection and decision-making (e.g., blood pressure, glucose, and heart rate monitors); and consumer-grade wearables, such as watches and rings, which account for the largest market share due to the growing use of smartphone applications (2).

WIoT is primarily used in health and safety monitoring, disease diagnosis, management, and rehabilitation. In health and safety monitoring, the main target population is older adults, aiming to support high-quality, independent living. For example, emergency call systems such as call pendants offer a quick method for seniors to

DOI: 10.1201/9781003624875-15

notify caregivers or emergency responders during a crisis. These devices typically feature a button and are worn around the neck or wrist; pressing the button allows the wearer to request assistance. Call pendants are especially crucial for elderly individuals with mobility limitations or cognitive impairments who may have difficulty accessing a phone in an emergency. In assisted or long-term living settings, the call pendant is considered a vital component, as it supports wander management (e.g., for persons with dementia who may leave safe areas unknowingly) and fall prevention. This enhances the safety and security of residents and families and also increases caregiver efficiency and productivity.

Wearable technology can be used to assess gait and fall rates in older adults, track daily activities in unsupervised home environments, and identify primary movement patterns (walking, standing, sitting, lying) to support independent living. Additionally, wearable devices have shown promising developments in tracking depressive symptoms in children and adolescents.

The primary functions of these devices include monitoring, screening, detection, and prediction. Wearables are ideal for continuous data collection, as they are worn throughout the day and track various biomedical processes depending on the type of sensors used. They monitor vital signs such as heart rate, physical activity, and oxygen saturation. Screening involves identifying specific health conditions based on the monitored data, while detection involves analyzing this data to alert individuals.

Wearable devices also support chronic disease management, including cardiovascular disease, pulmonary disease, hypertension, and diabetes, through active health monitoring. Furthermore, they assist in managing neurological conditions by providing early warnings during the pre-dementia phase of Alzheimer's disease, potentially delaying the onset of symptoms. Wearable technology is widely used in sports rehabilitation, cognitive rehabilitation, and support for individuals with impairments (3).

11.1.1 Categories and Applications of Wearable Devices

Medical-Grade vs. Consumer-Grade Wearables:

- **Medical-Grade:** Examples include glucose monitors and ECG devices
- **Consumer-Grade:** Smartwatches, fitness trackers, and rings

11.2 CORE APPLICATIONS

11.2.1 Health Monitoring: Continuous Data Collection of Vital Signs

The broad application of wearable devices in healthcare and research spans areas such as fertility tracking, chronic disease monitoring (e.g., Alzheimer's, diabetes, atrial fibrillation), and lifestyle factors (e.g., coffee intake, sleep, physical activity). The growing use of wearables in studies involving rare populations and conditions—such as fibromyalgia and Pompe disease—highlights their potential to provide valuable insights into underrepresented or underserved groups. Affordable, consumer-grade wearables may serve as cost-effective and user-friendly alternatives to specialized devices, making them accessible to diverse populations, including individuals of different ethnicities, nationalities, abilities, and those affected by rare conditions.

11.2.2 Disease Diagnosis and Management: Chronic Illness Tracking

Regular physical activity lowers the risk of cardiovascular diseases, chronic obstructive pulmonary disease, and obesity, while also reducing disability and functional decline in older adults. It enhances overall well-being, improves mood, and reduces anxiety and depression. Conversely, sedentary behavior—particularly screen-based inactivity—is associated with sleep disturbances, musculoskeletal pain, and depression in adolescents. Prolonged sitting increases cardiovascular risk in older women, and excessive sedentary time may diminish the benefits of moderate to vigorous exercise in youth (4). Wearable devices help monitor health behaviors and promote physical activity through real-time tracking, feedback, and goal setting. They transmit data to healthcare professionals and mobile applications using algorithms. Preliminary studies suggest that these devices increase activity levels in the short-term, with goal setting acting as a primary motivator and action cues aiding in the reduction of sedentary behavior (4).

Recent research in medical emergencies, such as fatal seizures, highlights that the time elapsed after the onset of symptoms is a critical factor in determining a patient's prognosis and likelihood of survival. Therefore, immediate treatment based on on-site diagnosis is essential. An ideal solution is a soft, implantable drug delivery device (SID) that enables rapid intervention for patients at high risk of status epilepticus (SE). A wearable device continuously monitors EEG signals without disrupting daily life. In the event of a life-threatening epileptic emergency like SE, the wearable sensor detects the condition and wirelessly triggers the SID to deliver an immediate drug dose (5).

11.2.3 Rehabilitation: Cognitive and Physical Rehabilitation Tools

Around 40 million people worldwide are in need of palliative care, yet only 14% of them receive it. According to the World Health Organization (WHO), "palliative care improves the quality of life of patients and that of their families who are facing challenges associated with life-threatening illness, whether physical, psychological, social or spiritual." Wearable devices play a crucial role in facilitating patient-centered palliative care, allowing for treatment adjustments and effective symptom management. They reduce the need for patients to travel to clinics by enabling continuous communication with healthcare professionals. In 2012, the United Nations acknowledged that human rights related to palliative care for older individuals had not been adequately addressed. As a result, the Council of Europe adopted a resolution in 2014 focused on the "Promotion of human rights of older persons." This resolution includes a specific section on palliative care, emphasizing the importance of access to care that meets patients' needs and their right to choose their own home as a potential care setting. This is where the role of wearable devices comes into play. While there have been significant advances in patient care for cancer patients, there remain areas for improvement. The use of wearable devices can offer added benefits, particularly for those opting for home care settings (6).

11.2.4 Mental Health Monitoring: Stress and Sleep Tracking, Depression Monitoring

Actigraphy is a non-invasive method used to monitor activity and sleep patterns through a wearable device, typically resembling a wristwatch. This device tracks movements and activity levels, providing valuable data on sleep onset, duration, and wake periods. Healthcare providers use actigraphy to detect sleep disorders like insomnia, sleep apnea, and circadian rhythm disturbances by analyzing movement patterns. The device measures accelerations to differentiate sleep from wakefulness, generating metrics such as sleep onset time, sleep efficiency, and total sleep time. It doesn't directly measure sleep but identifies the absence of movement as sleep. Unlike polysomnography, which requires a sleep lab, actigraphy can be used in a natural home setting, offering a convenient and cost-effective alternative for long-term monitoring. This device measures total sleep time (TST), sleep efficiency, wake after sleep onset (WASO), Sleep Fragmentation Index, which helps in research like extracting time and frequency domain features directly from raw data files and developing application-specific learning or pattern recognition algorithms. By providing objective data on sleep behaviors, actigraphy aids in accurate diagnosis and treatment planning, making it an essential tool for healthcare providers in managing sleep disorders (7, 8).

Sleep apnea refers to health conditions where airflow either ceases or decreases episodically during sleep. A systematic review showed that the global prevalence of obstructive sleep apnea (OSA) is between 9% and 38%. In the United States alone, the number of people struggling with sleep apnea may exceed 30 million, as per the American Medical Association (9).

Polysomnography, the gold standard for diagnosing sleep apnea, has several limitations: it is costly; access to sleep labs can be limited; it requires an overnight stay with sensors attached; it may not accurately reflect typical sleep behavior due to the first-night effect, and its analysis is subjective, relying on the clinician's experience. One of the promising solutions that have been used to address the limitations of polysomnography is wearable technology like actigraphy (9, 10).

Depression is the world's leading cause of disability within the youth population. As per a study among US adults, at 18 years of age, adults with depression had 28 more years of quality-adjusted life expectancy than adults without depression, resulting in a 28.9-year quality-adjusted life expectancy loss owing to depression. Stress significantly impacts mental health, leading to various physical and psychological issues. Stress management is important in workplaces to boost employee motivation and enthusiasm. Additionally, engaging in daily physical activity is crucial for improving mental well-being, as it helps reduce stress. Wearable devices play a key role in this by tracking parameters like body weight, calorie intake, and dietary habits, making it easier for individuals to incorporate physical activity into their routine to support mental health (10).

11.2.5 Elderly Care: Fall Detection, Emergency Call Systems, and Wander Management

In 2019, 9% of the global population was aged 65 years or above, and this percentage is predicted to increase to 16% by 2050. Older individuals living in rural areas often encounter extra challenges in accessing healthcare services, as these regions typically lack specialized care and do not offer the same level of healthcare quality as urban areas. According to the "Global Health Workforce Labor Market Projections for 2030," the world will soon experience a shortage of 15 million healthcare workers, which will exacerbate the current situation. Therefore, there is an urgent need for solutions to address these challenges. Digital health, which includes technologies like telemedicine, mHealth, and wearable devices, offers personalized care while reducing costs. It enables remote monitoring by healthcare professionals, preventing unnecessary emergency visits, and giving patients greater autonomy (5).

Elderly care institutions can highlight the benefits of wearable technology to older adults, ensuring regular maintenance and safety while emphasizing the effectiveness of consistent use. Building trust in the reliability of these devices will encourage continued use, ultimately improving nursing staff efficiency, reducing their workload, and enhancing the competitiveness of the institution in the long run (9).

11.3 BENEFITS OF WEARABLE TECHNOLOGY IN HEALTHCARE

11.3.1 Enhancing Quality of Life for Individuals with Disabilities or Chronic Illnesses

To make wearable devices more useful and user-friendly, they need to be designed in a way that fits naturally into people's lives while making the best use of current technology. A useful design should focus on the user's experience, allowing wearables to be more helpful and easy to use. To achieve this, wearable devices should not demand too much attention, should be comfortable to use while moving, should respond quickly to other media like screens and sounds, should be aware of the surroundings through sensors, and should allow users to easily connect with others and the internet. UNICEF has been using innovative wearable technology in its social projects, highlighting both the benefits and ethical considerations of such research. Wearables are not just making people more productive but are also improving lives and serving the public good. To ensure they are useful in different communities, UNICEF suggests that future wearables should be affordable and suitable for low-cost areas, energy-efficient with long battery life, strong and durable to withstand harsh conditions, and easy to expand, use, and maintain across different environments. Wearable devices need to be strong, long-lasting, and easy to use, especially in emergencies. They should also work well even in places with poor or no network connection. If designed with these things in mind, wearables can help protect people, support vulnerable communities, and improve everyday life. Instead of just focusing on modern technology for one specific purpose, wearables should be designed to fit into people's lives and surroundings. When done right, they can bring positive changes not just for individuals but for society (11).

11.3.2 Promoting Independent Living and Reducing Hospitalization Rates

There are many modern wearable devices that can help ill patients get treatment without being hospitalized. Initially, elderly people showed hesitation to use the wearables, but later they were designed to be small, comfortable, and user-friendly devices. A boon of wearable technology is that more than one sensor can be incorporated into wristbands, smartwatches, etc., which can gather information from the individual. Using wearable technology can help doctors track the patient's response to the medication, their progress, and can make necessary changes in the treatment without even seeing them. This is most convenient for the patients as they can avoid traveling to the hospital and waiting long hours to meet the doctor (12).

Wearables like a wristband, paired with a phone and a pulse oximeter, can track important health signs like heart rate, temperature, sweat levels, and oxygen levels. This data can be sent to a doctor every day. If something seems wrong, the doctor can call the patient to check in and give advice, especially if things look like they are getting worse. This system can help reduce COPD flare-ups and hospital visits by catching problems early and helping patients manage their condition better. It is a straightforward way to keep patients safer and improve their health (12).

Also, wearable cardioverter defibrillators (WCDs) can help monitor people who have had a heart attack or are at elevated risk of dangerous heart rhythms. These devices can spot and treat serious heart problems early, even while patients are at home, keeping them safe during recovery. WCDs are helpful for people at risk of sudden heart problems including death. It is found that the WCD can prevent many patients from needing a permanent heart device right away. It acts as a temporary safety net until physicians decide if a permanent solution is necessary. Thus, WCDs are a less invasive option to reduce the need for surgery. It has been easy for people to use and accept, with many sticking to wearing it regularly. This shows how wearable devices can be helpful, safe, and easy to use, making them a good option for both patients and doctors (12).

11.3.3 Cost Savings Through Prevention and Early Detection of Illnesses

Wearable devices possess the advantage of tracking important health signs like heart rate, blood pressure, and body temperature in real-time. Conventional methods like making an appointment and visiting a doctor can take time and thus there will be a delay in diagnosing disease on time. Wearable devices can continuously monitor basic vital signs like heart rate, blood pressure, oxygen saturation, and body temperature and physiological metrics like sleep patterns, respiratory rates, skin conductance, and even specific biochemical markers in sweat. This constant stream of data gives detailed and up-to-date information regarding the patient's health. The physiological metrics can provide a deeper insight into a patient's health status, lifestyle habits, and potential risk factors. For example, irregular sleep patterns indicate that the patient could be under stress, or they could have a sleep disorder. Change in skin conductance could be because of emotional or physical stress (13).

Continuous data tracking is helpful when something unusual happens; it can be noticed right away. For example, a resting heart rate that suddenly and consistently rises could be an early warning sign of a heart issue or an oncoming illness. By catching these changes early, the patient can see a doctor sooner and potentially avoid bigger health issues later (13).

11.3.4 Improving Productivity and Efficiency of Caregivers

Caregiving is something that many people do, and it is as common among men (37%) as it is among women (40%). It does not matter how much money someone makes, how much education they have, what their race or ethnicity is, or how old they are—at least 30% of people in every group are caregivers. What makes caregiving even harder is that most caregivers (70%) also have jobs. This means they must manage their work while also taking care of someone else. Almost half of all adults (47%) say they expect to care for an aging parent or older relative at some point in their lives. While many caregivers help with everyday tasks like cooking, cleaning, and shopping, more than half also must do medical tasks. These tasks can include giving medicines, taking care of wounds, giving injections, or helping someone who cannot control their bladder. Often, caregivers must figure out how to do these things on their own because they do not get much training or support from doctors or nurses. This can make caregivers feel scared or worried about whether they are doing things the right way (14).

Luckily, technology is starting to help. Big companies like Intel and GE, as well as smaller startups like Lively, have created tools to make caregiving easier. For example, they have made systems that let caregivers check on their loved ones from far away, especially if the person being cared for lives alone. There are also websites and apps that help families organize caregiving tasks. Innovative technologies, like wearable devices and cloud computing, are also making a significant difference. Wearable devices, like smartwatches, can now send information to the cloud, which means they do not have to do all the work on their own. Devices like Google Glass can show caregivers vital information right when they need it. In the future, there could be something called an "Intelligent Family Care Assistant." This would be a system that keeps track of all the caregiving tasks and health information for a family. It could remind family members about things they need to do, like giving medicine or going to a doctor's appointment, and even warn them if there is a problem or emergency (14).

We are living in a time where we do not always need brand-new inventions to solve problems. Instead, we can use technology that already exists and combine it in new ways to create helpful tools. Some of the new technologies that will make caregiving better in the future include systems that learn what we need and adjust themselves (called proactive computing), devices that are always connected to the internet and the cloud (called pervasive connectivity), tiny sensors that can monitor health very accurately (called high-resolution sensing), and devices that work together automatically (called orchestrated devices). All these ideas will help create better caregiving tools in the future, making it easier for families to take care of their loved ones and reducing the stress that caregivers often feel (14).

11.4 CHALLENGES AND BARRIERS

11.4.1 Data Privacy and Security

Health information is among the most sensitive types of personal data, with privacy centering on an individual's ability to control when, how, and to what extent their information is shared. As technology advances, data from wearable devices and electronic health records are increasingly combined to create comprehensive health profiles, raising significant concerns for users who often lack control over what data is collected, how it is used, and who owns it. Currently, the raw data generated by wearable devices is owned by the companies that produce them, not the users, and while individuals may access summarized versions of their data, the raw information can be sold to third parties, creating serious privacy risks. These concerns are further amplified by security threats, as data collected through these devices is typically stored in centralized databases, which, if breached, could expose vast amounts of sensitive information. A striking example of this vulnerability occurred when the fitness-tracking app Strava inadvertently revealed the locations of US military personnel in conflict zones like Syria and Iraq through its "heatmap" feature, exposing military facilities, troop movements, and even de-anonymized user details such as names, speeds, and heart rates. The security risks associated with wearable devices fall into three main categories: threats to the individual user, such as physical interference or device limitations; risks to data as it travels between the device and software programs; and vulnerabilities in the storage of aggregated data within databases, highlighting the urgent need for stronger privacy protections, greater user control over personal data, and more robust security measures to address the growing risks in an era of interconnected health technologies (15).

Wearable technology constantly collects sensitive health data, often without users fully realizing it, which can lead to misuse like fraud, extortion, or targeted advertising. The lack of strong safeguards and user control over how data is collected, stored, and shared makes these risks even worse. For example, there have been alarming cases of hackers targeting medical devices like insulin pumps and pacemakers, putting lives at risk. To address these issues, experts are calling for medical wearables to be treated as essential infrastructure, with strict security measures, regular risk assessments, and penalties for data breaches. The European Union's General Data Protection Regulation (GDPR) offers a strong model for protecting privacy, requiring companies to build privacy into their designs, collect only the data they truly need, and give users control over their information, including the right to correct or delete it. It also mandates that users be notified of data breaches and sets out rules for transferring data across borders. Expanding these protections to include health data as a "special category" could further strengthen user rights and limit how data is reused in risky situations. However, creating truly secure systems is technically complex, so collaboration among manufacturers, policymakers, and users is essential to treat privacy and security as shared responsibilities, not just individual goals. If we get this right, wearables can transform healthcare in ways that benefit everyone, but if we ignore these risks, public trust could be lost, and the technology's potential could be wasted. By prioritizing privacy, security, and ethical practices, we can ensure that wearables improve health outcomes while respecting individual rights. The decisions we make now will determine whether this technology becomes a force for good or a source of harm and distrust (16).

11.4.2 Device Accuracy and Reliability

Accurately tracking physical activity, like step counting, in real-life situations is challenging because current technologies have limitations. Smartphone apps work well in short-term, controlled tests but aren't reliable for long-term use since people don't always carry their phones with them. For example, phones are often left on desks or in other rooms during activities like cooking, cleaning, or visiting the toilet, and they're not carried during activities that could damage them, like swimming, gardening, horseback riding, or dancing. Over time, these gaps add up and make the data unreliable. Fitness wristbands, on the other hand, are less intrusive, don't disrupt lifestyles, and can collect accurate, long-term data. However, they're not perfect—they can underestimate energy expenditure during activities with little movement at the hip, and they might be removed when changing clothes, which can also affect data (17).

In 2016, a major activity tracker company was hit with a lawsuit because their devices were found to be inaccurate when measuring heart rate during exercises—sometimes off by more than 24 beats per minute on average. While these trackers are advertised as helpful tools for monitoring workout intensity, their reliability is a big concern, especially for people who might use them for medical reasons. For example, cancer survivors with heart issues—like those taking beta blockers, dealing with heart damage from cancer treatments, or managing other health problems—could be at risk if they rely too much on these devices. Since there hasn't been enough independent research to prove how accurate these trackers really are, it's important to be cautious. Cancer survivors and others with serious health conditions should avoid depending on these devices for important health decisions until they're proven to be reliable. This situation shows why we need better testing and standards to make sure wearable tech is safe and accurate, especially for people with complex medical needs (18).

Device reliability refers to a device's or system's ability to consistently perform its intended function without failure over a defined period. The design of the product is a key factor in its reliability. A well-developed initial design is likely to result in fewer errors during long-term use. The build quality, materials used, and environmental conditions also affect reliability, which in turn is linked to customer satisfaction (18).

In elderly living facilities, homes, and other treatment centers, the use of an emergency call system can alert staff to assist during an emergency. For example, the Igeacom EMU (Emergency Monitoring Unit) is a user-friendly Personal Emergency Response device that enables hands-free two-way voice communication between the resident and the monitoring center. When the Igeacom EMU is activated, it connects to a dedicated phone line and uses integrated voice annunciation software to identify the caller. A live two-way voice response is then initiated from the responder's fixed or portable phone to assess the situation, evaluate the event, and reassure the caller that assistance will be provided as needed. The Igeacom system is marketed by ATS, a company founded in 1975 that began as a small business. Through steady growth, consistency, and a focus on customer satisfaction, ATS has remained in business and continues to innovate. This reflects the reliability of both the product and the brand over the long term (18).

11.4.3 Patient Compliance

One of the biggest challenges with wearable technology in healthcare is getting patients to use these devices regularly and effectively. Many people find it hard to stick with wearables or understand the data they provide, which limits how helpful they can be for improving health. To tackle this, strategies like designing user-friendly interfaces that are easy to navigate, offering thorough training to help patients use the devices and interpret the data, and providing incentives like discounts or rewards for consistent use can make a big difference. However, even with these efforts, keeping people engaged over time is tough, as they might lose interest or find gadgets inconvenient. On top of this, wearable medical devices must meet strict safety, accuracy, and effectiveness standards set by regulators like the FDA. Developers must go through a complex and time-consuming process, including performance testing, clinical trials, and extensive paperwork, to prove their devices are reliable and safe. Balancing the need for user-friendly designs and patient engagement with these strict regulatory requirements adds another layer of difficulty. Solving these challenges is crucial to ensure wearable technology can provide trustworthy, useful information and earn the confidence of both patients and healthcare professionals (19).

For starters, some people may not know how to use the technology or don't have access to the necessary devices, like smartphones or computers, to make it work. Others might find wearing the device inconvenient or feel overwhelmed by the constant data collection. Staying motivated to change behaviors and follow the device's instructions can also be tough, especially when the excitement of using a new gadget wears off. Some people might feel self-conscious about being monitored in studies, stop paying attention to the feedback the device provides, or simply can't afford the technology in the first place. Even when these issues are addressed, wearable devices might not always be enough to drive meaningful, long-term changes in behavior. This shows that more personalized and engaging solutions are needed to help patients stick with wearable technology (20).

The costs of setting up, maintaining, and repairing these devices, along with teaching patients how to use them, can be high and often fall on patients themselves.

Another issue is that these devices tend to work better for people who are healthier and more active, but they're less accurate for those who move slowly, have limited mobility, or use walkers. On top of that, wearables often need to be charged frequently and require regular data syncing, which can be annoying and lead to missed data or inconsistent use. These problems make it harder for patients to stick with wearable technology and for healthcare providers to rely on it (21).

11.4.4 Compatibility with Current Healthcare Systems

The integration of patient data from wearable devices into Electronic Health Records (EHRs) is a growing challenge in healthcare. Many health systems lack the platforms needed to handle continuous streams of data from different devices, making it hard to integrate this data into EHRs. Currently, device manufacturers and EHR vendors use a variety of proprietary and closed communication methods, which create barriers to seamless data sharing and lead to a lack of interoperability. As a result, valuable patient data from wearables often ends up isolated and less useful because it can't be easily combined with the patient's full medical history. To solve this, researchers are working toward plug-and-play interoperability—a standard already common in consumer electronics—where devices and systems can automatically detect, communicate, and sync with each other without complex setup. For this to work in healthcare, systems need to be easy to use, compatible across devices, and scalable to accommodate new technologies. As the demand for better interoperability grows, third-party applications are emerging to bridge the gaps between devices, EHR systems, and healthcare providers. However, achieving true interoperability will require stronger partnerships and collaboration between health systems, device makers, and app developers. By improving these relationships, healthcare can become more efficient, ensure safer transitions of care, and ultimately reduce costs for patients and providers (22).

The challenges of using data from wearable devices start with the devices themselves. The quality, quantity, and accuracy of the data depend on factors like the sensors used, how often measurements are taken (temporal resolution), how far apart measurements are (spatial resolution), and external factors that might affect the readings. Since wearables are often low-cost, energy-efficient, and used by many people in different situations, the data they collect can vary widely in quality (23).

Once the data is collected, there are challenges in gathering it on a large scale. This includes figuring out how to transmit the data efficiently while keeping it secure, private, and trustworthy. After collection, the data needs to be cleaned and organized to make it useful. This involves fixing errors, removing outliers, and making sure the data is consistent, even though it comes from different devices with different settings (23).

Another issue is the lack of good datasets and the difficulty of labeling the data accurately, which often requires experts or input from the users themselves. Traditionally, this data is sent to the cloud for processing and storage, but this can cause delays and put a lot of strain on the network. To solve this, edge computing has become a popular alternative. It processes data closer to where it's collected (at the "edge" of the network), which reduces delays and makes the system faster. However, edge devices need to be powerful enough to handle the workload that the cloud usually manages, which is still a challenge. In short, making wearable data useful involves solving problems at every step—from collecting high-quality data and ensuring privacy to cleaning it up, analyzing it, and finding the best way to process it without overloading the system (23).

11.5 FUTURE TRENDS AND INNOVATIONS

The next generation of wearable technology, like smartwatches, will make it even harder to tell the difference between wellness gadgets and medical devices. This is because the sensors in these devices are getting better at analyzing health data without needing to invade the body. As these sensors improve, they can be built into everyday devices like smartwatches. At the same time, scientists are learning more about how certain biological signs (called biomarkers) are linked to serious illnesses. This means the sensors in wearables will become more accurate at monitoring health and detecting diseases (24).

It is moving toward a future where people will have what's like a small chemical lab on their wrist. Being able to access this health data will help people take better care of themselves and could improve health for people all over the world. These advances mean that wearable devices could do the same kind of medical tests that are usually done in clinics, but more often and from anywhere. This could help solve health problems much earlier (24).

Wearable technology isn't just for humans—it's also being developed for pets. These devices will help pet owners keep track of their pets' health, but they could also change how working animals, like sniffer dogs, are used. Dogs are incredibly good at detecting smells, like explosives, and can tell different scents apart almost instantly. However, training sniffer dogs is expensive, costing around £60,000 over the course of two years. Wearable tech could help reduce these costs. For example, when a sniffer dog finds something it's trained to detect, like an explosive, its heart rate and breathing increase because it gets excited about being rewarded. Wearable devices could track these changes and give handlers real-time information about the dog's physical and behavioral state. This could make training faster and more efficient, allowing more dogs to be used in important jobs like detecting explosives (24).

Improving energy efficiency in wearable devices is a big opportunity, and one way to do this is by using remote in-network computational offloading. This means shifting heavy computational tasks from wearables to other devices or systems in the network, like the Cloud (where tasks are done on remote servers), Fog (where tasks are handled by nearby network nodes), or Edge (where tasks are sent to the closest power-independent device). While these methods generally work in similar ways, they behave differently in systems with strict reliability or latency requirements, especially in challenging conditions like high mobility, low network coverage, or heavy system loads. Today, many companies, including Apple and Google, are using smartphones as the main solution for offloading tasks from wearables. Even though smartphones are energy-hungry and face growing power consumption limits, they're still a practical choice because they're close to wearables and have more processing power. This approach helps wearables save energy while still getting the job done (25).

Wearable technologies have a lot of exciting possibilities, but there's one big challenge: these devices need to work perfectly and consistently, which isn't always guaranteed. A big issue is that not all wearables meet the same standards. Many consumer wearables don't share information about how accurate they are, making it hard to fully trust them. In the U.S., the FDA only steps in if a device claims to have a medical purpose. For example, the Apple Watch has had a heart rate monitor since 2016, but because it's meant for fitness and wellness (not medical diagnosis), it doesn't need FDA approval. However, things changed in 2018 when Apple released the Series 4 Watch, which included an FDA-approved ECG feature. This was a big deal because it was the first time a consumer product had this kind of medical capability. Around the same time, Alphabet's Verily Study Watch also got FDA clearance for its ECG functions. These moves show that tech companies are serious about breaking into the healthcare market and are pushing to make wearables more medically reliable (26).

As wearables become more advanced, the FDA is working to keep up. They're updating their guidelines to make sure these devices are safe and effective while still encouraging innovation. This is important because wearables are starting to change how doctors and researchers work. For example, doctors are now seeing patients who've detected heart rhythm issues using their wearables. On the research side, the Apple Heart Study (which involves 500,000 Apple Watch users) is helping to understand how common conditions like atrial fibrillation are in the general population. This is just the beginning—wearables are opening new possibilities in medicine and could transform healthcare soon (26).

11.6 CONCLUSION

This chapter discusses how wearable technology is shaping the future, particularly in the field of healthcare. The application of wearable technology is commendable in areas such as health monitoring, disease diagnosis and management, rehabilitation, mental health tracking, and especially elderly care. Cost-effective and user-friendly wearables are becoming increasingly popular due to these core applications. Wearable devices can monitor physical activity and detect the onset of symptoms. These devices can be connected to smartphones, allowing data to be communicated with health professionals. This constant communication can reduce hospital visits, particularly for elderly patients. Wearable technology also supports mental and physical health by tracking parameters such as body weight, calorie intake, and more. Continuous monitoring and timely communication with healthcare professionals reduce the workload of nursing staff and improve their efficiency. If wearable technology is designed to be affordable, energy-efficient, long-lasting, and functional even in areas with weak network signals, it could bring significant improvements to society. Continuous tracking and communication with healthcare professionals from home not only reduce hospital visits but also promote independent living, thereby enhancing users' confidence.

The constant data stream provides a comprehensive view of a patient's health status, enabling early detection of abnormalities. This reduces caregiver stress and enhances their productivity at work. As wearable technology evolves, it is crucial to address emerging challenges. A lack of robust security and control can lead to data mishandling or loss. However, the European Union's General Data Protection Regulation (GDPR) is driving the development of strong security frameworks for wearable devices. Device accuracy and reliability are additional concerns. Since smartphones cannot always be carried, fitness wristbands are becoming valuable for collecting reliable data. In elderly care facilities, technologies like the Igeacom EMU, supported by ATS, help ensure data reliability. Patient compliance is another issue, which can be addressed by designing more user-friendly devices. Integrating data from wearables into electronic health records (EHRs) presents another challenge, but researchers are working toward plug-and-play interoperability solutions. Edge computing—where data processing happens at the edge of the network—is gaining traction, enabling faster responses with minimal delay. Looking ahead, the growth of wearable technology is expected to accelerate. Scientists are developing biomarkers linked to serious illnesses, making health data more accurate and enabling faster identification and treatment of health issues. Wearables are also being developed for pets, capable of detecting explosives based on physical and behavioral cues such as heart rate and breathing patterns. Since smartphones are energy-intensive, remote in-network computational offloading is being explored. This approach improves battery efficiency by transferring heavy computational tasks from the wearable to external systems. The Apple Watch Series 4 and Alphabet's Verily Study Watch have received FDA approval for ECG features, marking a significant step as tech companies enter the healthcare market. In response, the FDA is updating its guidelines to support innovation in wearable healthcare technology, opening new possibilities for the future.

REFERENCES

1. Alyssa Schroer. (2024, August 30). *15 examples of wearable technology in healthcare and wearable medical devices*. Built In. https://builtin.com/articles/wearable-technology-in-healthcare
2. Lu JK, Wang W, Goh J, Maier AB. A practical guide for selecting continuous monitoring wearable devices for community-dwelling adults. *Heliyon*. 2024 Jun 22;10(13):e33488. doi: 10.1016/j.heliyon.2024.e33488. PMID: 39035501; PMCID: PMC11259861. https://pmc.ncbi.nlm.nih.gov/articles/PMC11259861/
3. Rodgers MM, Alon G, Pai VM, Conroy RS. Wearable technologies for active living and rehabilitation: Current research challenges and future opportunities. *J Rehabil Assist Technol Eng*. 2019 Apr 26;6:2055668319839607. doi: 10.1177/2055668319839607. PMID: 31245033; PMCID: PMC6582279.
4. Yu S, Chen Z, Wu X. The impact of wearable devices on physical activity for chronic disease patients: Findings from the 2019 health information national trends survey. *Int J Environ Res Public Health*. 2023 Jan 3;20(1):887. doi: 10.3390/ijerph20010887. PMID: 36613207; PMCID: PMC9820171.

5. Joo H, Lee Y, Kim J, Yoo JS, Yoo S, Kim S, Arya AK, Kim S, Choi SH, Lu N, Lee HS, Kim S, Lee ST, Kim DH. Soft implantable drug delivery device integrated wirelessly with wearable devices to treat fatal seizures. *Sci Adv*. 2021 Jan 1;7(1):eabd4639. doi: 10.1126/sciadv.abd4639. PMID: 33523849; PMCID: PMC7775752. https://pmc.ncbi.nlm.nih.gov/articles/PMC7775752/
6. Sandic Spaho R, Uhrenfeldt L, Fotis T, Kymre IG. Wearable devices in palliative care for people 65 years and older: A scoping review. *Digit Health*. 2023 Jul 2;9:20552076231181212. doi: 10.1177/20552076231181212. PMID: 37426582; PMCID: PMC10328013.
7. Cleveland Clinic. (2025, March 19). *What is actigraphy?*. Cleveland Clinic. https://my.clevelandclinic.org/health/drugs/25196-actigraphy
8. About Us. (n.d.). https://theactigraph.com/about-us
9. Abd-Alrazaq A, Aslam H, AlSaad R, Alsahli M, Ahmed A, Damseh R, Aziz S, Sheikh J. Detection of sleep apnea using wearable AI: Systematic review and meta-analysis. *J Med Internet Res*. 2024 Sep 10;26:e58187. doi: 10.2196/58187. PMID: 39255014; PMCID: PMC11422752. https://pmc.ncbi.nlm.nih.gov/articles/PMC11422752/
10. Wang Y, Lu L, Zhang R, Ma Y, Zhao S, Liang C. The willingness to continue using wearable devices among the elderly: SEM and FsQCA analysis. *BMC Med Inform Decis Mak*. 2023 Oct 16;23(1):218. doi: 10.1186/s12911-023-02336-8. PMID: 37845659; PMCID: PMC10577990. https://pmc.ncbi.nlm.nih.gov/articles/PMC10577990/
11. Lee J, Kim D, Ryoo H-Y, Shin B-S. Sustainable wearables: Wearable technology for enhancing the quality of human life. *Sustainability*. 2016;8(5):466. https://doi.org/10.3390/su8050466 https://www.mdpi.com/2071-1050/8/5/466
12. Bonacaro A, Rubbi I, Sookhoo D. The use of wearable devices in preventing hospital readmission and in improving the quality of life of chronic patients in the homecare setting: A narrative literature review. *Professioni Infermieristiche*. 2019;72(2).
13. Ibrahim T, Ali H. The impact of wearable IoT devices on early disease detection and prevention. *Int J Appl Health Care Anal*. 2023;8. https://norislab.com/index.php/IJAHA/article/view/27/16
14. Adler R, Mehta R. Catalyzing technology to support family caregiving. National Alliance for Caregiving, 2014. https://ajuntament.barcelona.cat/familia/sites/default/files/arxius-noticies/Catalyzing-Technology-to-Support-Family-Caregiving_FINAL.pdf
15. Cilliers L. Wearable devices in healthcare: Privacy and information security issues. *Health Inf Manag J*. 2019;49(2–3):150–156. doi: 10.1177/1833358319851684. https://journals.sagepub.com/doi/full/10.1177/1833358319851684?casa_token=djofh5GbtcQAAAAA%3ABmdxdEnyQTKsHElfWx8sCdKcJ5NC9jpMO377WQbMkaEEjJ5g3CX8sYBnNtQSXyt1CCuKvE1ZWG84
16. Sivakumar CLV, Mone V, Abdumukhtor R. Addressing privacy concerns with wearable health monitoring technology. *WIREs Data Min Knowl Discov*. 2024;14(3). https://doi.org/10.1002/widm.1535
17. Piccinini F, Martinelli G, Carbonaro A. Accuracy of mobile applications versus wearable devices in long-term step measurements. *Sensors*. 2020;20(21):6293. https://doi.org/10.3390/s20216293. https://www.mdpi.com/1424-8220/20/21/6293
18. Walker RK, Hickey AM, Freedson PS. Advantages and limitations of wearable activity trackers: Considerations for patients and clinicians. *Clin J Oncol Nurs*. 2026;20(6). https://cjon.ons.org/system/files/journal-article-pdfs/WalkerDec2016.pdf
19. Phuyal S, Elvas LB, Ferreira JC, Bista R. Harnessing wearable devices for enhanced long-term care: Opportunities, challenges, and future directions. *Int J Comput Inf Syst Ind Manag*. 2024;16:502–514. https://cspub-ijcisim.org/index.php/ijcisim/article/view/722/607

20. Phillips SM, Bertram LC, Rosenberg D, Buman MP, Lynch BM. Wearable technology and physical activity in chronic disease: Opportunities and challenges. *Am J Prev Med.* 2018;54(1):144–150. ISSN 0749-3797. https://www.sciencedirect.com/science/article/pii/S0749379717304567?casa_token=XgqrF4xiL2UAAAAA:3ETi9dQXu5FbC7Qn-GwEG_kejTOpyxJP93bi5ZZe1W_ys91VOvn3lHHQ1hEbsQ_wkxU8GEkpgIg
21. Amin T, Mobbs RJ, Mostafa N, Sy LW, Choy WJ. Wearable devices for patient monitoring in the early postoperative period: A literature review. *Mhealth.* 2021 Jul 20;7:50. doi: 10.21037/mhealth-20-131. PMID: 34345627; PMCID: PMC8326951. https://pmc.ncbi.nlm.nih.gov/articles/PMC8326951/#sec8
22. Dinh-Le C, Chuang R, Chokshi S, Mann D. Wearable health technology and electronic health record integration: Scoping review and future directions. *JMIR Mhealth and Uhealth.* 2019;7(9):e12861. https://mhealth.jmir.org/2019/9/e12861. DOI: 10.2196/12861 https://mhealth.jmir.org/2019/9/e12861/
23. Ometov A, Shubina V, Klus L, Skibińska J, Saafi S, Pascacio P, Flueratoru L, Quezada Gaibor D, Chukhno, Olga Chukhno N, Ali A, Channa A, Svertoka E, Bin Qaim W, Casanova-Marqués R, Holcer S, Torres-Sospedra J, Casteleyn S, Ruggeri G, Araniti G, Burget R, Hosek J, Simona Lohan E. A survey on wearable technology: History, state-of-the-art and current challenges. *Comput Netw.* 2021;193:108074. ISSN 1389-1286. https://www.sciencedirect.com/science/article/pii/S1389128621001651
24. Brophy K, Davies S, Olenik S, Çotur Y, Ming D, Zalk NV, Hare DO, Güder F, Yetisen AK. The future of wearable technologies. Imperial College London. Institute for molecular science and engineering. Briefing Paper No. 6, 2021. https://www.guderesearch.com/wp-content/uploads/2021/12/IMSJ8878-Wearable-Tech-Briefing-Paper-210601.pdf
25. Ometov A, Chukhno O, Chukhno N, Nurmi J, Simona Lohan E. When wearable technology meets computing in future networks: A road ahead. In *Proceedings of the 18th ACM International Conference on Computing Frontiers (CF '21).* Association for Computing Machinery, New York, NY, USA, 185–190, 2021. https://doi.org/10.1145/3457388.3458614 https://dl.acm.org/doi/pdf/10.1145/3457388.3458614
26. Liao Y, Thompson C, Peterson S, Mandrola J, Beg MS. The future of wearable technologies and remote monitoring in health care. *Am Soc Clin Oncol Educ Book.* 2019 Jan;39:115–121. doi: 10.1200/EDBK_238919. Epub 2019 May 17. PMID: 31099626; PMCID: PMC8325475. https://pmc.ncbi.nlm.nih.gov/articles/PMC8325475/

Index

C

D

E

F

G

H

I

J

M

N

P

Q

R

S

T

U

V

W

For Product Safety Concerns and Information please contact our EU representative GPSR@taylorandfrancis.com
Taylor & Francis Verlag GmbH, Kaufingerstraße 24, 80331 München, Germany

www.ingramcontent.com/pod-product-compliance
Ingram Content Group UK Ltd.
Pitfield, Milton Keynes, MK11 3LW, UK
UKHW020201200926
475702UK00004B/563

* 9 7 8 1 0 4 1 0 3 6 8 7 6 *